THE AWARE BABY
(revised edition)

Aletha J. Solter, Ph.D.

Shining Star Press
Goleta, California

Revised edition 2001

Cover photo by Outi Knoff
Cover art/design by Frank Bucy, No Waves Press, Santa Barbara,California

Previous edition published in 1984 with the title *The Aware Baby: A New Approach to Parenting*.

Published by Shining Star Press, P.O. Box 206, Goleta, California 93116, U.S.A. Phone & Fax: (805) 968-1868
e-mail: publisher@awareparenting.com
web site: www.awareparenting.com

Publisher's Cataloging Information

Solter, Aletha Jauch
    The aware baby (revised edition)
    Includes bibliographical references and index.
    ISBN 0-9613073-7-4
    1. Infants. 2. Infant psychology. 3. Child rearing.
    4. Parent and child.

    Dewey Decimal Classification: 649'.122
    Library of Congress Card Number: 00-192346

Printed in the United States of America

Acknowledgments

I would like to thank the thousands of parents who have contributed to the revisions of this book. Their questions, comments, and experiences over the years have helped me to clarify my presentation of this material. Some of their experiences are included in the book. Special thanks goes to my three colleagues who took the time to read the manuscript for this revised edition, and give me insightful feedback and suggestions: Libby deMartelly from New Hampshire, Dr. Mary Galbraith from California, and Nancy Gibson from Iowa. Many thanks also to my mother, Tonia Jauch, for her careful editing, and to my husband, Kenneth Solter, for his ongoing help and support. Finally, I would like to thank my children, Nicky and Sarah, for teaching me so much by being themselves.

Table of Contents

Chapter 3: Food: Letting your baby become self-regulated

Chapter 4: Sleep: Letting your baby rest

Chapter 5: Play: Letting your baby learn

Chapter 6: Conflicts: Letting your baby feel respected

Chapter 7: Attachment: Letting your baby feel safe

List of charts

Preface to the new edition

When *The Aware Baby* was first published in 1984, I had no idea whether or not parents would welcome this new approach. I needn't have worried, because it has now been translated into French, German, Dutch, Italian, and Hebrew, contributing to a quiet, but powerful, revolution in parenting around the world. I am thrilled to be a part of it.

My children are now young adults, and I can personally attest to the fact that this approach does indeed work very well. Furthermore, I have received hundreds of letters from parents around the world describing the beneficial effects of raising their children this way. These children have no need to rebel during adolescence, and they grow up to be compassionate, cooperative, and extremely bright. They follow their own paths with strong determination and confidence, and become well-functioning, contributing members of society. Perhaps most importantly, they have no interest in drugs or violence.

There has been considerable research in child development since I first wrote this book, so I have updated every chapter for this new edition. In particular, I have included some of the recent findings from studies in prenatal psychology, attachment, and the effects of trauma. I have also incorporated more of the cross-cultural research that allows us to gain a broader perspective about our own child-rearing practices by comparing them to others around the world.

In 1990 I founded The Aware Parenting Institute, an international organization, to promote the concepts described in my books. There are now certified instructors of Aware Parenting in several different countries. For more information, please visit our web site at www.awareparenting.com. Together, we *can* change the world!

Aletha Solter
The Aware Parenting Institute
P.O. Box 206, Goleta, CA 93116, U.S.A.
Phone & Fax: (805) 968-1868
solter@awareparenting.com
web site: www.awareparenting.com

Warning/Disclaimer

This book is an educational resource focusing on the emotional needs of infants and toddlers, and is not intended to be a substitute for medical advice or treatment. Many of the behaviors and symptoms discussed can be an indication of serious emotional or physical problems. Parents and teachers are advised to consult with a competent physician whenever babies display behavioral or emotional problems of any kind, a sudden change in sleep, eating, or crying patterns, or when pain or illness are suspected. Furthermore, some of the suggested methods in this book may not be appropriate under all conditions or with babies suffering from certain physical or emotional problems.

The mention of specific therapies in this book is for informational purposes only and does not entail endorsement by the author. Some forms of therapy can be dangerous if carried out by improperly trained practitioners. If you are considering choosing a therapist for yourself or your child, it is recommended that you carefully review the therapist's credentials and references.

The author and publisher shall have neither liability nor responsibility to any person or entity with respect to any damage caused, or alleged to be caused, directly or indirectly by the information contained in this book.

"For in the baby lies the future of the world..."
-From a Mayan proverb

INTRODUCTION

The need for a revolutionary approach to parenting

The birth of a baby is a joyful event. Many new parents feel tremendous love and caring, sometimes at a depth never before experienced. Friends and relatives are eager to see what the infant looks like, and perhaps also to experience for a few seconds the feelings of love and hope that a fresh new human being elicits in all of us. Parents naturally want to do everything they can to insure that their baby will grow up to be loving, intelligent and happy, and contribute something to society.

The world is gradually becoming a better place for babies. Knowledge of nutrition has led to better diets for pregnant and breastfeeding women as well as for babies. This knowledge, combined with improvements in health care, allows babies to have a better chance than ever before of surviving and being healthy. The growth of developmental psychology has alerted parents to the importance of the first few years of life, and has resulted in a proliferation of parenting books and educational toys that can help babies develop their intellectual abilities. Infants with handicaps now stand an excellent chance in many countries of being encouraged to reach their full potential. Research on the importance of early attachments has further contributed to our understanding of the optimal conditions for emotionally healthy development. As a culture, we are gradually accepting the fact that babies are full-fledged human beings with the ability to think and feel.

All over the world, parents raise their children to become productive members of their specific cultures. Parents foster the development of different values depending on their religious or cultural beliefs, as well as the requirements for survival, whether these are cooperation or obedience, dependence or independence, creativity or conformity, sharing or ownership, humility or pride. Parents also emphasize the development of social, motor, memory, language, or reasoning skills depending on what will best serve the child later in life. Parents transmit these cultural values, expectations, and skills to their babies in a myriad of ways: by how the parents respond to crying, how much they hold their babies, what kinds of stimulation they offer, how often they feed them, where the babies sleep, and how they set limits. In most cultures, these traditions are assumed to be the "natural" and correct way to treat babies.

In the traditional hunter-gatherer !Kung San culture of the Kalahari desert in Africa, parents emphasize the development of motor skills so that the children will eventually be able to walk long distances, hunt, and carry heavy loads on their backs. Consequently, anthropologists found that the !Kung babies excelled in motor coordination tests.[1] The Yequana Indian mothers in the Amazon forest of Venezuela expose their babies to different water currents at an early age. Fish is a staple of their diet, and these people are some of the best white water canoeists in the world.[2] The Gusii of East Africa stress the development of obedience and responsibility so that the children can become productive members of society and help in the fields or tend livestock at an early age.[3]

However, no culture is perfect. In most cases, the cultural values and economic constraints force parents to impose certain restrictions on their children and ignore certain legitimate needs, such as the need to express emotions, to be fully accepted, or to explore freely in a safe environment. The fact that infants survive and grow up able to carry on the culture and reproduce does not imply that their basic human needs have been met, or that they have attained their human potential for intellectual, emotional, or spiritual development.

In Western, industrialized nations, parents have traditionally emphasized the development of independence and the acquisition of linguistic and cognitive skills. The idea is that children must become intellectually competent and self-reliant in order to succeed in an increasingly competitive world. In fact, scholastic achievement tests at all levels of education reflect this cultural bias. They measure primarily vocabulary, reading comprehension, and mathematics. Speed and superficial knowledge are also emphasized, especially in the

United States. This cultural emphasis is often at the expense of the development of deep thinking, creativity, cooperation, and empathy.

Furthermore, until recently, there has been little effort in Western cultures to raise children to become non-violent. Our children are exposed to violence on a daily basis, both in real life and in the media. However, because of the powerful weapons of destruction and the easy availability of guns, raising children to be non-violent is now of primary importance for everyone's survival. We must teach children alternatives to violence for solving conflicts. We must also raise children so they will be free of pent-up rage or fear, because these emotions are so often at the root of violence. This means paying close attention to the ways they get hurt, and helping them heal from stress and trauma. *We can no longer afford to ignore how children feel.*

Our child-rearing methods must therefore change drastically if we are to raise children to be not only productive, but also non-violent, citizens of our changing world. We still need to emphasize the development of linguistic and cognitive skills for economic survival in industrialized nations, but we must also focus on emotional health and self-esteem. We need to question our assumption that independence is a virtue, and raise children to be more interdependent. They need models of democracy in action and conflict-resolution skills so they will learn how to work cooperatively with others. Perhaps most important of all, we must allow them to express their emotions and heal from trauma.

This new approach is not based only on the requirements of our particular culture. It also recognizes deep and universal human needs that must be met if babies are to grow up emotionally healthy in *any* culture. According to psychohistorian Lloyd de Mause, there has been an evolution in child rearing throughout the ages, with a gradual shift from abusive methods to an approach that trusts children's inherent goodness, involves more dialog with them, more empathy to their emotions, a tolerance of their developing will and individuality, and encouragement for creativity and independent thought.[4]

This new approach has been gradually gathering momentum since World War II. It began with the popularization of natural childbirth and gentle handling of the infant after birth. It has further manifested itself by a revival of breastfeeding, the recognition of attachment needs, and a tendency towards less authoritarian child-rearing methods. However, we need to continue questioning some of our basic assumptions and beliefs about what is best for babies.

This book describes a comprehensive, revolutionary approach to parenting from conception to two-and-a-half years of age. The seven chapters each discuss a separate topic (such as crying, sleep, food, and play), and address babies' needs in regard to that particular area. This approach, that I call "Aware Parenting," does not involve quick solutions or simplistic methods. Instead, it represents an entirely new way of being with babies based on trust, empathy, and respect. It describes how to form a deep emotional connection with your baby, and how to help your baby stay connected to her true self and grow up as a whole human being. Aware Parenting is comprised of three basic aspects: attachment-style parenting, non-punitive discipline, and acceptance of emotional release.

The recommendations in this book may be quite different from other books you have read or from your cultural assumptions about what is a "normal" or "correct" way to raise a child. I encourage you to have an open mind, even though at first you may strongly disagree with some of the material. It is normal and healthy to question what you read. On the other hand, please don't accept this approach blindly as a new dogma or "system" for raising children. It will work well only if you keep thinking creatively about what is best for you and your family.

Four Basic Assumptions

There are four basic assumptions concerning human nature underlying the ideas presented in this book.

The first assumption is that human beings are born knowing basically what they need, not only for survival, but also for optimal physical, emotional and intellectual development. As an illustration, given choices between toys, babies will play with the ones that best foster their intellectual development on any given day. The idea is that babies know and indicate what they need, and we can therefore trust them to be in charge of their own lives as much as they are physically able. Babies will communicate their needs, if given a chance, and it is the caretaker's role to interpret their signals correctly.

The second assumption is that babies are conceived with the potential for both good and bad behavior, but how they are treated determines how they will act. If babies are not hurt or oppressed, and if all their needs are met, they will be good, cooperative, intelligent, joyful people with the ability to give and receive love. People act in hurtful and stupid ways only if they are suffering from unhealed trauma.

The third assumption is that experiences early in life can have a profound and lasting effect on feelings and behavior patterns later in life. Babies are vulnerable and can be easily hurt because of their extreme dependence and lack of information. Even in the best of families, babies will experience stress and emotional pain at times. In addition to contributing to negative feelings, painful experiences early in life may also be responsible for eating disorders, sexual dysfunction, addictions, insomnia, certain learning disabilities, relationship problems, self-destructive behavior, hyperactivity, depression, and violence. Throughout this book I explain how early experiences may lead to these and other negative consequences. Although later childhood experiences are also important, the first few years are by far the most important years of a person's life.

Some people disagree with this assumption, and feel that it places too much of a burden and responsibility on parents, so they prefer to believe that much of human behavior is determined by hereditary factors. There has been an ongoing debate between proponents of the "nature" theory, who believe that behavior is determined to a great extent by genetic factors, and proponents of the "nurture" theory, who place greater importance on environmental factors such as child-rearing. Nobody knows how much of our behavior is hereditary. However, there is ample evidence to suggest that the way babies are treated has a strong influence on their feelings and behavior later in life. In fact, early environmental influences can alter the very function of the brain.[5] It is therefore important to realize that even biological correlates of behavior may not be genetic at all, but rather the result of early environmental influences (including prenatal ones) on the developing brain.

The fourth assumption of this book is that, when optimal conditions are present, babies can heal from many of the effects of stress or trauma. Babies' natural biological tendency is to strive for health and physiological balance (homeostasis). In addition to describing an approach that avoids hurting babies as much as possible, this book also describes how to help babies heal from emotional trauma if it should occur. The fact that most of us adults still suffer from the effects of early trauma does not contradict this fourth assumption. It simply implies that we were not raised in an environment that allowed us to restore emotional health.

In summary, the four assumptions underlying this book are:

1) Babies know what they need.
2) If babies' needs are met and if they are not hurt, they will be intelligent, compassionate, and non-violent
3) Babies are extremely vulnerable, and early trauma and unfilled needs can have long-lasting, negative effects
4) Babies have the ability to recover from many of the effects of stress and trauma.

How to Do the Exercises

Following each chapter, there is a series of exercises consisting of three parts: exploring your childhood, expressing your feelings about your baby, and nurturing yourself. Being a parent brings many powerful emotions and wonderful opportunities for self-growth. These exercises can help you in your own healing and growth as you strive to be the kind of parent you would like to be.

The first part, exploring your childhood, will help you make important connections with your own past. It is not enough for a book to give information or advice, because you may find it hard to put new knowledge into practice as long as you are suffering from the effects of your own hurtful childhood. Most of us still carry around some "emotional baggage" from the past when we become parents. Remembering your own childhood is a first step in your own healing process. Talking about these memories with another person is better, and releasing emotions such as sadness, fear, or anger will help you even more.

The second part, expressing your feelings about your baby, will help you become aware of any current feelings that could be preventing you from being the kind of parent you want to be. These feelings may be directly related to the insights from your own childhood. As for the first set of exercises, you will benefit from sharing these feelings with another person and releasing any painful emotions through anger or tears, if you feel the need to do so.

When you share your responses to these questions with another person, you can choose to what depth you wish to explore your emotions. You can simply talk briefly about the topics that interest you, or you can use these questions to do deeper emotional healing work. Some of the questions will probably be more meaningful to you than others, so feel free to skip around. You may also think of topics to talk about that I have missed.

When it is your turn to listen, give your partner your full, undivided attention and try to refrain from interrupting, interpreting, analyzing, offering suggestions, giving advice, consoling, asking questions for your own information, or talking about your own experiences.

The third kind of exercise consists of suggestions for ways to nurture yourself. Many people forget about their own needs when they become parents. Hopefully, these exercises will remind you that your own life and well-being are just as important as your baby's. In fact, you can never adequately meet your baby's needs as long as your own needs are unmet and your life is out of balance. So I encourage you to try some of these suggestions.

With these guidelines, I hope that the exercises following each chapter will help you grow with your baby and nurture yourself as your family strives to maintain meaningful, caring relationships with each other.

Explanations of Terms Used

This book is not intended only for mothers. In fact, as long as mothers are expected to be the sole caretakers for babies, it will be extremely difficult to fill babies' needs in the manner that I recommend. When I use the word "parents" in the book, I imply anyone who assumes a parental role, whether male or female.

The term "baby" is used as a general term for a human being who is under two-and-a-half years of age. The term "infant," refers to a baby from birth to one year of age, and the term "toddler," refers to a baby between one and two-and-a-half years of age (regardless of whether or not the baby actually walks). In order to avoid sexual biases, the sections alternate between the use of feminine and masculine pronouns when referring to babies.

CHAPTER 1

BEGINNINGS: LETTING YOUR BABY FEEL LOVED

What can I do during pregnancy to enhance my baby's development?

One does not become a parent at the birth of a baby, but rather at conception. The most important way to show love to your unborn baby is to provide a healthy physical and emotional environment. This means that it is best to eat a good diet, obtain plenty of rest, and refrain from consuming drugs that can harm your baby. It is also advisable to minimize stress and loud noises as much as possible during pregnancy.

Maternal emotions can influence babies before birth. Researchers have found that the higher a mother's stress levels during pregnancy, the greater the likelihood that her baby will be born prematurely or will have physical and emotional problems, as well as crying spells.[1] If you are depressed during pregnancy, this can affect your baby biochemically. Researchers have found that the levels of stress hormones in newborns of depressed mothers are similar to those of their mothers, indicating a physiological state of depression in the infants. These babies also cry more than other babies.[2]

Even with the best of precautions, stress and unexpected events can occur. Furthermore, pregnancy itself can bring physical problems as well as powerful, unfamiliar emotions. If you become stressed, anxious, or depressed while pregnant, for whatever reason, do not hesitate to obtain the support you need. Meditation, massages, and relaxation exercises can be helpful in reducing stress during pregnancy. It is also important to release painful emotions through talking and crying, rather than block and repress them. Try to find a supportive person who can listen to you.

There is a growing body of knowledge about prenatal learning. We now know that babies are sensitive, intelligent, and receptive to stimulation before birth.[3] Ingenious experiments have demonstrated that newborn infants recognize stories that their mothers read to them before they were born.[4] Researchers have shown that when parents provide prenatal enrichment activities, this results in infants with a larger head circumference, and enhances the babies' motor, cognitive, language, and social development after birth, compared to control groups.[5] These children continue to have a developmental lead at six years of age.

Although some people recommend a structured approach to prenatal stimulation, I do not think this is necessary. Activities can consist of singing or talking to your infant, swaying or dancing to music, patting or rubbing your abdomen to massage your baby, and pressing your abdomen in response to your infant's kicks, thereby setting up a nonverbal "dialog" with your unborn infant. Both the mother and the father can engage in these activities. Fathers can also talk softly to the infant while placing their lips on the mother's abdomen. (See Thomas Verny's book, *Nurturing the Unborn Child*).[6]

Whatever prenatal stimulation you provide, it is important to keep it simple and natural, and not overstimulate your infant or attempt to arouse it when it is sleeping. The best time to interact with your unborn infant is when you feel it actively moving. The goal should be to establish a loving relationship with your child, *not* to produce a "super baby."

Prenatal stimulation and communication not only enhance the development of cognitive systems, but also help you learn to accept your infant as a family member before birth. Some parents find it easier to establish a positive relationship with an unborn, quiet infant than with a demanding, crying infant after birth. If you can begin to build a bond with your infant before birth, this will probably make it easier for you to cope patiently with the demands of your infant after birth.

Is birth a traumatic experience for infants?

Birth is an intense, powerful, and stressful experience for every-one involved, but it need not be traumatic. If your baby has a gentle, natural birth without complications or drugs, then he may not expe-rience any long-term, traumatic effects.

However, many births do cause the baby distress. Many people fail to recognize the emotional impact of birth trauma, which can affect a child's later feelings and behavior. Studies have shown that complications at birth correlate with later susceptibility to emotional and behavioral problems, including schizophrenia, drug abuse, de-pression, suicide, and violence.[7]

Any difficulty or complication during labor or delivery can have a strong impact because the infant is not used to coping with stress-ful situations and does not understand what is happening. Birth experi-ences are especially traumatic when the infant's life is in danger. Furthermore, even when the infant does not experience trauma di-rectly, he is affected biochemically (through the placenta) by the mother's physiological stress response.

Most obstetrical interventions can be emotionally traumatic, even though they may save the infant's life. Experts on birth trauma (such as Arthur Janov and William Emerson) have observed negative psy-chological effects following the use of anesthesia, forceps and vacuum extraction, induction and augmentation of labor, and Cesarean sur-gery.[8] Psychological distress can also be caused by a premature or breech birth, diminished oxygen supply, or an abnormally long la-bor.[9] It is therefore important for medical personnel to warn parents of the potential emotional impact on the infant of these medical pro-cedures and birth complications.

Studies have shown that many children can remember their birth, and that these memories are accurate. In his book, *The Mind of Your Newborn Baby*, David Chamberlain describes actual birth memories reported by children. Furthermore, many adults can remember their birth under hypnosis.[10] So everything that happens to your infant is being recorded somewhere in his brain, and can have an impact on him.

Painful or frightening experiences immediately after birth can be just as traumatic as birth itself. The immediate postpartum period is filled with exposure to many new experiences, and newborns strive to find meaning in the chaos. They do this by searching for similarities between new sensations and familiar, old ones, because that is how the human brain functions. The newborn will never again be bombarded with so much new information at once. Whether this transition, the most challenging learning experience in life, results in pleasurable and meaningful assimilation or in confusion depends on how you handle your infant.

In the womb, infants were familiar with the sound of their mother's body (heartbeat, digestive sounds, and her voice), other muffled sounds, dim light, and constant temperature and movement. After birth, therefore, it can be frightening and overwhelming for newborns to experience coldness, brightness, stillness, rough handling, loud noises, or separation from the mother. If the mother holds her infant close, he will hear her heartbeat and voice, and feel the familiar rocking caused by her breathing. This will be reassuring. If the infant is removed from the mother's presence, he will have more difficulty making a meaningful connection with all of the new sensations. This may overload his sensory system, resulting in confusion and panic. If the mother cannot hold her infant, then the father or someone else should do so.

It is important to observe your baby closely to determine what is best for him right from the start, by responding to his cues. If he squints, the lights are too bright. If he makes sucking movements, he may be ready for his first nursing. If he is sleepy, he will fall asleep, and when he becomes hungry, he will automatically awaken. There is no need to wake a sleeping baby to feed him, unless he is under the effects of drugs. There is no single, correct postnatal procedure. Each should be unique, since every newborn is different. The important thing is to be as loving and as gentle as possible, and to avoid overstimulating your infant.

Researchers have found that physical pain experienced by infants during the neonatal period can have long-lasting effects on future development by sensitizing the infants to pain. Infant boys who had been circumcised at birth cried more during routine vaccinations at four and six months of age than those who had not been circumcised. However, they cried less if they had been treated with an anesthetic cream before the circumcision to lessen the pain (but still more than those who had not been circumcised).[11] Before deciding to circumcise your son, therefore, you should be aware of the potential long-term emotional effect on your baby of this procedure. If your religion has a tradition of male circumcision, you may wish to consider an alternative ceremony that leaves your son's penis intact.

Newborn infants are also extremely sensitive to the mood of people around them.[12] If you are disappointed in the sex of your baby, for example, of if you feel rejecting of him for any other reason, your infant will probably sense this and feel anxious and confused. If you are very fearful for your infant's survival, this fear can be contagious. You cannot control your emotional state after your baby's birth, nor can you hide this from your baby. But if you are aware of the potential impact of your emotional state on your infant, you will be in a better position to help him recover from the psychological effects on him of these early traumatic impressions.

There are many kinds of psychotherapy that can help adults recover from birth trauma and other early trauma. Fortunately, infants can heal from the psychological impact of birth trauma while they are still infants (as described in Chapter 2), and this will reduce the need for therapy later on in life. So the negative impact of a traumatic birth need not cause lifelong problems. Only those infants who do not have opportunities to heal themselves are at risk for later emotional problems.

How can I prepare for a positive birth experience?

In addition to adequate nutrition and medical care, there are several steps you can take to increase the likelihood of a positive birth experience. Classes in prepared childbirth provide training in breathing and relaxation techniques, and often eliminate the need for medication. These classes also provide useful information about labor and birth, so you will know what to expect. I highly recommended them for all expectant parents.

A woman's state of mind can affect the course of her labor. If she does not feel ready or mature enough to care for an infant, she may unconsciously prevent her body from pushing her baby out. The pain of labor contractions can trigger memories of past physical pain, such as an illness or abuse, causing her to unconsciously interpret the situation as threatening. She will then mobilize her body's defense mechanisms for danger (a stress response), and this will interfere with the progress of her labor. Giving birth can also trigger unconscious memories of a woman's own traumatic birth, leading to difficulties.[13]

Labor can also be more difficult if the woman is made to feel powerless, frightened, discouraged, or rushed. A laboring woman needs to feel in control, supported in her decisions, and allowed to do whatever she needs in order to control the pain and relax. She should be permitted to labor and push her baby out in any position she chooses.

It is therefore important to have adequate emotional support during labor. Your support people should be calm, patient, encouraging, and confident in your ability to give birth. They should be strong enough to stand up for your rights in a difficult situation, and they should trust you to know what is best. Some women want to be held during contractions, while others prefer not to be touched. In between contractions, some women find it helpful to talk, laugh, cry, or shake. Others prefer to walk around, be massaged, meditate, or quietly relax in a warm bath. These are all tension-release mechanisms that can help deal with emotional or physical pain.

In many traditional cultures, a supportive woman called a doula helps the expectant mother during pregnancy, delivery, and the postpartum period. The doula's role is to "mother the mother" by attending to her emotional and physical needs. This is a different role from that of a labor coach (who is often the father). The concept of a doula is gaining popularity in industrialized nations. Studies have shown that the presence of a doula during labor and delivery reduces the need for pain medications and enhances women's perception of birth.[14] At six weeks after delivery, doula-supported women were more likely to be breastfeeding, and they reported less depression, greater self-esteem, and a higher regard for their babies compared to mothers who did not have a doula.[15] It is therefore definitely worth having a support person during labor and the postpartum period in addition to the baby's father.

If you are planning a home birth with a midwife, you will probably have no difficulty maintaining contact with your newborn baby. If a hospital birth is planned, you can inquire about hospital policies and explain your wishes well in advance of your due date. Most doctors and hospitals are eager to please their patients and are willing to discuss delivery and postnatal procedures ahead of time, so that an agreement can be worked out. It is important not to forget the possibility of a Cesarean birth, and to agree ahead of time on postnatal procedures in the case of such an emergency. If you have a choice, a local anesthetic is preferable to a general anesthetic, so that you can see and touch your newborn infant immediately after a Cesarean birth. Some couples have a written birth plan in which they clearly state their wishes. They show this to their doctor or midwife before the birth, and discuss it with them.[16] A written plan in your medical chart is especially useful in a large hospital where nursing shifts change frequently, and where you may not know ahead of time who your obstetrician will be.

Doctors and nurses are unlikely to change their routines if their patients do not make their wishes known. Many hospitals now allow fathers in the delivery room, but it is only because parents insisted that this change came about.[17] Before my daughter's birth, I made my wishes very clear ahead of time with my doctor. I requested no medical interventions of any kind unless they were absolutely necessary. I also asked to use the birthing room in the hospital (the same room for labor and delivery), and I requested that my five-year-old son be present at the birth, as well as my husband, mother, and sister. My requests were granted, and my daughter had a beautiful birth surrounded by her family.

It is obviously more convenient and less risky for medical personnel to maintain routine procedures than to try innovations. However, if you cannot reach an agreement with your doctor, it is definitely worth looking for a different doctor or hospital, or considering a home birth. You do not want to risk having disagreeable surprises when you are in labor.

There is no reason to feel guilty if your baby had a difficult birth, or if it did not go as planned. You certainly did your best. If something made you feel powerless, angry, or frightened, you will benefit from talking about your birth experience and telling the story many times to an attentive listener. You may also need to cry or express rage in order to work through these emotions. Many mothers find that they cry easily during the postpartum period. It is important to allow yourself to release your tears.

In the following interview, a father tells about his feelings of disappointment during and after the Cesarean birth of his daughter:

> They gave Jane a Cesarean. It was an emergency. I had wanted to be there to see her born, and I was sort of left out in the hall, alone, sitting on a table. That was a big disappointment, that we weren't able to share the experience together. The pediatrician and the nurse wheeled Jennifer on a cart into the elevator and into the nursery on the next floor. So I didn't get to touch her. Then, immediately, she was behind this glass. I didn't think of asking to be able to touch her. I didn't think I had the right, or that it would be important. If we have another baby, I wouldn't allow that to happen. I would do it a lot differently. If they tried to do that, I would say something. I don't know why I didn't say anything at the time. They all seemed so efficient and I really felt like an outsider. I didn't know how to assert myself, or what I would say or who I would say it to. It didn't occur to me that I could touch her and hold her. Everything happened so fast. Furthermore, I had had no experience in holding or handling babies, and I thought they were so fragile. I thought that, being a man, I should keep my hands off and leave this to the women nurses ... I remember coming home and crying.

Although birth trauma can have a life-long impact on your baby, *the emotional impact of birth trauma is reversible* and it is possible for babies to heal emotionally while they are still infants. So if your baby had a traumatic birth, this need not damage her for life, because you have the means to help her recover. Chapter 2 describes how to recognize and assist babies' natural tendency to heal themselves.

It is important to obtain adequate rest after giving birth, and to wait until you have fully recovered before resuming your usual activities. In Western cultures, women are expected to resume normal activities quickly, and to think of giving birth as a temporary interruption and inconvenience. It is better for your health to resist this attitude and to view birth as a major physiological and emotional transition that requires many weeks of recuperation and adjustment. While making your birth plans, don't forget to plan for adequate support after the birth. Arrange for a network of people to help with cooking, cleaning, laundry, emotional support, and occasional respite from your baby. The more help and support you have, the less likely you will be to suffer from postpartum depression or health problems.

How can I bond with my infant after birth?

Bonding is the process by which a parent falls in love with his or her baby. Both parents can become very bonded to their infants. The importance of early, close contact with the newborn infant has received much attention as a potentially crucial factor in mother/infant bonding. During the first hour after birth, most babies born to undrugged mothers are in a quiet, alert state with their eyes open. Some research seems to indicate that this is a sensitive period for bonding in the human mother, similar to the sensitive periods found in mothers of certain animal species.

In an extensive study of the effects of early contact between human mothers and infants, reserchers found that mothers who had early contact with their infants after birth were more reluctant to leave their infants with another person when the infants were one month old, compared to mothers who had not had early contact with their infant. The early-contact mothers also showed more soothing behaviors when their babies cried during a physical examination, and they were more likely to look at their babies face to face and caress them more during feedings. Additional findings were that the mothers with early contact breastfed their babies longer, and the children had higher IQ's at five years of age. These researchers concluded that there is a sensitive period in the first minutes and hours after an infant's birth, which is optimal for bonding with the infant.[18]

More recent studies have shown that a crucial factor in this early bonding is whether or not the infant's lips touch the mother's nipple.[19] From an evolutionary point of view, strong maternal-infant bonding has been necessary for the survival of our species. In some animals, such as monkeys and apes, the young can cling to their mothers' fur. In others, such as ducks, the young become attached to their mother (or whatever they see first), and follow that figure around. This phenomenon is known as imprinting. In such species of animals, it is not as important for the mother to develop a strong feeling of love towards her infant to insure its survival.

Human babies, however, are extremely helpless and can neither cling to nor follow their mothers. Nature has provided another mechanism to prevent neglect of the human infant, thereby guaranteeing survival of the species. This mechanism is maternal bonding or love. It is similar to imprinting, but in reverse, because the mother is the one who becomes attached.

In the following interview, a mother described to me her feelings towards her newborn son who had been born without any drugs:

> When he was born I had a very warm feeling. I was just delighted. He was beautiful and perfect, and I held him all night and spoke to him. I felt very loving right away towards him. My pregnancy was a very positive experience and I was really sure that this was what I wanted. I was so glad he was okay. When I looked at him I was really moved by this little human being. It was hard for me to take my eyes off him. I was filled with awe and excited, and I wanted to tell everybody.

In a study of the impact of newborn infants upon their fathers, researchers found that fathers usually begin feeling a bond towards their babies during the first three days. This is characterized by feelings of preoccupation, absorption and interest in the newborn.[20]

In observations of home births, researchers have noted that people who are present during the labor and birth, whether or not they are related to the baby, become more attached to the infant than friends of the family who do not witness the birth.[21] A father's presence at the birth of his baby, therefore, is an essential factor in paternal-infant bonding. Fathers, like mothers, need to feel a sense of control during the birth of their child. If they are overpowered by events beyond their control, they will feel helpless and perhaps guilty, and have a negative impression of the birth. This could adversely affect their ability to bond with their baby.

There is evidence that contact between father and infant during the days after birth is important in further increasing the father's feelings of attachment.[22] Fathers who were asked to undress their infants twice during the first three days and to establish eye contact with them for one hour, showed more care-giving behaviors during the first three months than fathers who were not asked to do those things.

During the following interview, there were tears of emotion in the father's eyes as he talked about his feelings during and after the birth of his son. This example shows the strong bond that can occur between father and infant after a positive birth experience:

> I could see Randy's head crowning with a tuft of black hair, all wet and matted down. When he finally came out, my feeling was overwhelming. I can't describe it. Here was this event that we'd been waiting for so long. After we both held him, they put him under a bright light. I went over to him and he had his eyes closed because of the intensity of the light. I put my hand over his eyes to shade them from the light, and I sat there and looked at him. I guess I talked to him, too. Pretty soon he opened his eyes, and he just lay there and looked at me. I had an incredible feeling of communication with him that was very powerful. It went on for maybe half an hour. I had a distinct feeling that he could see me. I remember feeling a really strong attraction to him. It was a private time between us, even though we were right there in the delivery room. People were moving around near us, but I was completely oblivious to what was going on. We were just there the two of us.

It is therefore highly advisable for fathers to witness the birth and have contact with their infant during the hours and days after birth so that the bonding process can occur. This will make fathers more likely to *want* to care for their baby.

Mothers are not necessarily more bonded to their babies than are fathers, but hormonal and other physiological factors influence a mother's relationship with her baby, especially if breastfeeding, and it is definitely *different* from a father's relationship with his baby.

If you were denied contact with your infant immediately after birth, it is normal to feel sad about the fact that you missed that early opportunity to bond with your infant. However, rest assured that this will *not* automatically make you more rejecting or abusive. It takes much more than that to produce rejecting or abusive parents. Many mothers and fathers feel a strong bond towards their babies and are excellent parents even though they were denied early contact. In fact, not all researchers agree with the conclusions from the bonding research, and some studies have failed to find any negative effects resulting from lack of close contact after birth on a mother's feelings of love for her baby.[23]

Some parents experience delayed bonding when the natural, early bonding process has been disrupted. In fact, a strong bond can grow between parent and child at any point in the child's life, and the relationship always improves when this occurs. Before this attachment can be felt, however, the mother and father may need to grieve about the postnatal separation from their baby. One mother wrote: "My son was fifteen before I cried about not having him with me right after birth. It took us fifteen years to bond the way I wanted to. My sorrow was in the way, even though I had plenty of love to give."[24]

Close physical contact can help the bonding process, even if it is not immediately after birth. There is a practice called kangaroo care in hospital nurseries for premature infants. The mothers (and sometimes fathers) are asked to hold their infants in skin-to-skin contact against their chest for several hours a day. The kangaroo-care method was first developed in Colombia, and then spread to Europe and the United States. Researchers have found that mothers asked to practice kangaroo care feel more bonded to their infants, and also more competent compared to mothers whose premature infants receive traditional incubator care. The infants also benefit: they sleep longer and have fewer interruptions of breathing.[25]

Breastfeeding can also help you bond with your infant. By necessity, breastfeeding promotes close and intimate contact between mother and infant many times each day. It also contributes to a mother's feelings of attachment towards her baby by means of certain hormones. Lactating women have high levels of prolactin and oxytocin, the "mothering hormones," which cause women who nurse their babies to have a great desire for physical contact with them.[26] Furthermore, the act of nursing causes some mothers to experience pleasurable contractions of the uterus similar to mild orgasms. (It is important to know, however, that these contractions can be quite painful during the immediate postpartum period, when they serve the purpose of reducing hemorrhaging and helping the uterus return to its original size. Also, many women experience painful nipples at first. But these are usually only temporary discomforts.) Breastfeeding, like sexual intercourse, is meant to be pleasurable, because both of these activities constitute the acts of reproduction that insure continuation of the human species.

Although close contact after birth and breastfeeding can help you bond with your baby, those factors are not absolutely necessary. For many parents, knowing that their baby is biologically related to them is enough to insure a strong bond. However, even that is not necessary because many parents are able to feel a very strong bond to their adopted babies. It is clear that bonding is a complex process that does not depend on only one factor.

Babies differ from one another in several ways right from birth because of hereditary factors and prenatal experiences. These differences can have a strong influence on the parent-infant relationship. An active baby may thoroughly delight you if you yourself are an active, athletic person. But if you prefer to sit quietly and read or listen to music, you would probably feel closer to a baby who loves to spend hours calmly looking and listening. You may find it especially difficult to bond with your baby if she cries a lot or does not settle into a predictable feeding or sleeping routine.

Other factors that can influence your feelings may be the sex of your baby, your baby's physical appearance (who she looks like), and the presence of health problems or handicaps. You might need to grieve about the loss of the ideal imagined baby that you did not have. Try to find a supportive listener who will not shame you for admitting that your baby has not met your expectations.

If you feel guilty for not loving your baby enough, remember that any unloving feelings you may have are not your fault. When the entire situation is taken in account, all parents are doing their best. It is important for you to appreciate yourself and focus on your strengths as a parent. Think of how well you are taking care of your baby in spite of possible birth complications, lack of early contact, an inability to breastfeed, health problems, or other sources of stress in your life.

If you don't feel a strong bond to your infant, for whatever reason, you may think that your baby does not need or want you to hold her. This is not true. Your baby needs you very much, and you, the parent, are the most qualified person to take care of her needs. So don't withdraw from your baby. The more you hold her the more loving you will probably feel.

What does my newborn infant need?

The human species has a very large brain that requires a large skull, and this causes the human fetus to be born at an early stage in its development. The fetus could not pass through the birth canal if birth were to be postponed until the brain was larger. This would result in possible fatal consequences for both mother and infant.[27] Survival of the human species has therefore entailed the helplessness of babies at birth, to a greater extent than in most other mammals. Some paleontologists consider the first year after birth to be a period during which gestation is completed while the brain continues to grow rapidly, implying that the human species actually has a 21-month gestation rather than a nine-month one.[28] Despite the fact that newborn infants can see and hear well and are ready for social interaction, they must nevertheless rely totally on others for warmth, protection, and nourishment.

Postnatal life should therefore be considered a direct extension of prenatal life. The needs that babies have after birth reflect this developmental continuation: newborn babies thrive on any stimulation that is similar to what they experienced in the womb. These needs include warmth, stimulation of the skin, pressure against the body, movement, a heartbeat sound, the mother's voice, and nourishment from the mother's body. The best way to fill these needs is to carry babies around and to let them nurse on demand. Thus, although babies are technically separated from their mother's body once the umbilical cord is cut, they are not yet ready for a total separation from another human body. It is important to point out that it does not always have to be the mother who fills these needs. The biological mother is needed primarily to fill the infant's need for breast milk, but there is no reason why other loving people cannot help fill an infant's needs for physical contact.

NEEDS OF NEWBORNS

- Warmth
- Physical contact (touching and holding)
- Gentle movement (rocking)
- Heartbeat sound
- Mother's and father's calm voices
- Sensitive attunement from adults
- Prompt responsiveness to crying
- Breastfeeding when hungry
- Protection from overstimulation

During the years of human prehistory, mothers probably carried their babies most of the time. In fact, our very early pre-human ancestors probably clung to their mothers in the same way that baby monkeys and apes cling to their mothers. Modern human infants have two reflexes during the first few months that may be remnants of such clinging: the Moro reflex and the palmar grasp reflex. If the baby is frightened or jolted, his arms curve around in a sudden gripping motion (Moro reflex). The palmar grasp reflex is elicited by placing an object in the infant's hands. Both reflexes can be elicited simultaneously. When infants formerly clung to their mother's fur, any sudden movement would have triggered these two reflexes, causing the infants to grip tighter, thereby reducing the likelihood of being dislodged. This had obvious survival value. With the loss of fur, human babies can no longer cling to their mothers. Instead, strong parental bonding insures that babies receive the human contact and protection they need for their survival.

Studies of infants in institutions have shown that individual mothering care is essential for survival. In 1915, ninety percent of the infants in Baltimore orphanages died within a year of admission.[29] In the 1940's a third of infants in United States orphanages were still dying in spite of good food and meticulous medical care. During this period, child-rearing methods in the United States were influenced by the leading expert of the time, Dr. Luther Holt, who warned of the dangers of holding babies too much.

Infants in these institutions who survived often failed to grow normally, a condition known as "deprivation dwarfism." Scientists now believe that infants who fail to grow (or who die), even though they are receiving adequate food and health care, are suffering from the effects of prolonged stress caused by lack of physical contact.

Researchers have discovered some of the mechanisms by which stress inhibits growth.[30] One of the hormones secreted during stress is cortisol. This serves the purpose of mobilizing energy reserves to help the body defend itself in case of physical danger. But in the long run, excessive amounts of cortisol are counterproductive, because it also inhibits growth and lowers the immune response. This helps to explain the high mortality rate in orphanages with inadequate mothering care.

Other studies have shown that bottle-fed infants who are held during feedings digest their milk better than those who are not held.[31] This is another contributing factor to the phenomenon of "deprivation dwarfism" in institutionalized infants, who are often propped up with a bottle for feeding because of insufficient staff.

Inhibition of growth is only part of the problem for children who survive these institutions. It has been known for decades that children raised in insufficiently staffed institutions with very little physical contact show developmental delays in cognitive and social skills.[32] This is caused partly by another side effect of the stress hormone, cortisol. In excessive amounts it can damage a part of the brain called the hippocampus, leading to impairments in learning and memory. Romanian orphans who have suffered from severe neglect have high levels of cortisol, and the children with the highest levels of cortisol have the lowest levels of language, motor, and social skills.[33]

In addition to elevated cortisol levels, animal researchers have discovered many changes in the brains of infant mammals that are separated from their mothers, including a decrease in certain neurotransmitters (catecholamines and serotonin), and a decrease in the number of opiate receptors.[34] It is likely that early experiences of neglect (with insufficient holding and mothering care) can cause a permanent shift in neurobiological systems in human infants, making them vulnerable to depression, anxiety, drug abuse, and perhaps even violence later on.

In societies where adults frequently touch, hold, and carry the infants, there is generally less violence than in societies where infant care is restricted to merely feeding, bathing, and changing diapers.[35] Jean Liedloff lived with the Yequana Indians of Venezuela, and attributed their peacefulness as adults to the practice of filling their babies' early needs for being held. In her book, *The Continuum Concept*, she wrote of the first year after birth as the "in-arms phase" of development during which infants have an innate, biological expectation for continuous physical contact and mothering.[36]

In the following sections, the various early needs are discussed separately and in greater detail.

How can I best fill my infant's need for touch, rocking, and a heartbeat sound?

A baby's sense of touch is fully developed long before birth. The baby's skin was constantly stimulated and massaged by the amniotic fluid in the womb, and, through that, by the uterine wall. Stimulation of the skin is one of the first means by which an infant becomes aware of her own body. Being touched is essential for a baby to develop a sense of reality of her own existence. It literally brings babies to life. Skin stimulation can take many different forms, including touching, holding, patting, caressing, massaging, and nursing.

Studies have shown that touching can dramatically affect the development of infants. In one experiment, institutionalized infants were touched for two ten-minute periods for ten days, in addition to their usual routine care. They made better progress in areas such as language and social development than infants who did not receive this extra handling.[37]

Premature infants can also benefit immensely from being touched. In another study, premature infants who received ten days of extra touching (for three fifteen-minute periods a day) gained weight nearly 50% faster than premature infants who did not receive this extra touching (the control group). Interestingly, the number of feedings and calorie intake was the same for both groups.[38] Researchers have also discovered that the cortisol levels of premature infants decrease during massages, indicating that touching has an immediate beneficial physiological effect on the body.[39]

Touching and holding can also reduce the effect of pain. Infants who were held by their mothers in whole body, skin-to-skin contact during a standard heel lance procedure cried significantly less than infants who were not held.[40]

During the first few months, babies benefit from being lovingly caressed or stroked over their entire bodies. From about three months of age until the baby can roll over or crawl, deeper massages are a wonderful way to provide tactile stimulation. The book *Loving Hands* by Leboyer describes how to massage babies of this age.[41] After your baby learns to crawl, she may no longer want to lie still for very long, but you can still offer to massage or caress her if she lets you. You can also continue to provide plenty of holding and cuddling. No child is ever too big for a cuddle. People need to be touched and held throughout their lifetime.

Some people unknowingly touch babies in ways that make the baby feel powerless, for example by tickling or playful pinching. Although babies often laugh when tickled, this could be an indication of mild fear rather than pleasure. Most young babies react to tickling by tensing their bodies, squirming, pulling up their legs and swiping with their arms in an attempt to get away or to remove the person's hand. Their reaction is quite different when they are lovingly caressed: the whole body relaxes with pleasure. It is important to take cues from babies and to let them be the guide to appropriate touching. (See Chapter 5 for more on tickling.)

The art of aware touching is not easy for those adults who were deprived of physical contact during their own infancy. Very few adults received enough aware touching as infants. Perhaps you were left for long periods of time with no human contact, only to be followed by unaware touching, rough handling, or even sexual abuse. If so, you may find it difficult to relate physically to your infant in a loving, supportive way, and you may feel anxiety or even repulsion at the sight of your infant's helpless, naked body. It is important to be aware of these feelings and look for connections with your own past so you will be able to touch your own infant lovingly.

In the past in some cultures, mothers used to immobilize their infants for many months after birth by binding them tightly with long strips of cloth. This practice, called swaddling, is now considered to be unnecessary and even harmful. However, some newborn infants seem to enjoy being wrapped up tightly in a blanket, which is a modern form of swaddling. In the womb towards the end of pregnancy, babies do not have much room to move around, and they become accustomed to the pressure of the uterine wall against their body. After birth, many newborn infants panic when confronted with the unfamiliar freedom of space. Pressure against their bodies accompanied by some restriction of limb movements seems to help them feel more secure. Experiments have shown that swaddled infants (who are wrapped in a blanket) from two to five days of age remain calmer and have a lower heart rate under stressful stimulation than unswaddled infants.[42]

Some babies do not like to be wrapped up tightly, however, and even those who do enjoy it at first eventually yearn for more freedom of movement. It is important for infants to be free to move and develop motor skills. Babies who are wrapped tightly in blankets against their will may develop problems later on. Any later confinement situation, such as sitting in an airplane seat, may trigger early memories of being restricted, and the person may panic. Tight wrapping should therefore be discontinued as soon as your baby objects to it. Instead, you can provide a sense of security and gentle pressure by holding her closely against your own body.

Before birth babies experience continual movement because, even when the mother is asleep, her breathing gently rocks them. Rocking babies is an ancient practice that has been shown experimentally to be beneficial, especially for premature infants. Studies have shown that gentle rocking of premature infants results in better neuromuscular development, and helps to regulate breathing.[43]

Even for full-term infants, a certain amount of movement stimulation (also known as "vestibular stimulation") is beneficial.[44] Rocking, swinging, dancing, romping, and bouncing are all ways of providing vestibular stimulation, and babies normally love to be handled in these ways. It is also beneficial to give babies opportunities to adjust their bodies to the pull of gravity when held in various positions. Babies will benefit most from vestibular stimulation if you offer it at times when they are happy and alert. When babies are crying, they usually benefit more from other kinds of attention (as described in Chapter 2).

The sound of a heartbeat is a continual stimulus before birth and appears to be important for infants after birth. In one study, researchers found that an artificial heartbeat sound at 72 beats per minute improved weight gain and reduced crying in newborn infants compared to a control group that did not hear a heartbeat sound. But when the heartbeat frequency was speeded up to 128 beats per minute, the infants cried more than those in the control group! The study also showed that both right- and left-handed mothers tend to hold their babies more on the left side than on the right.[45] Perhaps women do this unconsciously so that the babies will benefit by hearing their mother's heartbeat.

Modern infants in Western cultures spend a considerable amount of time in cribs, infant seats, or playpens. This does not adequately meet their needs for touch, movement, or a heartbeat sound. The best way to fill these needs is to hold or carry your baby much of the time, both when she is awake and asleep. There are many different kinds of baby carriers available for sale that allow you to "wear" your baby comfortably.

How should I talk to my infant?

In addition to these physical needs for touch and movement, infants also become aware of themselves and the world by looking at and listening to those around them. Infants benefit from seeing the faces of their delighted parents, and hearing loving voices speaking to them (even though they may not understand the meanings of the words at first). One of the most important skills for the human species is communication competence, and infants have an inborn tendency to seek social interaction. They actively attempt to engage their parents in reciprocal communication by looking at them, moving excitedly, vocalizing, and, after six to eight weeks of age, smiling at them. In research studies where the mothers were asked to be unresponsive, their three-month-old infants quickly became distressed.[46]

In those traditional, tribal cultures, where infant mortality rates have been very high, the parents speak to their infants very little. Instead, the parents strive to keep their infants calm and well fed, with a minimum of stimulation until the vulnerable period of infancy has passed.[47] The top priority in these cultures is to insure the infants' survival. In Western cultures, probably because of lower infant mortality rates, parents usually strive for meaningful communication right from the start, by talking to their babies and responding to their cues for social interaction.

Infants begin to understand what we say long before they can respond with words. At first, however, the pitch, volume, and rhythm of your voice are more important than the actual words you use. Sensitive attunement involves mirroring your baby's level of excitation in your own movements and voice, and then respecting his need for a lower level of stimulation if he stops responding or looks away.

Newborn infants can recognize their mother's voice, and prefer it to the voice of other women.[48] This is not surprising because they have been hearing their mother's voice in the womb. Adults of both sexes spontaneously use a higher pitched voice and simpler sentences when speaking to infants than when speaking to older children or other adults. People intuitively know that infants will attend better this way. Your baby will learn best if you use simple, but correct sentences, such as "Are you hungry?" or "Do you hear the music?" or "I love you." If you don't know what to say to your baby, you can talk about what you are doing.

Routines such as diaper changes, bathing, dressing, and feeding offer important opportunities for social interaction. It is important and helpful to explain to your infant what you are going to do. If it is time for a diaper change, you can say, "It's time to change your diaper, so I'm going to pick you up now. Okay, let's get this dirty diaper off. Can you pull your leg out of that? Oh dear, it looks like you have a rash. I'll put some soothing lotion on your bottom. Maybe that will feel better now. Here's a clean diaper for you..." and so on. This approach not only helps infants develop language skills, but it also makes them feel like a respected partner during the caretaking routines, and they will be more likely to cooperate.

You can also sing to your infant, as this is an important form of stimulation. Even if you don't consider yourself to be a good singer, your baby will probably love being sung to. Just sing whatever tunes come to mind, with or without words. In addition to helping you bond with your infant and communicate your love, music can help your baby relax, and it can drown out other sounds that may startle or overstimulate your infant. It is also possible that the rhythms inherent in music help babies develop some of the cognitive skills necessary for learning mathematics.

Whatever you say or sing to your infant, the important thing is that he hears your voice. This will enhance his emotional and intellectual development.

Should I worry about "spoiling" my baby?

The notion of spoiling is all too prevalent. It is impossible to spoil a baby. Some parents have been led to think that babies must learn to be alone part of the time, and that they must not be overindulged so they will become independent. The parents fear that too much loving and cuddling will only make babies want more. They are afraid their babies will become demanding monsters who do not give the parents a minute of peace. This reasoning is completely backwards. Babies ask for only as much as they need. When a need has been filled, they are content.

In an interesting study of mother-infant interaction, researchers found that infants whose mothers held them for long periods of time during the first three months tended to be fairly independent by the end of the first year. Although they enjoyed being held, they did not mind being put down, and were able to play independently at times. On the other hand, infants who were held for only brief periods at the beginning showed ambivalence towards the end of the first year. They did not seem to enjoy being held very much, yet protested when put down, and did not readily play independently.[49] It is clear from this study that those infants who were acting spoiled were the ones who had not been held enough.

What about responding to crying? Child-rearing "experts" used to warn parents not to go to their babies every time they cried for fear of producing "spoiled" and demanding children. Many people still believe that one must not reinforce crying behavior because they fear that the baby will only cry more and more just to get attention. They claim that if you ignore some of the crying, the crying behavior will eventually decrease. This is precisely what happens with insti-tutionalized infants whose demands are never responded to. They stop crying altogether. They also become extremely passive, retarded in almost all aspects of development, and they fail to form healthy attachments. They are the prototype of human beings who have given up.[50]

In family-reared babies, researchers have found that mothers who were the most prompt and responsive had babies who became less fussy and demanding, but not at all passive. Instead, the babies de-veloped other modes (besides crying) of communicating their needs at an early age.[51]

There are several reasons why it is extremely important to fill all of a baby's needs promptly when she cries. During the first few years of life, babies form an opinion of themselves, other people, and the world in general. A baby whose cries are ignored may come to be-lieve that the world is unpredictable, and that she cannot reliably count on other people to meet her needs. She may grow up never fully able to trust anybody. She may also learn that she has no power to determine what happens to her, and may grow up feeling power-less and helpless, as well as unworthy, unlovable, or unimportant. If, on the other hand, someone responds to her every time she cries, she will develop a basic sense of trust, and feelings of powerfulness and self-esteem.

Babies do not try to manipulate their parents, and have no con-cept of power struggles. All they know is that they have needs, and that, when they cry, somebody either comes or does not come. When babies do not receive a response to their cries, they are totally unable to interpret the situation in terms of other people's motives, for ex-ample, "My mother really loves me, but is feeling tired today." All they can do is understand from their own point of view, and draw conclusions about themselves ("I am not important," "I have no power," "Nobody loves me."). Thus, to ignore a baby's cries is to give her incorrect information about herself on which her whole fu-ture outlook will be based.

Some parents, in an attempt to spare their baby needless frustra-tion and effort, try to anticipate their baby's needs. They feed her before she gets hungry, turn her over before she indicates any dis-comfort, and offer her toys before she reaches for them. It is true that babies whose needs are always anticipated may rarely become frus-trated. But unfortunately such babies will miss opportunities for de-veloping a sense of their own powerfulness. They will not readily learn to form a link between their own actions and external events. The best way that babies learn this is by having people respond to their needs *after* they have indicated a need.

When parents are extremely sensitive to their babies' signals, and keep them close to their own bodies, the babies may not cry at all to indicate their needs. They will learn to communicate with subtle movements and grunts, as the following example illustrates:

> When my son was an infant, he slept in a separate bassinet, and I would be awakened in the night by his crying for his night feedings. However, when my daughter was born five years later, she slept in physical contact with me right from the start, and never cried for a night feeding. I would be eased out of my sleep by her gentle and eager grunting noises, and I would feel her squirming and rooting

around for my breast. She learned that eager grunting noises obtained what she wanted. This carried over to daytime feedings as well. I did not anticipate her needs, but neither did I wait for a full-blown cry.

It may well be that crying for a present need, such as food, occurs only when the baby's more subtle signals have been ignored. Crying then occurs because of frustration, impatience, and discomfort, as the baby feels the need more acutely.

It is important to realize, however, that not all crying indicates an immediate need, and this can be frustrating and confusing for parents. Babies also use crying as a way to release stress, often at the end of the day. But in either case, you will not spoil your baby if you pick her up whenever she cries, because she needs your prompt responsiveness and attention, whatever the reason for the crying might be. (See Chapter 2 for more on crying.)

What about my own needs?

Babies do not need to be held or touched all the time, but they do require a considerable amount of holding and attention, especially during the first half year. Many mothers and fathers do not feel like giving their babies as much tender loving care as they need. There are several possible reasons for this.

A possible cause for resentment may be that your baby interferes more than expected with your career, lifestyle, or other relationships. Another reason may be that you did not have a chance to bond well with your baby because of circumstances at birth. Fatigue from childbearing and working, combined with lack of sleep, can also contribute to an inability to give your baby as much attention as he needs, as can depression or anxiety.

A major reason, however, is probably the fact that most of us did not receive enough tender loving care when *we* were babies. Having to give constantly to our babies is tremendously difficult because many of us are still longing for the loving parents we never really had. This, of course, is through no fault of our own.

All parents can therefore benefit from exploring their own past unmet needs for closeness and attention. If you suspect that caring for your baby is triggering some unmet needs from your own childhood, you can try the following exercise. Hold your baby and try to become aware of any emotions that are interfering with complete delight and love. These may include resentment, anger, anxiety, grief, or guilt. (An effective way to do this exercise would be to have another adult present who can support and listen to you.) Here is my own experience:

> I experienced a strong bond to my infant at birth, and I naturally wanted to be physically close to him and to hold and touch him, but when I did so, I would be overwhelmed by tremendous grief. I am the youngest of three children very close in age, and I was held and touched very little as a baby. The grief I felt while holding my infant was for my own unmet infant need to be held. But I was determined not to treat my baby the same way I myself had been treated. So I held him anyway, even though I would occasionally burst into tears when I felt my deep love for him.

Another reason why parenting can be difficult is that many parents do not have enough help from others. Caring for a baby is an extremely demanding job, and no one person can be expected to give good quality attentive care to an infant all day long (and at night too!). The desire to have time away from your baby does not imply that you are a rejecting parent. Women are often expected to be the sole caretakers for their babies. This places a tremendous burden on women, because caring for a baby is an extremely demanding job. If you feel overburdened or exhausted, it is therefore important to find some respite away from your baby.

However, getting help does not necessarily mean that you must separate from your baby. Perhaps part of the problem may be that you are feeling isolated from other adults. Another valuable form of help is therefore to have someone give you companionship and support while you care for your baby. It is important to remember that we are a social species, and we evolved in family clans where no woman was ever left alone with her baby. If you do not have an extended family nearby or a group or friends or neighbors, then you will probably benefit from a community program such as a playgroup or discussion group for new parents.

If you are working at a job outside the home, you may feel torn between wanting to spend time with your baby and wanting time just for yourself. There is no simple solution, but don't hesitate to ask for as much help and support as you need. Try to avoid being a "super" mom (or dad)! You don't have to be perfect. Also, be sure you have your priorities straight. Is an outside job really something you need to do right now? Or can it wait a year or two until your child is older?

EXERCISES TO DO BEFORE THE BIRTH

Explore your childhood.

1. Tell everything you know about your own mother's pregnancy and your own birth. How do you feel about the way you were born?
2. What memories do you have associated with doctors, hospitals, and physical pain?

Express your feelings about your baby.

1. How do you feel about the way your baby was conceived?
2. What feelings do you have towards your unborn child (tenderness, worry, resentment, love, etc.)? Talk about any negative feelings with someone else, or write them in a journal (but try not to direct them towards your baby). Caress your abdomen and try to visualize your unborn child. Talk to your child and welcome him/her into your life.

Nurture yourself.

1. Do one thing every day to pamper yourself and relax, such as obtaining a massage, walking in nature, meditating, a taking a relaxing bath.
2. If you are very stressed or anxious, for whatever reason, find someone to listen to you while you talk, cry, or figure out a way to reduce stress in your life.

EXERCISES TO DO AFTER THE BIRTH

Explore your childhood.

1. Do you have memories of being held lovingly as a little child? Were you held enough? Who do you wish had held you more?
2. Does your baby remind you of anyone from your past (for example, a younger sibling, yourself as a baby, your mother, father, a grandparent, or in-laws)? How is your baby similar? How is he or she different? What expectations do you have about your baby's personality or your relationship with your baby because of this resemblance?

Express your feelings about your baby.

1. Recount the birth of your baby with all the details that you can remember, and spend extra time on anything that was painful, frightening, or made you feel angry or powerless. How do you feel towards your baby because of your birth experience (for example, guilty, angry, resentful, or worried)?
2. In general, how do you feel towards your baby (loving, resentful, anxious, indifferent, etc.)? What pleases you the most about your baby? What displeases you the most? How do you feel during each of the following caretaking situations: holding, feeding, changing diapers, bathing, dressing, or undressing your baby?

Nurture yourself.

1. How have you been feeling since your baby was born (exhausted, depressed, elated, serene, etc.)? Talk about your feelings with a supportive listener, or write them in a journal. Allow yourself to have a good cry from time to time. If you are very depressed, be sure to obtain professional help.
2. Try to find enough help and support from other people. If you need time away from your baby, be sure to ask for that. But if you would benefit more from help with shopping, cooking, house cleaning, or laundry, don't be afraid to ask for that as well, as this will allow you to spend more relaxed time with your baby.

CHAPTER 2

CRYING: LETTING YOUR BABY RELEASE TENSIONS

Why does my baby cry even when all her needs are met?

During the first three months, infants in Western cultures cry on the average of two hours a day for no apparent reason. The amount of crying typically peaks around six weeks of age, and is more common in the evening. After the first three months, the average amount of crying is about one hour a day throughout the first year, although there are wide variations in the amount of crying at all ages.[1]

These infant crying patterns are fairly universal. Anthropologists have observed this same phenomenon in the !Kung infants of Africa, a hunter-gatherer society, although the total amount of crying was less.[2] Other researchers observed that babies in a small rural town in India cried as much as babies in London, with a similar peak at around six weeks of age.[3] These observations are interesting in view of the fact that maternal responses to crying differ greatly between Western and non-Western cultures.

Some babies cry more than two hours a day. In a survey done in England, 29% of mothers reported that their infants had cried more than three hours in a 24-hour period during the first three months. Twenty percent reported being upset by their baby's crying, and 21% had sought the advice of a health professional.[4] The term "colic" is generally used for extensive crying during the first three months. It is defined as irritability, fussing, or crying lasting for a total of more than three hours a day, on more than three days in any week.[5] In Western cultures, 20% to 25% of babies meet this criterion at around six weeks of age, and those who cry extensively at six weeks also cry more than average at five months of age.[6]

Traditional explanations for extensive crying in infants focus primarily on possible physiological causes. The most common of these explanations is that babies cry because of abdominal pain caused by an immature digestive system. The expression "three-months colic" is used to describe the phenomenon of extensive crying occurring during the first three months when the digestive system is assumed to be immature.

However, researchers have failed to find any gastrointestinal disorder in most babies who cry extensively.[7] Furthermore, these babies often prosper and gain weight, in spite of hours of crying,[8] hardly what one would expect from a marginally functional digestive system. To further counter this "colic" theory, not all babies stop crying after three months of age. It seems unlikely that the digestive system would still be immature at nine months, when many infants still cry for an hour or more a day. The explanation of crying being the result of pain due to an immature digestive system is therefore inadequate.

Another theory for colic is that infants cry because of an allergic reaction or sensitivity to something in the milk. When infants are bottle-fed, an immediate suspect is an allergy to cow's milk protein. This possibility should be considered in all cases of extensive crying. Switching from cow's milk to a hypoallergenic formula milk has resulted in less crying for some "colicky" infants.[9]

Some mothers report that their breastfed babies cry less when the mothers eliminate certain foods from their own diets. The most commonly cited foods are cow's milk, caffeine, alcohol, eggs, nuts, citrus fruits, legumes, onions, broccoli, strawberries, grapes, and wheat.

If your baby cries a lot, first have a pediatrician examine him to eliminate a possible milk allergy or other medical condition. If there are no physical problems detectable by medical tests, you can then try eliminating certain foods from your diet if you are breastfeeding. If your baby cries less, however, be careful not to fall prey to superstitious behavior, depriving yourself needlessly of some food item. Unless you reintroduce the food back into your diet as a test, you will never be certain that your consumption of the food actually caused the crying in the first place. Remember that most babies begin to cry less after two months of age, regardless of what you do.

In addition to the physiological theories of crying, there is also a psychosocial theory. Proponents of this theory claim that babies cry because their mothers lack love or confidence, or are anxious or hostile. Although researchers in the 1950's found a correlation between mothers' lack of confidence and the amount of crying by their infants,[10] it is quite likely that a mother's lack of confidence or anxiety could be the *result* of having a crying baby, rather than the cause, as more recent studies seem to suggest.[11] In fact, researchers in London have found that persistent infant crying in the early months often occurs in spite of high quality maternal care. In most cases, therefore, the crying is probably not caused by inadequate parenting.[12]

If these traditional explanations for extensive crying during infancy are unsatisfactory, then why do healthy babies cry? Many people are baffled by infant crying because they assume that crying is always caused by an immediate need or discomfort. This assumption is incorrect. Crying can also be an important stress-release mechanism, a way to reduce tensions caused by past trauma or an accumulation of stress.

It is therefore important to distinguish two main functions of crying during infancy. The primary function is to communicate immediate needs and discomforts that require a caretaking intervention, such as feeding, holding, a diaper change, a different position, or an extra blanket. The secondary function is that of stress-release mechanism. Infants sometimes cry for long stretches of time even though they have no immediate need other than to be held and loved. They are releasing pent-up tensions through crying, and this helps them to relax. Brazelton supports this theory by writing, "The cyclic timing of ... crying periods, plus the infant's 'determination' to cry them out, are strong evidence to me that he is expressing some inner need to cry or let off tension."[13]

William Frey, a biochemist, has studied the chemical composition of human tears, and has detected the presence of certain hormones and neurotransmitters (specifically ACTH and catecholamines). These substances play an important role in the stress response, preparing the body to defend itself physically in case of danger. After the stressful event is over, these chemicals would maintain the body in a state of needless tension and arousal. Frey has suggested that the purpose of shedding tears when we cry may be to eliminate these chemicals from the body, and thereby restore our chemical balance (homeostasis).[14]

During a crying spell, an infant's heart rate increases. However, on closer examination, researchers have found that, following a frightening event (such as the sudden appearance of a stranger wearing a mask), a baby's heart rate increases *before* the onset of crying. This indicates that physiological arousal comes first, and is then followed by crying.[15]

Researchers have also measured physiological changes after crying in adults, and have found that there is a greater reduction in blood pressure, pulse rate, and body temperature after crying than after the same length of time engaged in vigorous exercise. The brain waves are also more synchronous after crying, indicating a relaxed state.[16] The conclusion from these studies is that crying serves to reduce tension.

Although infants cry from birth on, they typically do not shed tears until they are several weeks old. However, they do sweat considerably and exert energy, often appearing to be very relaxed and content after a good cry. Crying to release stress is probably as important for healthy development as eating, sleeping, or being held. A mother I interviewed described the crying of her baby during the first few months:

> The first two months he cried a lot. Every night at roughly 6 or 7 o'clock he began to cry, and he cried from one to three hours solid. He would close his eyes really tightly and clench his fists and he'd cry like that really hard for half an hour or so. Then he'd open his eyes and look around and look up; then he'd close them again tightly and get back into some real hard crying, just crying, crying, crying. Then he'd stop in a little while, look up and around, then go back into it again. He wouldn't be interested in food during those crying spells. Usually he would just cry, or else he would nurse and cry, but the crying was the predominant thing. We noticed that at the end of these crying sessions, he was so relaxed. He would unclench his fists and his eyes would relax. Either he would be really alert and awake, but calm and relaxed at the same time, or else he would just fall asleep. There was a real change in him after this crying.

It is extremely unlikely that evolution would have spent millions of years perfecting a process that is useless and purposeless. Although crying probably evolved as a signaling system to keep the mother nearby, thereby guaranteeing sufficient warmth, protection, and nourishment, continued crying by well-fed infants in their mothers' arms serves another purpose. Frey points out that none of the other excretions from the human body are purposeless. Exhaling, urinating, defecating, and sweating all serve a definite purpose, so why wouldn't the excretion of tears? Crying would not exist as a reaction to stress and trauma unless it served a definite function enhancing our well-being and survival.[17]

TWO REASONS FOR CRYING IN BABIES

1. Communication: the baby needs something
- holding
- food
- stimulation, etc.

Parent's role: try to fill your baby's need as accurately and promptly as possible.

2. Healing: the baby has been stressed
- physical hurts
- emotional hurts

Parent's role: Eliminate source of hurt, reduce stress, hold your baby lovingly, and allow the crying to continue.

What kind of stress causes babies to cry?

It is tempting to think of infancy as a stress-free stage of life. However, this is far from the truth. Because of their helplessness and lack of experience, babies are extremely sensitive, vulnerable, and easily stressed, even with the best of parenting.

Researchers use the amount of cortisol present in the saliva of infants as a measure of stress. During stressful events, the pituitary gland produces large amounts of a hormone called ACTH (adreno-corticotropic hormone). This, in turn, stimulates the adrenal cortex to produce another hormone, cortisol, that plays a crucial role in helping the body mobilize energy resources to cope with stressful or threatening events. Cortisol levels are high in infants at birth and during the immediate postpartum period. The amount of cortisol then gradually declines until about six months of age, after which there is very little change (except for daily fluctuations).[18] This implies that infants are very stressed at birth, and become gradually less stressed.

SOURCES OF STRESS FOR BABIES

- Prenatal stress
- Birth trauma
- Unfilled needs
- Overstimulation
- Developmental frustrations
- Physical pain
- Frightening events (e.g. loud noises, separa-
  tion from parents, parental stress)

These high stress levels help to explain why most infants have crying spells that are unrelated to any apparent cause. Researchers have found that crying itself does not activate the stress response in infants (as measured by cortisol levels), whereas other factors do, such as medical interventions and separations from the mother.[19]

Crying is therefore the result of stress, rather than the cause. The goal, therefore, is not to stop the crying, but to look for ways to prevent stress, thereby reducing your baby's *need* to cry.

There are six major categories of stress during infancy that can cause babies to cry. These are: 1) prenatal stress and birth trauma, 2) unfilled needs, 3) overstimulation, 4) developmental frustrations, 5) physical pain, and 6) other frightening experiences.

Prenatal stress and birth trauma

As mentioned in Chapter 1, researchers have found that maternal stress levels during pregnancy correlate with the amount of crying in the infant. Studies have shown that newborns born to mothers who had been anxious or depressed during pregnancy cried more than infants born to mothers who were not anxious or depressed.[20] In one survey, almost half of the mothers whose babies cried extensively reported having been under considerable ongoing stress during pregnancy. These stresses included living in poverty, frequently quarreling with a spouse, caring for a dying parent, being pressured to have an abortion, or excessive worrying about the baby. None of the mothers whose babies cried less frequently reported any unusual stress during pregnancy.[21]

Crying also correlates with birth trauma. Babies whose mothers experienced a difficult delivery tend to cry more than babies whose mothers had a more pleasant delivery. In one survey, mothers whose babies cried the most were significantly more likely to have had obstetrical interventions or made to feel powerless during birth.[22] Others studies have shown that babies who have experienced birth complications have longer crying spells at three months of age and are more likely to wake up crying frequently at night during the first 14 months.[23]

The extensive crying that occurs in babies following a traumatic pregnancy or birth can be considered a biological stress-release mechanism. It allows excess chemicals to be excreted from the body (through sweat and eventually tears), and also provides a release of energy, resulting in deep relaxation. If the birth trauma was severe, the baby may have long crying spells every day for several months before the trauma is completely resolved and homeostasis is attained.

A mother reported to me how she helped her baby release birth trauma:

> My son had periods each day when he cried a lot, but there was no
> medical problem. One morning, when my son was four months
> old, I was doing my usual morning activities. All of his needs had
> been met: he had comfortable clothes, had recently nursed and
> burped, and I was carrying him around. He started to fuss and then
> to cry. I sat down with him on the rug in the warmth from our
> southern window. I held him so he could see my face, and I smiled
> and nodded my head, telling him that he was doing a great job of
> crying. After a few minutes, his crying started to taper off. I thought
> about his birth trauma and gently laid my hand on the part of his
> head where the metal vacuum extractor had bulged out his scalp
> and had even caused a significant laceration. (It all had visibly healed
> in a couple of weeks after birth.) While my fingers were on his
> head, his crying exploded forth once again. We did this ebb and
> flow about four or five times, lasting a total of 45 minutes. I felt
> very deeply connected to him during this time, and I was crying
> too, tears of joy and sadness. He fell into a deep sleep and woke up
> about an hour later, so alert and happy for the rest of the day. And
> from that day on, his crying episodes were markedly shorter.

Unfilled needs

A second source of stress during infancy results from unmet
needs, specifically the need to be touched and held, as described in
Chapter 1. The more babies are held, the less they cry. In one study,
researchers asked a group of mothers to carry their infants an extra
two hours per day, while another group (the control group) was asked
to provide more visual stimulation for two hours per day. The mothers who had carried their infants more reported one hour less crying
per day at six weeks of age than the control group.[24]

If a baby has had insufficient touching and holding, he may need
to cry to release the emotional pain resulting from the early, unmet
needs. This can be confusing to parents, because such babies often
continue to cry even though they are being held. Some parents interpret this crying as an indication that the baby does not want to be
held. This is probably not the case. I recommend holding babies as
much as possible, even if they continue to cry while being held, because holding creates the emotional safety that allows babies to heal.

Babies who are adopted from foster homes or orphanages often suffer from early deprivations, as well as from the trauma of multiple separations. It is common for these babies to begin having long crying spells after they are adopted into loving families. Although difficult for the adoptive parents, this is usually a good sign that the baby feels secure enough to begin a beneficial healing process.

Overstimulation

Every day babies are exposed to an overwhelming number of new sensations that have little or no meaning to them. Over a hundred years ago, the psychologist William James described the newborn's world as follows: "The baby, assailed by eyes, ears, nose, skin, and entrails all at once, feels it all as one great blooming, buzzing confusion."[25] Newborn infants attempt to make sense of these new experiences, but when they fail to do so, become easily overwhelmed and upset. Overstimulation occurs when the infant cannot make a meaningful connection between new information and familiar experiences. Most of the information that young babies take in is of this nature because of their limited experiences.

Appropriate stimulation is vital for optimal development, but more stimulation is not necessarily better. Premature infants, those who were stressed prenatally, and those who are more sensitive by nature are especially vulnerable to overstimulation, which can cause increased crying. Research with premature infants has found that stimulation similar to the womb experience (gentle rocking and a heartbeat sound) is the most beneficial, whereas stimulation that is different from the womb experience (loud noises and bright lights) is most likely to be overstimulating.[26] This is probably also true for infants born at term (as described in Chapter 1). Dr. Brazelton has observed that fussy periods tend to occur after active efforts by infants to maintain alert and responsive states, and he wrote: "This period of active fussing could be seen both as a period for discharging overstimulation and reorganization toward homeostasis."[27] Studies have shown that reducing stimulation reduces infant crying.[28]

In many traditional cultures, there is a period after childbirth, sometimes lasting several weeks, during which the new mother stays with her newborn in a quiet, dark place, while other women tend to her needs. This special time protects the newborn from overstimulation and allows the mother to bond with her infant, while recovering from the birth. We would do well in Western cultures to provide newborns with similar protection from overstimulation.

If your baby cries a lot, I strongly advise you to look for ways to minimize stimulation. It is common for babies to fuss and cry more at the end of a stimulating day than following a quiet day at home. But even a home can be overstimulating for a newborn, with the sounds of televisions, radios, telephones, doorbells, toilets, dishwashers, and vacuum cleaners, in addition to the loud voices of older children or adults.

If you must take your infant to a stimulating place, such as a party or festival, you can reduce the impact of overstimulation by keeping him close to your own body with its familiar smells and sounds. If possible, it is best to postpone trips or other major changes until your baby is at least six months old, especially if he already cries frequently. This is not always possible, of course, but it is important to be aware of the emotional impact on your infant of too many new experiences, and to recognize this as a cause of increased crying. As your baby grows older, the risk of overstimulation will gradually decrease. (See Chapter 5 for more on stimulation.)

Developmental frustrations

Another important source of stress for babies is the frustration caused by their helplessness and lack of competence. It is human nature to yearn for competence and self-sufficiency, but the intent to master a new skill always precedes the ability to learn it. This discrepancy is a continual source of frustration for babies. A three-month-old baby may want to grasp a toy, but be unable to coordinate his arm and hand muscles. He will be unsuccessful and very frustrated for many weeks. A six-month-old baby may want to crawl, but be unable to figure out how to move his legs and arms to propel himself forward. An 18-month-old toddler may become frustrated at attempts to make herself understood by talking.

You can try to minimize your baby's frustration as much as possible, for example, by providing immobile toys instead of swinging ones if your infant is learning to reach and grasp. But it will never be possible to eliminate all frustration because it is an inevitable part of development. It gradually builds up and is then released as anger in periodic bouts of crying, raging, kicking, and thrashing. These are the infant version of temper tantrums. Here is an example:

> One morning, when my son was seven weeks old, he nursed and then spent twenty minutes looking at and swiping at a toy dangling from a string. The toy kept swinging back and forth as he hit it. Then he began to whimper and cry. I picked him up and held him, and he proceeded to cry quite hard for twenty minutes, kicking his legs and flailing his arms. Then he fell asleep. Perhaps he was expressing his frustration at not being able to grasp the toy.

It is interesting that periods of increased crying often precede the acquisition of a new skill, such as the ability to roll over or crawl.[29] Many parents notice that their babies typically become repeatedly frustrated and cry more during the weeks of intense struggle to learn a new skill, and then seem much happier once the skill is mastered. (See Chapter 5 for more on this topic.)

Physical pain

Crying can be an indication of illness or physical pain, and a physician's opinion is always advisable if you have any concerns about your baby's health. But sometimes it is difficult to tell whether crying is caused by physical pain, emotional stress, or a combination of the two.

I stated earlier that the colic theory has been overused to account for all crying that seems to have no other cause. However, it is possible that stress can lead to abdominal discomfort because it causes the baby to be tense, and the stress hormones can interfere with digestion. Anything that helps a baby relax will be beneficial, and there is certainly no harm in trying a change in position, a hot water bottle, a feeding, or a gentle massage. However, if you suspect that emotional stress is playing a role (resulting perhaps from prenatal or birth trauma), then crying will probably be the most effective long-term remedy for this kind of physical discomfort. Hold your crying baby and allow him to cry in your arms as long as he needs to.

After three months of age, many people attribute crying to teething pain. As with the colic theory, I think that the teething theory has been greatly overused. Parents understandably feel the need for explanations based on physical pain when they lack information about sources of emotional stress. Teething may cause discomfort in some babies, and lead to whining and fussing. But teething is not likely to make a baby cry inconsolably for an hour.

There are other possible sources of physical pain or discomfort, including heat, cold, rashes, physical injuries, and illnesses. If you suspect physical pain or discomfort, it makes sense to do whatever seems to help your baby feel better. In addition to increased crying, physical discomfort usually also causes an increase in attachment behaviors, such as clinging. So be sure to hold your baby as much as he wants when he is sick or in pain. Remember, too, that emotional pain always accompanies physical pain because babies probably feel frightened and confused when they are in pain. Realize that the crying resulting from these emotions can sometimes last longer than the actual physical pain itself.

Frightening events

The illness or death of a parent can cause much terror, confusion, fear, and grief in even very young infants, and separations of more than a day can lead to similar emotions. Even short separations can be traumatic, especially after six months of age, when most babies have formed strong attachments to their primary caretakers. Researchers have found that nine-month-old infants who were separated from their mothers in a strange place and left with an unresponsive caretaker for half an hour had increased saliva cortisol levels, indicating a physiological stress response.[30]

Babies are very sensitive to the mood of the people around them, and they thrive in a relaxed home where the adults are reasonably happy and responsive to the infants. When parents are depressed, anxious, angry, or preoccupied with their own problems, babies can become anxious and stressed, even in the absence of overt abuse or neglect. As mentioned in Chapter 1, infants become very quickly distressed when their mothers simulate depression and fail to respond to their attempts to engage the mother in social interaction.[31]

Researchers in Germany have found that extreme crying in infants was more likely in homes where there were partnership conflicts or a mother who had serious psychological problems.[32] Even if these factors did not cause the crying, any parental stress becomes worse with a crying baby in the home, thereby further frightening the baby. This can create a vicious cycle leading to more and more crying. It is therefore important to take care of your own emotional health, and to obtain the help you need in order to keep yourself and your family in good shape.

Even in homes that are fairly stress-free, there are many minor upsets in babies' lives. Babies are born with different temperaments that affect how they react to stressful events. Some babies are more sensitive than others and become very distressed by loud noises, changes in routines, or transitions from one activity to another. If your baby is very sensitive, strive for predictable routines, gentle transitions, and a peaceful environment.

Additional sources of fear and stress are being yelled at or ridiculed, picked up with no warning, treated like an object or a doll, or ignored. Babies need caretakers who are loving, gentle, and sensitively attuned to them. Babies probably also experience anxiety and frustration every time they are forced to do something against their will or prevented from doing what they want to do. All forms of punishment are frightening and stressful (and unnecessary). The following chapters in this book give suggestions for how to treat babies without causing needless anxiety.

Here is an example of a minor, frightening event that could occur in the everyday life of an infant. Mother and baby are engaged in a cooing game, making loving sounds at each other. Baby is touching mother's face. Suddenly the telephone rings, and mother puts baby down abruptly to answer it. This sudden withdrawal of mother's attention is upsetting and confusing for the infant. One infant in such a situation might cry immediately, while another might cry later. Perhaps when mother returns from her telephone conversation she will find a fussy baby instead of a calm and contented one.

Babies are extremely sensitive and vulnerable. By being aware of the various sources of stress, you can strive to keep your baby's stress level to a minimum, and reduce your baby's need to cry.

What should I do when my baby cries?

If your baby cries excessively one day, or if the crying sounds different from usual, this could be an indication of a serious medical condition, even in the absence of a fever.[33] High-pitched crying can indicate an anomaly or disease affecting the central nervous system.[34] It is therefore important to take your baby to a doctor.

However, if your baby is healthy, and the crying is considered normal "colic," then the first thing to do is to see if she needs anything. (There is more information in a later section about how to tell if your baby has a specific need, or just needs to cry). Once you have ruled out all immediate needs, medical problems, physical pain, or discomforts, and your baby is still crying, you can then assume that she is releasing tensions caused by past hurts.

The most helpful thing to do at this point is easy to describe but sometimes difficult to put into practice. It is best if babies are never left alone to cry. It is therefore important to hold your crying baby, no matter how long she needs to cry, while communicating love, empathy, and reassurance.

In the following interview, a mother described to me how she learned to let her baby cry and to give him loving attention during his crying spells:

> To begin with, I tried to do things to make him feel better and to stop him. I would walk him around, but nothing helped. Then a friend came to visit us one evening when he was going through one of his long crying spells, and she just held him. She was really relaxed with him. She just sat there, held him, and told him, "You're doing just fine." Also I began to notice how relaxed he was after those crying spells, so I figured this was really doing something for him. So then we started to let him do it. We just held him and let him cry for as long as it lasted. Every evening it was like that.

This approach for handling crying should not be confused with the school of thought that claims it is good to "let babies cry it out." The use of that expression implies that parents should not pay attention to babies during crying spells.

There are three reasons why it is best never to leave babies alone to cry. The first reason is that they have a great need for being held and touched (as mentioned in Chapter 1). That may be the reason they are crying in the first place. For any given crying episode, it is impossible to know until you have picked up your baby. She may stop crying, in which case you will have successfully and promptly met her need. If she continues to cry, it indicates that she was not crying just to be picked up. But you can continue holding her, trying to figure out what she needs, and then support her crying if you think she needs to release tensions.

The second reason it is important to hold a crying baby is that the presence of another human being seems to be necessary for the effective release of tensions. It creates the emotional safety for deep healing to occur.

The third reason is that babies need to know they are cherished and accepted at all times, no matter how they are feeling or what they are doing. This is surely the best way to give your baby unconditional love. If you repeatedly ignore your crying baby, she may grow up to believe that she is lovable only when she is happy, and she may learn to suppress her painful emotions in order to be accepted and loved. Babies need the reassurance that their feelings of sadness or anger are not going to destroy the bond with their parents, and the best way to communicate this is to hold babies when they cry. However, they should never be held in a spirit of anger, resentment, or punishment.

Once your baby can crawl well, it is not necessary to pick her up every time she cries (unless she is in a crib or playpen). Instead, if you are in the same room, you can reassure her that you are paying attention to her and let her know that you are available if she wants to be held. She may surprise you by choosing to stay on the floor while she cries. Or you can go near her and reassure her by your touch, attention, and words. ("I'm right here," "I'm listening," or "I see that you are upset. I'll stay with you while you cry.")

Even when your older baby or toddler wants to be held, you may find that she sometimes struggles while crying, almost as if she wants to escape from your arms. This can be confusing. If this occurs, I recommend letting her go to see what she does. If she is happy and content away from you, it probably means that she is done crying and no longer wants to be held. However, if she comes back and clings to you, while continuing to whine or cry, then you can try holding her again (assuming you have already checked for other possible needs).

At these times when it seems as if your baby wants to get away (but then returns to you), it is possible that she is looking for a stronger force to push against while crying. Struggling against a stronger force is sometimes a necessary part of the stress release process. This physical exertion can accompany your baby's attempts to work through the emotional impact of prenatal or birth trauma, when there was indeed very little room in which to move around. It can also accompany the release of accumulated frustrations. Or perhaps she is releasing anger directed at you. No matter what the source of her rage, your baby needs to know that it will not cause you to reject her. You can provide gentle resistance to your baby's feet so she has something to push them against, and lovingly but firmly hold her to provide a safe "container" in which to cry and rage.

It sometimes requires more energy to prevent a baby from crying than to allow her to cry. The following example illustrates this, and also shows how babies can learn to turn their crying on and off at will at an early age:

> When my son was eight months old, we went to visit some friends. While we were there, he became clingy, whiny, and squirmy. I knew he wasn't hungry, so I thought he might need to cry. I excused myself and took him into another room, held him, and said, "Okay, you can cry now." He immediately burst into tears and cried very hard for twenty minutes. When he had finished, we returned to the other room where he played quietly and contentedly for the rest of our visit.

What are the benefits of crying while being held?

Allowing babies to cry while holding them has many benefits. An immediate one is that babies who release stress in this manner become much easier to live with. In between crying spells, they are generally calm, content, and alert, with very little fussing. They also sleep for longer stretches at night. In fact, this approach is one of the best ways to help babies sleep through the night without ever leaving them to "cry it out" alone (as described in Chapter 4).

Releasing stress through crying during infancy can also help prevent later psychological problems that could otherwise result from early trauma. Psychologists are gradually coming to recognize early trauma as a major contributing factor in mental illness, depression, anxiety, phobias, violence, attachment disorder, hyperactivity, and some cases of autism.

Although there is a correlation between complications at birth and later susceptibility of people to emotional and behavioral problems (as mentioned in Chapter 1), the people in these studies probably did not have the opportunity as infants to cry freely in the arms of an empathic witness. If they had been allowed to cry, these correlations would probably no longer hold true. This does not mean that your birth-traumatized baby is automatically going to have serious emotional problems if he fails to cry enough as a baby. It is never too late to begin healing through crying. But your baby will lead a much happier and rewarding life if he can heal from early trauma as soon as possible after it occurs. During infancy the natural and spontaneous healing mechanism of crying is readily accessible and has not yet become repressed.

Following a major traumatic event, children (and adults) sometimes suffer from a condition known as "post-traumatic stress disorder." Anything related to the original trauma can trigger a reliving of the event with a full-blown, physiological stress response. Nightmares, phobias, and anxiety attacks are common. When a child is allowed to cry sufficiently following a traumatic event, this reduces the likelihood of these problems later on. It appears that crying uses the energy that was originally intended for a flight or fight reaction in response to the trauma, while also allowing the body to rid itself of the stress hormones through tears. Perhaps crying thus "convinces" the brain that the danger has been dealt with, and this allows the child to relax.

Even mild frightening events can cause later repercussions. For example, if a barking dog has frightened a toddler on a swing, the child might acquire a fear of swings because he associates them with barking dogs. If he is offered protection and reassurance, but allowed to cry immediately after the dog has frightened him, it is less likely that he will have a fear of swings later on.

As adults, we tend to over-react frequently to situations that are completely innocent and unthreatening, simply because they remind us in some way of past hurtful events in our lives. In fact, much of what upsets us as adults can be traced back to early trauma. For example, as a young adult I felt extremely anxious in hospitals because I had experienced a traumatic hospitalization at five years of age for two weeks during which I was separated from my family. It took considerable therapy, during which I cried about that early hospitalization, before I could enter a hospital without experiencing a feeling of panic.

There are several kinds of therapy that help adults relive early experiences and release the pent-up emotions that are continually triggered by current events in people's lives. It is never too late to heal from early trauma. However, our lives could be much more pleasant, with less need for therapy later on, if we had been allowed to release these painful emotions while we were still young.

Another long-term benefit of allowing babies to heal from early trauma through crying is that this helps them be more attentive and alert for learning. When children have an accumulation of stress, it is hard for them to think clearly or learn new things. When there are chronically high levels of stress hormones in their bodies, they become tense, irritable, and unable to concentrate for very long. In a study of 4000 seven-year-old children, researchers found that the children with the highest levels of stress had the lowest IQ's.[35]

Cortisol, one of the stress hormones, seems to be a possible culprit (as mentioned in Chapter 1). Researchers found that Romanian two-year-old orphans had cortisol levels twice as high as those of U.S. babies of the same age, and those with the highest levels of cortisol had the lowest social, motor, and language skills.[36] Cortisol can affect the ability to learn by damaging a part of the brain called the hippocampus, and studies with traumatized people have found a reduction in the volume of the hippocampus.[37]

It is possible that crying could help eliminate excessive amounts of ACTH through tears, thereby lowering the cortisol levels in individuals who have chronically high levels caused by stress. (Remember that ACTH stimulates the production of cortisol.) Allowing traumatized babies to cry may therefore help prevent the brain damage caused by excessive cortisol, thereby enhancing their ability to learn.

From my own experience and work with parents, I have observed that babies who are allowed to cry freely as needed (while being held) are extremely bright and alert, quick to learn, and they also have very a long attention span. They become very "aware babies."

In addition to the psychological benefits of crying, there are also physical health benefits. Allowing your baby to cry freely (in your arms) will help him form a habit of crying when he needs to, instead of suppressing his emotions. This healthy habit will continue into childhood and adulthood, and can help your child heal from stress as he grows older. This will help him stay healthier, because pent-up stress is a contributing factor to many illnesses. Ulcers, cardiovascular problems (high blood pressure and arteriosclerosis), adult onset diabetes, tumors, and osteoporosis are all illnesses known to be at least partly caused by stress. In addition, chronically high levels of cortisol suppress the immune system, resulting in a lower resistance to infections and a susceptibility to allergies and other immune-related disorders.

Men are more prone to stress-related illnesses than are women. Men also cry less than women. Dr. William Frey, who did the biochemical analysis of human tears, has suggested that this lack of crying in men may be one of the reasons that men are more prone to stress-related illnesses and live shorter lives than women, on the average.[38]

Further evidence for the benefits of crying comes from clinical data with severely disturbed children. Crying is an important component of certain forms of therapy with autistic children and also with those who suffer from attachment disorders.

Two kinds of therapy have been successful with some autistic children: holding therapy and behavioral therapy. It is interesting that in both of these approaches there is considerable crying. In mother/child holding therapy, the mother holds her autistic child and insists on eye contact, while the child screams and rages.[39] In behavioral therapy, the therapist also makes demands on the child, by repeatedly insisting that he perform some task, even taking and guiding the child's hand, if necessary.[40] The child often resists strongly while crying and raging, sometimes for weeks, before beginning to comply.[41] Although behavioral therapists do not recognize crying as a therapeutic factor, much of the success of this approach can probably be attributed to the crying that occurs. Whenever early trauma is a contributing factor to autism, these forms of therapy are likely to be successful. However, when the cause of autism is biological (the result of defective genes, brain damage, or other biological factors), crying would probably not be as effective.

Children who suffer from a rupture in attachment with their parents, through parental illness, neglect, or abuse, sometimes develop attachment disorders. These children are unable to trust or develop a bond with their foster parents, and are prone to violence, lying, and stealing. People describe them as children without a conscience. Holding therapy (involving considerable raging and crying) has proven to be successful with many of these children in reducing aggression, anxiety, depression, and delinquent behavior.[42] Proponents claim that holding teaches these children that closeness does not always have to involve pain. This is a useful corrective learning experience for children who are victims of parental abuse. The crying that occurs is probably a crucial component of the therapy, because it allows the children to release stress from the trauma they have been through, without being rejected.

By holding your crying baby and allowing him to cry as long as needed, you will help him heal from early trauma and stress while he is still a baby. This will enhance his physical and emotional health, as well as his ability to learn.

How do babies learn to suppress their crying?

Most books for parents state, incorrectly, that all crying indicates a present need or discomfort, and they offer a list of methods to try in order to stop the crying. This is called comforting, soothing, or settling a baby. This usually involves some form of movement or noise, or putting something in the baby's mouth. Some of the recommended methods are jiggling, patting, rocking, bouncing, swinging, walking the baby, taking her for rides, nursing, giving a pacifier or bottle, singing, making noises ("hush hush"), or distracting with a toy or picture. Some books even recommend putting the baby on top of the clothes dryer to be soothed by the continuous noise and jiggling. When these methods fail, some parents decide that there is nothing they can do, so they leave their baby to "cry it out" alone, while others hit or shake their baby out of desperation and frustration. (Shaking can be very dangerous.)

None of these methods is beneficial for babies when they need to cry, because the babies learn to hold their feelings inside themselves instead of releasing them. These methods are sometimes effective, and they do stop the crying temporarily. This reinforces the behavior of the parents, who then use the same method when the crying begins again, as it inevitably will.

When these methods are used repeatedly, babies become dependent on them to repress their crying because they learn that people are unable to listen and accept their emotions. I use the term "control pattern" to refer to any behavior that represses crying. For example, a mother could mistakenly interpret her baby's crying as a need to suck, and give him a pacifier. If she does this frequently, her baby will begin to demand a pacifier every time he is upset, frightened, overstimulated, sad, angry, or confused. He will learn that nobody wants to listen to him when he needs to cry, so he will become dependent on the pacifier to suppress the crying.

Another control pattern could originate if a father mistakenly interprets fussiness as an indication of sleepiness instead of a need to cry. Instead of holding his baby and allowing her to cry in his arms, he puts her in a crib and leaves the room. In response to this withdrawal of attention, the baby may console herself by clutching a corner of her blanket or sucking her thumb. If this occurs frequently, these will become her control patterns, and she will want to hold the same blanket and suck her thumb each time she needs to cry.

Objects such as a special blanket have traditionally been called "security objects," or "transitional objects." Some professionals believe that it is a good sign when babies learn to "comfort" themselves with the help of a special blanket, a pacifier, or thumb sucking. I disagree, because I consider these behaviors a means of shutting off feelings and suppressing the need to cry in an environment that does not understand or encourage crying. In my experience, babies who are given loving attention when they need to cry, and who are allowed to cry as long as needed, do not acquire any of these habits or attachments to objects.

Almost anything can become a control pattern, and most babies have well-established control patterns by six months of age. Even though I was aware of the importance of crying, my son developed a few control patterns. This made me realize how easy it is to mistake a baby's need to cry for other needs:

> I wanted my son to share my love of books, so I began showing him picture books at an early age. But I must have read to him many times when he really needed to cry (thinking he was bored), because he eventually began to ask frantically to be read to whenever he was upset. Because of my preoccupation with the importance of reading, I failed to see any control pattern there, and would dutifully read to him. Not until he was over two years of age did I discover what was going on. I was able to see it then, and to give him my full attention at times when he needed to cry, instead of distracting him with a book.

Two common control patterns in toddlers are a desire to be held frequently and a desire to be entertained. A one-year-old may scream every time she is put down. Her parents may think that she needs to be held and distracted all the time, but in reality she probably needs to cry while being held. Perhaps her parents picked her up and held her many times when she was fussy, but then distracted her in some way instead of giving her full permission to cry. Some people describe such babies as spoiled, and make the parents feel guilty for having "given in" to all of their baby's demands. If your baby is very demanding of your attention, this does not imply that you have spoiled her. You have probably only misinterpreted her needs, thinking she needed to be entertained, when all she needed was to have a good cry in your arms.

HOW STRESS-RELEASE CRYING IS REPRESSED IN BABIES AND COMMON CONTROL PATTERNS

- Bouncing, jiggling, rocking, walking, swinging:
  - Baby could become overly demanding.
  - Baby could become a head-banger, self-rocker, or a hyperactive toddler.

- Nursing for "comfort" (rather than for hunger):
  - Baby could want to nurse frequently when upset.
  - Baby could become overweight.
  - Baby could become addicted to sweets later on.

- Giving a pacifier or a bottle:
  - Baby could become addicted to the pacifier or bottle.

- Distracting with toys, books, music, or games:
  - Baby could demand constant entertainment.

- Putting baby in crib, ignoring:
  - Baby could suck his thumb or become attached to an object in crib (blanket, stuffed animal, etc.).

- Giving sedatives or other drugs:
  - Baby could seek relief from stress through drugs later on.

Control patterns do not usually disappear by themselves unless a child begins to cry, but they can become modified later on. For example, a thumb-sucking control pattern during infancy can develop into a nail-biting habit as an older child and a smoking habit as an adult. This is because the need to put something in one's mouth when upset will become a strong habit.

Parents often pass on their own control patterns (addictions) to their babies. If you frequently drink beer when you are depressed, you may tend to misinterpret your baby's crying as an indication of thirst. Instead of allowing your baby to cry in your arms, you may keep offering juice, even though she shows little interest in it. Your baby may later develop a drinking habit, just like you.

When control patterns are operating, babies are feeling tense and stressed, but are not able to release the stress. The control patterns seem to calm the baby down, but this is only a temporary effect. In fact, researchers found that non-nutritive sucking on a pacifier during routine physical procedures reduced the amount of crying but not the plasma cortisol levels.[43] This implies that the babies had a physiological stress response even though they were not crying. When we artificially repress an infant's natural urge to cry out in distress, we must therefore not delude ourselves into thinking that we have reduced the infant's stress level or pain.

Control patterns produce mild dissociation (psychological numbing) that prevents active learning, exploration, or genuine interaction. You can see this in the blank, dull expression of babies with a pacifier or thumb in their mouth. Rather than assume that these babies are content, I assume that they are holding in painful emotions and waiting for an opportunity to release them.

What can I do if my baby has already learned to suppress his crying?

There is no need to be overly concerned or feel guilty if your baby uses a control pattern, such as thumb sucking, to suppress his crying. This probably means that he has not felt quite safe enough in the past to release stress through crying. He can always catch up.

The first step to take, if your baby frequently suppresses his own crying by means of a control pattern, is to change the way you normally react to him when he needs to cry (assuming you are fairly sure that all immediate needs have been met). Hold him and allow him to cry for as long as you can do so with loving attention, while reassuring him of your love and understanding. If he puts his thumb in his mouth, I do not recommend taking it out or even commenting on it. Instead, you can gently touch his arm or head, to let him know that you are right there with him. Try to make eye contact, and reassure him that you are willing to listen. Often, this will cause a baby to remove his thumb spontaneously from his mouth in order to cry. When babies need to cry, they will do so spontaneously if they feel safe enough.

Laughter is also an important stress-release mechanism, and eliciting laughter is an effective way to help your baby stop using a control pattern. If your baby is old enough, you can engage him in a game of peek-a-boo whenever he sucks his thumb and seems lost in his own world. This will probably cause him to take his thumb out of his mouth in order to laugh. (See Chapter 5 for more on laughter.)

If you yourself have given a control pattern to your baby, such as a pacifier, you can stop offering it. However, it is always wise to explain why, no matter how young your baby is. The following example illustrates this.

At 22 months of age, Daryl had a pacifier in his mouth most of the time, and was frequently clingy and whiny, but did not cry much. His mother asked me for help. I waited until he started crying spontaneously one morning, and then gave him my full attention. Soon after he began crying, he asked for his pacifier. I said to him, "You'll feel much better if you let yourself cry. We'll both stay with you." His mother and I reassured him while he screamed, cried, and thrashed around. Every time he asked for his pacifier, I repeated my explanations. I kept reminding him that it was okay for him to cry and kick, and that he was doing just fine. After about 30 minutes, he became very calm and happy, and seemed to have totally forgotten about his pacifier! He did not even mention it. His mother reported to me later that he was in an unusually good mood the entire day, and did not ask for his pacifier at all.

A single crying session will probably not cure a baby permanently of a control pattern that has been in use for a long time. Such a baby will probably ask for the pacifier again when he needs to cry. But if you make it safe for him to cry, he will eventually be able to cry spontaneously without feeling the need to stop himself with his pacifier.

Be prepared to accept the crying if you refrain from giving a usual control pattern to your baby. If you decide to remove a control pattern, such as a pacifier, without providing the emotional safety for your baby to cry, he may adopt a new control pattern, such as thumb sucking or overeating. Another possible consequence is that your baby will begin to develop behavior problems. For example, if you think that your toddler's bedtime bottle is acting as a control pattern, and you suddenly decide one day to remove it (but without allowing the crying that needs to happen), your toddler may begin to become excessively rebellious or hyperactive at bedtime. Such behaviors are often the result of accumulated, painful feelings that have no healthy outlet.

Babies with control patterns have to catch up on many hours of crying. If you do not have the time or attention for this, then your baby may be better off with his control pattern until the time is right. You can assess your resources and come to your own best decision as to when and how to start helping your baby catch up on his crying. A gradual approach is perfectly fine. Remember that the most important thing is to create an atmosphere of emotional safety in which crying is welcome. If you work towards that goal, your baby will eventually stop using control patterns to repress his crying.

Many adults do not cry as much as needed because nobody was available to listen to them as babies and children, and they have therefore learned to repress their emotions. Adult control patterns are very common, and include smoking, consuming alcohol or caffeine, taking drugs, nail biting, overeating, muscle tensions, and addictions such as frequent TV viewing. We live in a "non-cathartic" culture where the expression of strong emotions is discouraged, so our tensions and painful emotions accumulate over the years. With sufficient emotional safety, however, we adults can find relief and healing through tears.

COMMON CONTROL PATTERNS IN ADULTS
(Behaviors that repress crying)

- Consumption of mind-altering chemicals
- Overeating
- Nail biting, nervous tics, and other habits
- Muscle tensions and rigidities
- Excessive activity
- Distractions (ex: television, computer games)

How can I tell if my baby needs to cry?

Many genuine needs, such as nursing, can become control patterns. This makes it difficult to determine when a baby needs to cry. There are no easy answers, but there are some guidelines that may be helpful.

First of all, some control patterns are never real needs. Examples of these include pacifiers, thumb sucking, and security blankets. These are the most apparent control patterns. Furthermore, some of the frantic remedies that parents try in attempts to stop babies from crying are not genuine needs. For example, there is no such thing as a need to be jiggled.

One guideline for detecting a control pattern is to see whether or not the baby tends to do it or request it when she is obviously upset. For example, if your baby asks for her bottle when she is physically hurt, then her bottle is probably a control pattern. Anything that a baby does to "comfort" herself is a control pattern when it prevents her from releasing her feelings. You can note how your baby asks for things. Any sudden, frantic, full-blown cry is not likely to be a cry from need. If your toddler frantically throws herself on you in an attempt to cuddle, then cuddling is probably a control pattern for her at that moment. It is not likely to be a control pattern if she comes to you with a relaxed look on her face, while snuggling close.

As a toddler my son liked to have a drink of juice from a bottle first thing in the morning. But I became aware that his morning juice bottle was sometimes a control pattern. On some days he would wake up full of smiles and ask for his juice in a relaxed tone of voice. But on other days he would wake up whiny and fussy, and then frantically demand his bottle of juice. When he asked for his juice in that way, I would not give it to him right away. Instead, I would offer him juice in a cup (in case he was really thirsty), and give him my full attention. He would usually refuse the juice and have a good cry, from which he would emerge calm and happy. Only then did I offer him his bottle of juice. (But he was not always interested in it, which made me realize that he hadn't wanted it to begin with!) After this experience, it was obvious to me that the act of sucking on his bottle had become a control pattern for my son.

Another guideline is how your baby looks while doing the behavior in question. Does she look passive or listless when you rock or nurse her? If so, those behaviors may be control patterns for her. When babies are not crying or sleeping, you can expect them to be happy, aware, and alert. If this is not the case, the two most likely possibilities are that they are not feeling well, or they have a control pattern operating.

During the first month, the only immediate needs are the need to be held and those resulting from physical discomforts, such as hunger, thirst, coldness, and pain. Any other crying is probably an indication of a need to cry. There are many other needs, of course, such as the needs for movement (vestibular stimulation) and other forms of stimulation (as described in Chapter 1). Newborns need a certain amount of these things, but they are unlikely to cry for those *specific* reasons, because these needs are not experienced as immediate discomforts. For example, if your baby goes a day or two with very little rocking, she is not going to cry because of a desperate need to be rocked, bounced, or jiggled. If a baby's basic and primary needs for food and physical contact are met, then it is best to respond to any crying that occurs with calm holding. If she needs to continue crying to release stress, she will then be able to do so with your loving attention. Artificial rocking movements, bouncing, or jiggling may calm your baby down temporarily by putting her in a sort of trance, but the crying will only be postponed until a later time. There is plenty of time during a baby's non-crying, alert states for rocking, playing, and other forms of stimulation.

As your baby grows older, she will acquire a greater need for different kinds of stimulation and interaction, as well as opportunities to exercise motor skills. At times she will need less stimulation. It is therefore best to check for all possible needs before assuming that your baby simply needs to cry.

In the following chapters of this book I offer additional guidelines for determining when babies need to cry. Chapter 3 deals with distinguishing hunger from a need to cry, and Chapter 4 offers suggestions for distinguishing sleepiness from a need to cry. Chapter 5 has a section on determining whether a baby needs additional stimulation when she cries, and Chapter 6 has a section to help you determine which forms of inappropriate behavior may indicate a need to cry. (Toddlers who are harboring strong, pent-up feelings sometimes hit, bite, or act in rebellious or obnoxious ways.) Finally, Chapter 7 offers guidelines for interpreting your baby's crying during separations.

The first few months will be especially difficult in learning to interpret your baby's cues. Don't worry if you make a few mistakes from time to time, because this will not cause extensive damage to your baby. What you want to avoid, however, is to repeatedly repress your baby's crying. As you get to know your baby, you will gradually become more confident in your ability to interpret her different cries and meet her various needs. Hopefully, you will also learn to relax while holding your crying baby, and to detect any control patterns that may be developing.

Toddlers who have cried as much as needed since birth are delightful to be with. They are joyful, relaxed, alert, curious, and eager to explore and learn. They are kind and gentle and they do not hit or bite. They love to be held, but are able to play alone at times, and do not demand constant attention. Provided their needs are met and they are allowed enough autonomy and freedom, they are eager to cooperate. These children do not have any control patterns (such as a pacifier, special blanket, bottle, thumb sucking, nursing just for "comfort," or overeating). They cry hard when they need to, and, unless they are ill, generally sleep through the night. Be advised, however, that these toddlers are not passive or docile. Instead, they are very persistent in getting their needs met, and will strongly resist disrespectful treatment. This is healthy and normal.

How much can I expect my baby to cry?

The amount of crying time is determined by the amount of stress and trauma the baby has experienced. Some babies may need to cry for several hours a day, especially if there were birth complications or prenatal stress, while others may need to cry for only a few minutes a day. If there is a lot of stress, overstimulation, or a major change in your baby's life, this will increase his need to cry. He will probably also cry more at times when you are going through difficult or stressful times. Perhaps you will also notice that your baby cries more before developmental milestones such as the ability to crawl or walk. Some babies are more sensitive than others and therefore more easily stressed. Those babies will need to cry more than others.

The most crying generally occurs during the first three months, peaking at about six weeks of age, and then gradually declining. During the first few days, it is typical for newborns to spend most of their time nursing and sleeping. Because of this, some parents are surprised when their infant begins to have crying spells after a few days. By six weeks of age, it is common for a baby to have one long crying session a day, lasting for one or more hours. This often tends to occur in the late afternoon or evening, but can happen at any time of the day or night. Some infants develop this pattern of one regular crying spell per day, while others never do. Infants who had a traumatic birth sometimes begin their crying spell at the same hour of the day (or night) that they were born.

As babies grow older, they tend to cry less, and they can save up their crying for longer periods of time. Your one-year-old could still need to cry for thirty to sixty minutes a day, but he might save up his crying and then let it all out in a long crying spell or temper tantrum every few days. He will make use of times when you are relaxed, attentive, and available to pay attention to him. Many parents who work outside the home find that their babies cry more on the weekends than on weekdays. This is because the babies sense their parents' availability on the weekends and make use of this to catch up on their crying.

When toddlers start to talk, many parents hope that the crying will be replaced by language, and some of it is. However, as stated previously, there are two reasons why babies cry: to communicate a need and to release tensions caused by stress. They eventually learn to ask for what they need by talking, so it is true that crying to communicate becomes replaced by language. The stress-release type of crying, however, does not become replaced by language. Talking about one's painful emotions is not the same as releasing them through tears. Crying is therefore not a "babyish" thing to do, and it is not helpful to get a crying two-year-old to talk when he obviously needs to cry.

Your child will continue to need to cry as he grows older and experiences new forms of stress. It is important to remember that even loving and attentive parents cannot shield their children from pain and stress. Your job is to offer reasonable protection so your child will not get hurt, but also to give him opportunities to heal when something traumatic or stressful has occurred. If you establish a healthy, listening relationship with your child right from the start, he will continue to come to you as an adolescent to talk about his problems and cry in your arms. This ongoing acceptance of your child's emotions is one of the greatest gifts you can give him.

What if I find it hard to hold my crying baby?

A baby's crying can bring up many intense emotions in parents, including feelings of incompetence, powerlessness, anger, anxiety, or grief.

If you think that all crying is an indication of an immediate need or discomfort, you will probably feel inadequate as a parent when you are unable to stop your baby from crying. It is true that crying very often is an indication of an immediate need in infants, and this is one reason for the confusion and misunderstanding of the function of crying. When your baby is trying to release stress through crying, however, then the crying itself becomes the need, and your baby will not feel better until she cries. It is important to remember that when your baby cries, this does not imply that you are incompetent. Your baby may not need anything at all, except to be held and loved. Hopefully this information about crying will help relieve the pressure to have a quiet baby in order to feel confident as a parent.

A mother reported to me how her self-confidence as a mother had been dependent on whether or not her baby cried:

> Sometimes it felt as if my baby's crying was cutting through me like a knife. I was trying to attend to every need, never leaving him alone, but also doing a lot of patting, rocking, walking, nursing, bouncing, denying the need ("You're all right"), distracting, turning up the stereo, or even vacuuming. Deep inside me, there was a voice saying, "You are not a good mother if your baby is crying. Stop the crying, stop the crying..." And the truth of the matter is that all these activities only postponed the crying for brief periods, and it started again later. It could eventually last for hours.

Even if you do not feel this pressure from yourself to stop your baby's crying, you will probably feel it from others. People will ask you if you have a "good" baby, meaning an easy, quiet baby who rarely cries. Experienced parents will be eager to show you how to stop your baby from crying.

Another feeling you may have is anger. It is only normal to feel resentful when you have done everything you can think of to meet your baby's needs, and all she does is cry. Furthermore, she chooses to do so at the most inconvenient times, just as the family is sitting down to dinner, or in the middle of the night. This can be extremely frustrating and disconcerting. A mother remembers how she felt:

> The one time her crying really got to me was when she was about ten days old and it had been intermittent all day long. By about 7 o'clock that night I was ready to get out. I had to get out of the house, and I did. I just left. I couldn't take it any more. It made me angry, not knowing what I could do for her.

Some parents feel angry because they think their baby is rejecting them. This is more likely for people who were rejected or neglected in some way by their own parents. They begin to feel unwanted, unloved, and powerless, just as they felt when they themselves were small. These feelings of anger can lead to abuse, especially if the parents were themselves abused while crying. Crying is a potent trigger for abuse.[44] In one survey, 80% of abusive parents admitted that their baby's crying was the trigger that led to their abusive behavior.[45]

If you are feeling very angry with your baby, and afraid that you might hurt her, it may be best to put her down for a few minutes until you can regain your composure. Tell her that it's okay for her to cry, but that it's hard for you to hold her. This is not ideal, but it is better than hitting your baby. Then, when you are feeling calmer, go to your baby and pick her up. If you frequently feel anger towards your crying baby, you should seek help through therapy or a support group. You were probably hit or ignored when you yourself cried as an infant. Remember that your baby is not trying to manipulate you, nor is she rejecting you by crying, and her crying does not imply that you are inadequate as a parent. She is simply letting off steam, and she needs you very much, just as you yourself might welcome a shoulder to cry on after you have had a hard day.

You may also feel very anxious when your baby cries inconsolably. Perhaps you think your baby is suffering terrible pains, or that the crying itself is bad for your baby. Perhaps you are afraid your baby will stop breathing, have a heart attack, or never be able to stop crying. These worries are understandable in our society where the display of strong emotions is taboo. People are not accustomed to seeing others let themselves go to the point that babies naturally do. It may be helpful to remember that babies, as well as adults, are meant to cry as a normal response to stress. It is a natural healing mechanism, which a normal, healthy baby is fully equipped to handle. Babies do not continue crying indefinitely, although it is not at all unusual for them to cry for an hour or more at a time. They do stop eventually on their own. But don't immediately dismiss your anxiety. If you suspect pain or illness, or if the crying lasts longer or sounds different from usual, it is important to consult a doctor. (Be aware also that hard crying may be dangerous for babies suffering from certain medical conditions.)

Even with reassurance from your baby's doctor and an understanding of the stress-release function of crying, it may still be difficult to hold your crying baby and let her cry without trying to stop her. One reason for this difficulty is that hearing a baby cry reminds us of our own need to cry. Most of us were not held and allowed to cry as much as needed when we were little, so we carry around a load of pent-up emotions. If you have not experienced the great relief that follows a good cry, you will probably find it hard to allow your baby to cry, even though you might theoretically agree that it is important for babies to cry. You will feel a strong urge to stop or ignore the crying, just as you yourself were stopped or ignored when you cried as a baby.

If you can begin to allow yourself to cry more, this will probably make it easier for you to accept your baby's crying. If you normally hold back your tears while watching a sad film, try to let them out instead. This will be much healthier for you. Ask your spouse or a friend to listen to you after you have had a hard day, and tell them that you might need to cry. Perhaps you can find a support group or form of therapy that encourages emotional release. It is important to talk and cry about your childhood traumas. The questions at the end of this chapter will help you explore how your own crying has been repressed, and how this affects your feelings towards your crying baby.

EXERCISES

Explore your childhood.

1. Do you remember times when your needs were promptly filled as a child? How did you feel? Do you remember times when your needs were ignored? How did it make you feel? Did anyone ever tell you that you were "spoiled"?

2. What did your parents usually do when you cried (ignored, punished, distracted, consoled, etc.)? What words did they use if they tried to stop you from crying ("Shut up," Don't be such a baby," "Big boys don't cry," "There, there, it's all right," "If you don't stop crying, I'll *give* you something to cry about," "You're giving Daddy a headache," "Look at the pretty picture," etc.)? How did it make you feel? Can you recall specific times when you were stopped from crying?

3. As a child, did you ever experience a good, liberating cry in the arms of someone who loved you and was able to accept your tears? Describe how you felt.

Express your feelings about your baby.

1. Do you worry about "spoiling" your baby by responding to every cry and picking your baby up? Describe your fears and try to figure out where these feelings come from.

2. How do you feel when your baby cries and you can't find anything he/she needs (angry, worried, powerless, incompetent, guilty, frustrated, sad)? What do you feel like doing? The next time your baby cries for no apparent reason, hold him/her lovingly and just listen without interfering. How does it make you feel?

3. How do you feel if your baby cries when other people are around? Has anyone ever tried to give you unbidden advice, ask whether you have a "good" baby, or comment on your baby's temperament? How did it make you feel?

Nurture yourself.

1. The next time you feel the need to cry, allow yourself to do so, preferably in the arms of someone who loves you.

2. If your baby cries a lot, you deserve all the help you can get. Take steps to reduce stress in your baby's life and your own life, and find other people to help care for your baby from time to time. Realize that this stage will pass and your baby will eventually cry less as he/she grows older.

CHAPTER 3

FOOD: LETTING YOUR BABY
BECOME SELF-REGULATED

What are the advantages of breastfeeding?

There are many advantages to breastfeeding. A major one is that breast milk helps protect infants against infections through its anti-viral and antibacterial agents. Studies show that breastfed infants have fewer gastrointestinal disorders, respiratory infections, and ear infections than bottle-fed infants, and they are also less likely to have eczema and diaper rash.[1] In addition, human milk is high in certain substances that are important for the development of the brain (such as the amino acid cystine and certain fats). Cow's milk is low in these substances.[2] This may help account for the fact that children who are breastfed as babies have higher IQ's, on the average, than those who are bottle-fed.[3]

From the psychological point of view, breastfed infants are better off than bottle-fed infants because they do not have to wait long for their milk (assuming the mother is nearby). Breast milk is immediately available and always at the right temperature. A bottle-fed baby may have to wait for his bottle to be prepared and warmed, and then it may be too hot or too cold. Breast milk is also easier to digest than cow's milk. Furthermore, breastfeeding guarantees close physical contact with the mother many times a day. Lactating women have high levels of the hormones prolactin and oxytocin, which help contribute to their desire to be close to their baby.

Breastfeeding is certainly easier for the mother than bottle-feeding. There is no need to spend time purchasing milk and preparing the bottles, worry about refrigeration while traveling, or get up in the night to fix a bottle. It is also less expensive, although breastfeeding mothers do need to eat (and drink) more. The cost of eating additional food, however, is much less than the cost of buying baby formula and bottle-feeding equipment. Although more convenient than bottle-feeding, producing breast milk does require energy, so be sure to obtain sufficient rest if you are a breastfeeding mother.

It is important to let newborns nurse as soon as they are ready to do so, preferably within the first hour after birth. However, it is not necessary to force a nipple into your newborn's mouth immediately after birth. When healthy, undrugged newborns are placed on their mother's chest, they rest for about a half hour at first, in a quiet, alert state with open eyes. Later they begin to make mouthing movements and body movements, indicating a desire to find a nipple. It is then appropriate to offer your breast. The survival instinct is so strong that, in the absence of being placed at the breast, newborns placed on their mother's abdomen will actually maneuver themselves to reach their mother's nipple, latch on, and suck. In fact, researchers have discovered that infants use smell and taste cues from the amniotic fluid on their hands to make a connection with their mother's nipple, which is coated with an oily substance similar to the amniotic fluid.[4] This instinct to reach the breast would have had survival value in prehistoric times in cases where the mother was too ill to bring her newborn to her breast. But there is no need to let your newborn struggle by himself to find your nipple.

The antibody content of colostrum (the liquid excreted before the first milk appears) is at its highest during the first twelve hours after delivery. Colostrum also has a laxative effect, which helps evacuate the meconium (first stools) from the baby's intestines. This will tend to make your baby hungry, causing more vigorous sucking, which in turn will stimulate milk production. The more frequently your baby nurses, the more milk there will be.

Immediate suckling after birth is also beneficial for the mother, because it releases oxytocin, which helps to contract the uterus, expel the placenta, and reduce excessive bleeding. These contractions can be quite painful during the first days, and this can interfere with the pleasure of breastfeeding at first. But try not to let any temporary discomfort discourage you from continuing to nurse your baby.

Except in rare cases, any healthy woman who really wishes to breastfeed her baby will be able to do so, provided she is given enough encouragement and support and has an adequate diet. Women can successfully breastfeed even though they have inverted nipples, a premature baby, a Cesarean delivery, or twins. The size of the breasts makes no difference in a woman's ability to produce sufficient milk.

However, breastfeeding is a learned activity, so unless you have observed other women breastfeeding, it is unrealistic to expect to know instinctively how to do it effectively. It is therefore important to seek the help and advice of other women, a breastfeeding support group, or a book about breastfeeding. There are many "tips and tricks" to be learned. For example, some women experience sore nipples during the first few weeks. The advice and support of experienced breastfeeding women can help you find ways to alleviate the soreness. In traditional cultures all over the world, new mothers learn how to breastfeed and care for their babies from other, experienced mothers.

Because of ways in which some women have been brought up, they may feel uncomfortable or embarrassed at the idea of nursing a baby. Some women feel that breastfeeding is too animal-like or that it will restrict their freedom too much. Western cultures overemphasize breasts as sex symbols, and this attitude leads some women to feel that the use of their breasts as a milk factory is inappropriate. This is an unfortunate attitude, because the biological function of breasts is to feed babies.

Although there are many advantages to breastfeeding, you should decide to nurse your baby only if you feel comfortable doing so. Mothers who are not happy with the idea of breastfeeding may not be very successful. Studies show that a woman's attitude towards breastfeeding affects her milk supply. Mothers with a positive attitude have more milk than those with a doubtful or negative attitude.[5] Therefore, it may be better for a baby to have a relaxed bottle-feeding mother than a tense and unhappy breastfeeding mother. If you do not breastfeed your baby, it is important to hold him during every feeding, even though you may be tempted to put him down when he is old enough to hold his own bottle. Studies have shown that babies who are held during feedings digest the milk better than those who are not.[6] If you choose not to breastfeed, or are unable to do so, it is nevertheless possible to give your baby good nutrition and good mothering.

How often should I nurse my baby?

The only logical time to feed a baby is when she is hungry (or thirsty). This means using a self-demand approach and letting the baby indicate when she is hungry. It is possible to make two mistakes in this regard: waiting too long between feedings and feeding too frequently (overnursing).

Babies who are forced to wait for their feedings, even though they are crying from hunger, will learn that they have no control over what happens to them, and may grow up feeling powerless and unable to trust that their needs will ever be met.

Overnursing can occur when a mother interprets every cry as a hunger cry, or thinks that nursing for "comfort" is an appropriate way to calm a crying baby, even though the baby has nursed recently and could not possibly be hungry. When the stress-release function of crying is not well understood, it is easy to assume that nursing is an appropriate way to calm a fussy baby. Nursing does have a temporary calming effect, which serves a biological purpose. The pacifying effect of sucking is probably a built-in mechanism designed to quiet infants temporarily when their stomachs are full, so they do not become too active and regurgitate their food. However, if you nurse your baby when she needs to cry, this will serve only to postpone the crying until a later time. Nursing babies frequently for "comfort" can cause them to be chronically fussy and demanding throughout the day (and night), because they never have a chance to release pent-up stress through crying. Nursing can therefore easily become a control pattern that the baby learns to depend on to repress crying, just as some babies suck their thumb or a pacifier (see Chapter 2).

Infants do not need to suck as much as many parents believe. Although repetitive sucking does have a calming effect on infants, there is no evidence that they need to suck for non-nutritive reasons. The sucking urge is very strong to insure survival through adequate food intake. Infants with a weak sucking instinct would not have survived in prehistoric times. But the fact that infants will eagerly suck on anything does not imply that they need to do this for emotional health.

There is a wide variety in nursing frequency among traditional cultures of the world. In tribal cultures where people live in extremely hot climates, the mothers nurse their babies very frequently, sometimes several times per hour. This is the case, for example, of the !Kung San mothers of the Kalahari desert.[7] This pattern of frequent nursing has obvious survival value when there is a high risk of dehydration due to heat and diarrhea (a common cause of infant death in hot climates). In fact, in some parts of Africa, infant mortality has been as high as 50% as recently as the second half of the twentieth century, much of it caused by dysentery. The major goal in these cultures is therefore to protect the health and survival of the infants.[8] When babies nurse briefly at frequent intervals, their nutritional requirements for fluids are met, and they will be less likely to become dehydrated and die from illnesses that cause diarrhea.

Frequent nursing in traditional cultures with high mortality rates is also adaptive because, by repressing crying, it helps babies avoid excessive energy expenditure and overheating. As mentioned in Chapter 2, infants do cry less in these cultures than in Western cultures.[9] Although this is not adaptive for an infant's optimal psychological development, when illness and dehydration are major threats, it is important to help babies conserve calories and avoid any activity, such as crying, that causes overheating. This is probably why mothers in these cultures have learned to keep their infants calm and quiet. Furthermore, the mothers need to be reassured that crying is not caused by illness or pain. If it can be stopped with nursing, they assume that all is well. However, if nothing can pacify their infant, this could be an indication of a serious health problem.[10]

It is interesting that the children in these cultures that practice frequent nursing sometimes cry a great extent when they are weaned several years later. Anthropologists have observed this crying to last for weeks or even months.[11] The children in these cultures do not normally wean themselves. Instead, the mothers gradually reduce the number of feedings. Sometimes, however, they smear their nipples with bitter herbs or even slap their children to break them of the nursing habit.[12] Anthropologists interpret the weaning experience to be traumatic, not realizing that much of the crying is probably due to the fact that the recently weaned children are simply "catching up" on crying that has been repressed through frequent nursing for several years. These children are finally able to release accumulated tensions resulting from a build-up of emotional stress.

Another potent power struggle and crying trigger for children in some traditional cultures occurs when the adults refuse to carry them, and force them to walk by themselves.[13] So once the child has survived the vulnerable period of infancy, the parents in these cultures are no longer concerned when their children cry, and they sometimes treat the children in ways that Westerners would consider to be uncaring or even abusive.

In colder climates it is not necessary to nurse babies as frequently as in hot climates. When babies nurse longer at each feeding, emptying out at least one breast completely, they obtain more of the hind milk, which is higher in fat.[14] This full stomach of rich milk slows down their digestion and provides sufficient calories so they can go several hours until the next feeding. This style of feeding fills babies' nutritional requirements for fats, proteins, and carbohydrates, while keeping their fluid intake to a minimum. Because there is less of a need to nurse at frequent intervals in cold climates, mothers in the northern indigenous cultures are less likely to keep their babies close to their bodies. Instead, they place them in cradles or hammocks, and strap them to cradle boards, animals, or sleds for transportation.[15]

A further advantage of less frequent nursing in colder climates is that the lower fluid intake results in a lower need for frequent diaper changes. This is much more convenient when the baby wears many layers of clothing. Furthermore, frequent undressing could put infants at risk by exposing them to the cold, as could leaving them in wet clothing.

Less frequent nursing is also common in some traditional cultures where the mothers contribute to the economy by farming. For example, the women of Alor, an island of the Lesser Sundas, return to the fields within two weeks after childbirth, leaving their infants with a relative during the day, but sleeping with their infants and nursing them at night.[16]

Infants in Western, industrialized nations can thrive whether they are nursed frequently or at intervals of several hours. Unless you live in an extremely hot climate, I recommend a pattern of less frequent, but longer, feedings. There are several advantages to this. One is that your baby will probably sleep longer stretches at night. Another is that you will be less likely to nurse your baby when she needs to cry. This will give her opportunities to heal from birth trauma and other stress at an early age (while you hold her during crying spells).

With modern health care and sanitation, we no longer worry as much that our babies will die. We are therefore free to focus on optimal psychological development right from the start. This requires an empathic, listening relationship with infants, allowing them to release stress through crying in our arms. This, in turn, will make them more receptive to the kinds of stimulation that will enhance their ability to think and learn.

It is sometimes difficult to interpret babies' cues correctly, especially during the first few weeks, when automatic reflexes cause infants to turn their heads and suck vigorously on anything that touches their cheeks. I recommend nursing your baby every time she cries during the first week or two in order to establish your milk supply. Then you can begin to look for signs of a possible need to cry. I offer some guidelines in the next section on how to tell whether your baby is really hungry, or whether she needs to cry (while being held).

By the time your baby is three weeks old, if you offer both breasts at each feeding and encourage your baby to suck as long as she wants, she will fill her stomach at each feeding and probably settle into a rhythm of nursing about seven to ten times in a 24-hour period. This is about two-and-a-half to three-and-a-half hours from the beginning of one feeding to the beginning of the next. You can expect these intervals to increase gradually to four hours or more as your baby grows older and is able to take in more milk at each feeding.

Your breast-switching style is an important consideration. Frequent hunger is more likely if you allow your baby to nurse at only one breast at a feeding, so be sure to offer both breasts at each feeding if you want the intervals between feedings to be longer. If you allow your baby to empty one breast completely and then offer the other one, she will obtain more of the hind milk, which is higher in fat and takes longer to digest.[17] If your baby needs more fluids, however, then feeding her for a short time (about five minutes) at the first breast before switching to the other breast will better meet her nutritional needs. You can then put her back on the first breast after she has emptied out the other one, if she is still hungry. This would also be a good nursing strategy for a baby who tends to fall asleep while nursing at the first breast, but before her stomach is full.

When mothers become aware of the possibility of overnursing, and look for cues of their baby's need to cry, they are often amazed at the results. Here is what a mother reported to me:

> A turning point for me was going to a weekend workshop where people were real supportive of letting Sylvia cry when she needed to. I realized from that how little she really needed to nurse. I couldn't believe it. During the workshop, I'd go looking for my baby, thinking she really must be hungry. Somebody would be playing with her and she'd be laughing and giggling, and I'd get near her and let her know I was available to nurse her. I expected her to stop whatever she was playing and grab on to my breast and nurse, because I thought she must be starving. But instead, she nursed very little, not nearly as much as she usually did when we were at home. So that was one of my first clues. I thought, wait a minute, if she can go a whole weekend like this, a lot of times she must be nursing just as a distracter at home.

Babies do need to be held when they cry, but they do not always need to nurse. Your job is not necessarily to stop the crying. This will be difficult to understand if you have never cried in the arms of someone who loves you. Many mothers confuse food with love, thinking that offering their breast is the only way to show love to their babies. There are many ways of responding to your baby and showing love without offering your breast. One of them is by holding and listening.

What are the consequences of nursing for "comfort"?

If you choose a style of very frequent nursing that includes nursing your baby more for comfort than for hunger, be prepared, not only for frequent night awakenings, but also for considerable crying, temper tantrums, and sibling squabbles after your child is weaned from the breast. These behaviors represent your baby's repeated attempts to heal by crying. The question to consider, therefore, is whether you want to allow your baby to heal from early trauma while still an infant, or later on.

Another possible consequence of nursing babies when they are not really hungry is obesity. Contrary to popular opinion, it is possible for a breastfed baby to be overweight (although this is more likely for a bottle-fed baby). One study found that 19% of breastfed babies in the United States were obese, which is almost one out of five.[18] It used to be fashionable for babies to be fat, with chubby cheeks and creases in their thighs. Many advertisements for baby food or diapers still display pictures of overweight babies, thereby propagating the attitude that bigger babies are better babies. In some cultures plumpness is a status symbol, and a thin baby would imply either poverty or neglect. However, when the fat baby becomes a fat child, we do not consider this to be attractive, and fat children often suffer from ridicule by other children. Moreover, fat children are at greater risk for health problems later on.

If you repeatedly nurse your baby when he is not hungry, but needs to cry, he may become dependent on nursing to repress his emotions. Every time he is upset, he will act as if he needs to nurse, because that is what he is used to. This leads to cases in which older babies (over six months of age) seem to want to nurse every two hours or more, day and night, or at times when they are physically hurt or frustrated. This is an indication that nursing has become a control pattern, similar to a thumb-sucking control pattern. The only difference is that your baby sucks on a part of your body instead of his own.

A nursing control pattern can generalize to a sugar addiction, because breast milk is very sweet (as are breast milk substitutes). If a toddler always seems to prefer sweet foods (even though other foods are offered simultaneously), a history of overnursing could be the cause. A preference for sugar in toddlers is not universal. Those who have been nursed only when they are hungry are less likely to become addicted to sweet foods, and enjoy eating vegetables and other wholesome foods later on.

Overnursed babies may grow into adults who tend to eat, drink, or smoke instead of crying when they need to. They may feel compelled to put something in their mouth every time they become upset, in order to dissipate temporarily the painful feelings and to keep themselves from crying. Many adults comfort themselves with cookies, chocolate, or other sweets when they are feeling depressed or anxious. Others reach for a beer or a cigarette. Without a support group and the opportunity to release painful emotions, breaking these habits by oneself is quite difficult.

A possible consequence of repressing crying by nursing is that your child will fail to heal from early trauma (such as birth trauma). This could put him at greater risk for all the emotional problems that can be caused by trauma (as described in Chapters 1 and 2). One such problem that may become evident early on is aggressive behavior. When toddlers frequently hit or bite other children, it is almost always because they have not had sufficient opportunities to cry. These are distorted expressions of anger. Mothers who have nursed their babies frequently for several years have consulted with me because their toddlers were aggressive with other children or even with the mothers themselves. This problem is usually solved quite rapidly when the mothers stop using nursing as a way to repress their child's emotions, and encourage a healthy release through crying and temper tantrums. (See Chapter 6 for more about aggressiveness.)

In spite of these possible consequences of overnursing, there is no need to be overly concerned if your baby has acquired a nursing control pattern and uses nursing to repress crying. He can easily catch up on his crying, and will do so once you stop using nursing as a pacifier. Hold your baby lovingly, and be prepared for some long crying sessions. You will eventually be rewarded with a baby who is happier, more alert, less demanding, and who sleeps better at night. Remember, however, that your baby should never be left alone to cry.

How can I tell when my baby is hungry?

It is not always easy to distinguish between hunger and a need to cry. Every baby is different and each mother must learn to interpret her own baby's signals. Nevertheless, there are a few guidelines for determining whether or not your baby really needs to nurse.

One guideline that you can use (with certain exceptions) is the amount of time since the previous feeding, provided your baby has taken a full feeding and sucked at both breasts, which can take a half hour or more. If your baby then begins to cry less than two-and-a-half hours after the beginning of the feeding, she is not likely to be hungry again so soon. Perhaps she just wants to be held and to interact socially with you. If you suspect that she might need to cry, then holding her without nursing her will allow her to do so.

The time periods between feedings normally increase as babies grow older, because their stomachs can hold more milk. If your baby seems to want to nurse more frequently rather than less frequently as she grows older, this could be an indication that she has a backlog of crying to do, and is beginning to use nursing as a control pattern. However, it could also be an indication that she is having a growth spurt, is not getting sufficient milk, or is ready for solid foods if she is over four months of age. She could also be thirsty because of hot weather, or prefer small, frequent feedings because of illness. Some babies are "grazers," perhaps due to a small stomach. They do not take in very much milk at each feeding, and may need more frequent feedings. As a general guideline, however, a normal, healthy baby who is at least one month old does not need to nurse more often than eight to ten times in a 24-hour period, provided she is allowed to suck as long as she wants at both breasts at each feeding. Any fussiness in between feedings is probably not caused by hunger, and may indicate a need to cry.

Another guideline is the *type* of crying. A true hunger cry does not usually begin as a cry at all, but rather as grunts of discomfort or a whine. It builds up to a full-blown cry only if the baby is not fed. This makes sense because hunger is not something that happens suddenly, but rather gradually, beginning as a mild urge. Some parents never hear a true hunger signal because they never wait until their baby is hungry before feeding her. If your baby is crying loudly and vigorously in your arms, and it has been less than two-and-a-half hours since a full feeding, it is probably not a hunger cry.

In a study of mothers' interpretations of infant crying, researchers recorded three types of crying (pain, hunger, and startle), and played them back to the mothers without telling them which was which. The mothers did not interpret all of the cries correctly, thinking that most of the cries were from hunger.[19] This tendency to interpret crying as hunger when it is not may be an evolutionary remnant of times when infant mortality was high and infant survival was the most important concern for parents. At any rate, it helps to explain why many mothers tend to overnurse their babies. However, some mothers do learn to distinguish the different types of crying quite successfully.

A third guideline is to observe your baby's behavior carefully after you offer your breast. If she does not latch on eagerly, she is probably not really hungry. If she does begin to suck, but soon starts crying again, this may be an indication that she is not really hungry, but needs to cry instead. There is no point in trying to insist that your baby nurse. Instead, you can continue to hold her and pay attention to her. Some mothers overlook their baby's cues when the baby does not really want to nurse, and they keep trying to offer their breast. If babies could talk at those times, they would probably say, "Please stop trying to put that in my mouth. I need you to pay attention to me so I can have a good cry!" (Note that crying after starting to nurse *can* be an indication of nursing problems, such as choking on too much milk, difficulties in getting milk out of the breast, or difficulty breathing through the nose. Be sure to check into these reasons first.)

Other possible signals of a need to cry include squirming, kicking, biting, grunting, or sucking sporadically and irregularly while nursing. A baby who is truly hungry and ready to nurse will do so calmly (unless it is hard for her to breathe, suck, or swallow, or unless there is a lot of noise or other distractions). If your baby is not nursing calmly because of accumulated tensions, removing her from the breast and holding her lovingly will allow her to do the crying she needs to do. This crying will then be followed by calm sucking, sleep, or happy alertness.

GUIDELINES FOR DETERMINING WHEN YOUR BABY IS HUNGRY

- Time since previous feeding (with certain exceptions). Intervals will increase with age.

- Careful attention to your baby's signals.

- Baby's behavior after you offer breast or bottle.

I encourage you to experiment a little, which is what I did with my son. On the days when I offered my breast every time he began to cry, this stopped the crying temporarily, but he would begin to cry again and again all day long. When I allowed him to cry (in my arms) instead of nursing him, I was always amazed at the results. Here is an example:

> One morning at three months of age, my son nursed extensively on both breasts and stopped by himself. After 90 minutes of playing happily, he began to cry very hard. I did not nurse him again, but gave him my full attention while holding him. He cried very hard for 20 minutes, and then fell into a deep sleep for about an hour. He woke up very happy and was extremely alert and active for about a half hour. He then gradually began to make little sounds of discomfort, which slowly increased in intensity. I interpreted this as hunger, and offered my breast. He nursed calmly and steadily. He had no more crying spells that day, and wanted to nurse only about every four hours. In between feedings he was calm and content.

Your interpretation of your babies' cries will be influenced by the manner in which you yourself were treated as a baby. If you were made to wait for your feedings because of a rigid schedule, you may be tempted to overreact and err in the opposite direction, by nursing your baby more frequently than necessary. If you were left to cry alone, you will feel that your mother abandoned you when you were crying. This may make it difficult for you to respond to your own baby every time she cries. On the other hand, you may feel a strong pull to hold, comfort, and nurse your baby in an attempt to compensate for your own past unmet needs for closeness when you cried as a baby.

In the following interview, a mother admitted that her fear of causing her baby to suffer made her overnurse him:

> I never knew whether he really needed the milk or whether he didn't, whether he was really hungry, or what was going on. So mostly I let him nurse because I didn't know. I would always give him the benefit of the doubt and give him milk. I would just wonder what it would do to him psychologically if his mother didn't give him what he needed. How is he going to feel about his mother? If this person who's supposed to love him doesn't give him what he needs, it's going to be horrible. So I was never sure if he really did or if he really didn't need to nurse, and I thought, well maybe he does. I'd end up giving it to him so that it wouldn't create other problems. And he nursed *constantly*. People were surprised when I would tell them how much he nursed. He was often more on the breast than off, just constantly wanting to nurse. Now, looking back, I think that he needed to cry more, that a lot of the problems like sleeping through the night probably would have been better if I had just held him and let him cry in my arms at times, instead of always giving him my breast to suck on.

The guidelines in this section are not absolute prescriptions. A few mistakes from time to time are not going to damage your baby. So don't be afraid to experiment a little as you learn to interpret your baby's needs and discover her natural rhythm. The important thing to remember is that your baby will need to cry at times, and she will indicate this. So try to be aware of this possibility and realize that nursing your baby at those times is not the best way to meet her needs. However, although your baby may not need your breast then, she definitely needs your love and attention.

When shall I wean my baby, and when shall I offer solid foods?

The longer you nurse your baby, the more he will benefit from the immunological and nutritional benefits of breast milk. You and your baby will also benefit from that special feeling of closeness that breastfeeding provides. In most traditional cultures, babies are breastfed for at least two years, and sometimes for as long as five or six years. So don't be surprised if your baby is not ready to give up the breast until he is several years old. If you and your baby enjoy your nursing relationship, there is no harm in continuing for several years. Unfortunately, Western society expects babies to be weaned early and considers six months to be a long time to nurse a baby. Some people are even shocked to hear of a toddler who is "still" nursing, not realizing that this has probably been the norm in human prehistory for millions of years.

When nursing is not a control pattern, toddlers will eventually lose interest and wean themselves, assuming they are receiving sufficient alternative food sources. But even when babies are taking in solid foods, it is rare for spontaneous weaning to occur before one year of age. If nursing has become a control pattern, however, toddlers are likely to continue nursing for a longer time and to strongly resist being weaned.

I recommend nursing your baby for at least a year if possible. After that, you can continue to nurse as long as you are both enjoying it. It is not a good idea to continue nursing if you no longer find it pleasurable or are beginning to feel resentful. If you decide to initiate the weaning process before your baby loses interest in nursing, try to do it very gradually, while making sure your baby's needs for closeness and nourishment are met in other ways. A gradual weaning will be easier on you too, as it will minimize the possibility of painful breast engorgement and sudden hormone shifts.

If we speculate from an evolutionary point of view, we can find some clues to the age at which solid foods should be introduced. While our ancient ancestors were being carried around as babies by their mothers, they learned to grasp objects and bring them to their mouths, just as all babies do today. These prehistoric babies probably grabbed and ate whatever food their mothers happened to be eating. That was their introduction to solid foods.

By four or five months of age babies can grasp objects, and all normal babies put everything they can into their mouths for many months thereafter. Could this strong tendency be a remnant of times when babies had to fend for themselves more than they do now, because mothers knew nothing about nutrition? It would be nature's way of supplying babies with additional nourishment at an age when breast milk is no longer a sufficient food. Just as with the sucking instinct, the putting-in-the-mouth instinct may have had definite survival value. So if a baby's grasping ability indicates a possible readiness for solid foods, this would imply that such foods should not be introduced before four months of age.

There are several additional indications that babies are not ready for solids until they are at least several months old. A study of 57 infants showed that babies do not readily accept solid foods from a spoon until around three months of age. Salivary secretion (drooling) does not appear until three or four months of age, and teeth do not usually appear until around six months.[20]

Introducing solid foods too early could be one factor leading to food allergies. Dairy products, wheat, eggs, and chicken are more likely to cause allergic symptoms in very young infants than in older babies. In one study, children who had been introduced to solid foods before 15 weeks of age were more likely to be overweight and have wheezing problems (asthma).[21]

Another disadvantage of offering solids too early is that this decreases the intake of valuable milk by lessening the baby's appetite. Furthermore, some manufacturers of commercial baby foods add sugar and starch to their products, which tend to fill babies up on "empty" calories. Feeding such foods to infants under four months of age could be one factor leading to obesity.

By the time your baby is five or six months old, you can begin to look for indications of readiness for additional foods besides milk. Perhaps he will try to grab food that you yourself are eating, or indicate that he is still hungry after you nurse him, or want to nurse more frequently, but still seem unsatisfied. At five months of age, my daughter started looking for a third breast after emptying both breasts during her feedings! This was a clear indication to me that she was ready for solid foods, and she accepted them eagerly. If your baby is not yet ready for solid foods, he will reject them.

What foods should I offer my baby?

Infants have the ability to select a good diet by themselves, if they are given the chance. Evidence for this is from a famous nutritional study with three seven- to nine-month old babies, who had been fed nothing but breast milk. The babies were offered a wide variety of wholesome, unrefined foods to choose from at each meal for a period of six months. They were not fed anything unless they indicated in some way that they wanted a particular food. Furthermore, nobody encouraged, praised, or reprimanded them for eating or not eating. In fact, the topic of food was never brought up during mealtimes. All of the babies chose a well-balanced diet, and none of them became too fat or too thin. One baby, who had poor bone structure (rickets), drank cod liver oil many times of his own free will until his bones were healthy and normal. All three babies went on food "binges." They would eat huge quantities of only one food for several days and then taper off. This did not cause any regurgitation, discomfort, diarrhea, or constipation, and none of the babies developed allergies.[22]

Some parents think that they should use nutritional knowledge based on scientific research as a guide to feeding their baby. Even though they themselves may have problems eating correctly, they think that at least they can give their baby a good start in life by making sure she gets the correct vitamins and a sufficient number of protein grams each day. This is certainly a praiseworthy attitude, but unfortunately the parents are bound to run into problems. This is because scientific research is based on averages. It can determine what the average 14-month-old needs to eat on an average day. Such research, however, says nothing about what little Susie needs to eat on any given day. This depends on how much exercise she has had, how much stress she is under, whether her brain or her bones are undergoing a growth spurt, or whether she has been exposed to the flu. All of those factors and many more can have a profound effect on her nutritional requirements.

There is considerable individual variability in nutritional needs, some of which is genetic.[23] Some adults, for example, need much more calcium than others, and many people have allergies or intolerances to certain foods. It is important to have some knowledge of nutrition, because this can guide you in selecting a wholesome and well-rounded diet for your baby. (No baby will develop well on a diet consisting only of spaghetti, bread, and potatoes, no matter how much choice she is given among those three foods.) But the usefulness of such knowledge goes no further than that, because the only person who knows what and how much the baby needs to eat on any given day is your baby herself. One of the assumptions of this book is that babies know what they need and will indicate these needs if given a chance. The study mentioned above shows that this assumption also applies to nutrition, so don't be afraid to give your baby plenty of autonomy in deciding what she wants to eat.

When you first start to offer soft foods to your baby, you can hold the spoon in front of her so she can see what is on it and decide whether she wants to eat it or not. If she wants it, she will probably open her mouth and perhaps even grab the spoon or your arm in an attempt to bring the food closer to her mouth. If she does not want the food, she will probably not open her mouth or make an attempt to bring the food closer, and she may even push it away or turn her head aside. You can then try another food. A different method is to set out several foods simultaneously in front of your baby, and to let her reach for what she wants. Some parents skip the spoon-feeding stage entirely, and begin by offering foods that their babies can grab by themselves and put in their mouths. You can put pieces of soft food on your baby's high chair tray and let her feed herself. Either approach can work very well. If you use spoon-feeding, try to let your baby be an active participant from the start, encouraging her to feed herself as soon as possible, so she can become fully autonomous. Letting your baby feed herself will be messier than if you feed her, but your baby will become more self-sufficient.

It is not necessary to supply your baby with an entire cafeteria of foods at every meal, but it may be a good idea to have at least one food available from each of the major food groups. If you offer a wide variety of wholesome foods over a period of time, your baby will have ample opportunity to choose an adequate diet. If your baby eats ravenously of one particular food, you can continue offering that food every day (along with other foods), until she has had her fill of it. Babies may have high physiological requirements for one particular nutrient for a while, because of growth spurts in various parts of their body, or because of illness. It is probably best not to combine foods, in case your baby wants only one of the foods in the mixture and not the others. Some babies refuse mixtures, but will eat each food served separately. Most babies go on food binges, and it is usually nothing to worry about.[24] Here are some examples of my son's food binges:

> At 13 months of age my son developed a craving for fatty foods. He would greedily lick the butter off the bread I gave him. So I began offering him more fatty foods such as mayonnaise and nut butters. This craving for fats lasted a few days and then tapered off. On other days he would eat nothing but grain products such as cereal, bread, crackers and noodles. Sometimes he would eat a whole bowl full of grapes at one sitting, and then go for weeks without touching a grape. He would often go for days without eating much of anything, and then gobble down everything I put in front of him for a day or two. He hardly ever had any digestive upsets, was very healthy, and was neither too fat nor too thin.

It is better to offer choices simultaneously, rather than one after the other, because babies have no way of knowing that other foods will follow. Babies normally eat until they obtain an adequate number of calories. If you begin with a sweet or starchy food, your baby may fill up on that, obtaining the calories she needs, and have no room left for foods high in protein, for example. This problem will not arise if you offer a variety of foods simultaneously at each meal. In this case, your baby will not fill herself up on the sweet foods, unless she has a specific nutritional requirement for them. The one exception to this, as I have already mentioned, is if your baby has already developed an addiction to sugar from being overnursed. If so, if may be wise to offer non-sweet foods first at mealtimes.

It is best not to influence what your baby eats, or even to comment too much about it. Some parents praise their babies for eating well, or reprimand them for not eating. Some trick their baby into eating a food that she does not want, by placing a small amount of desired food on the spoon that contains the undesired food. Others use games or humor to entice their babies to eat, by pretending, for example, that the spoon is an airplane flying towards the baby's mouth. None of this is necessary because you do not want your baby to lose the ability to know which foods her body needs. Many of us adults have lost touch with this knowledge because our natural inclinations were interfered with when we were little. In order for this self-regulation method to work well, it is best to apply it right from the start, as soon as you introduce solid foods.[25]

Even after you begin to offer your baby solid foods, milk (preferably breast milk) will remain the mainstay of her diet for quite a while. Gradually there is a shift, and eventually solid foods make up the bulk of the diet, with milk being a supplemental beverage. This shift may occur more rapidly for some babies than for others, and the change may occur unevenly. One day your baby may want only solid foods and liquids such as juice or water. Another day she may want only milk. If you have not interfered with your baby's self-regulation, she will probably know exactly what she needs, and will communicate that to you. As a toddler, for example, she may go to the refrigerator when she wants solid foods, but reach for her mother's blouse when she wants to nurse.

What if I have already interfered with my baby's self-regulation?

If your baby or toddler has developed a preference for sweets from having been overnursed, and if he is overweight, it may be necessary to restrict his consumption of sweet foods. If he still nurses very frequently, and you think this is a control pattern, you can begin to offer your attention and empathy, rather than your breast, at times when he is fussy. Choose times when you know your baby is not hungry, but only upset, because that is when he will probably benefit from a good cry. Be sure that you yourself are relaxed, with plenty of time. Explain that you do not think he really needs to nurse right then, and offer to hold him instead. Be prepared for his crying and anger, and stay with him until he has finished crying. These are tensions he has been carrying around for a long time, but which his nursing dependency has prevented him from releasing. You can give further explanations, as needed, such as, "When you nurse so much, it stops you from crying. It's much better for you to cry and to get all your sads and angries out."

If you begin to interrupt your child's nursing or eating addictions, but fail to create enough emotional safety for him to cry, he may substitute new habits, such as thumb sucking or nail biting. The only way to help him overcome the need for any of those behaviors is to allow him to do the crying he has needed to do for a long time.

Another way that babies can lose healthy self-regulation regarding food is when parents attempt to trick or encourage them to eat specific foods, such as vegetables. Some children develop a strong distaste for vegetables because of this. After 15 months of age, when toddlers typically enter a stage of autonomy and independence, they can become quite stubborn, and this is often when feeding conflicts arise. If this occurs, it is best to stop trying to control what your baby eats. Perhaps you can offer some new vegetables, or serve familiar ones in a new way. You can offer these vegetables along with other wholesome foods, and then remove any leftover food without saying anything about it. The use of praise or comments will only aggravate the situation. Trust that your toddler will become self-regulated and will eat enough foods to stay healthy. There is no point in turning eating into a power struggle because you will lose the battles. You cannot *make* your child eat.

Sometimes babies squirm, cry, or scream in their high chairs, or throw food, spoons or dishes on the floor. This problem has several possible causes. Perhaps you are keeping your baby in the high chair too long because you think he should eat more. Babies' appetites are often overestimated, especially after they are a year old and their rate of growth slows down considerably. Some toddlers are able to grow normally and stay healthy on what appear to their parents as very small quantities of food. A hungry baby with a desired food in front of him is not likely to squirm or throw food on the floor, because he will be too busy eating.

Once your baby has finished eating, he may be ready to get out of his high chair, even though it might be more convenient for you to keep him there. During the second year especially, toddlers become very resistant to being controlled in any way and may resent being cooped up in a high chair for any length of time. It is too much to expect a baby to sit still with nothing to do. The solution is to let him down as soon as he has eaten his fill, or else give him something interesting to play with. Perhaps he just wants closeness, in which case you can let him sit on your lap. High chairs are not really necessary. Some parents find that it is easier to feed their baby while he is sitting on their lap.

Another reason for fussing at mealtimes may be that you are not giving your baby enough autonomy during the feeding process. Perhaps he is ready to hold a spoon by himself, but you are still spoon-feeding him. Perhaps he would like to pick up pieces of food with his fingers and feed himself that way. Or maybe you are trying to coax him to eat something he does not want.

If these explanations do not seem to apply, there is always the possibility that your baby may need to cry. If so, he will not be ready to eat anything or sit still until he has completed the crying he needs to do. It does little good to reprimand your baby or try to feed him under such conditions. Give him empathy and attention so that he can release his pent-up emotions. Then, when he is feeling better, he will be ready to eat or play calmly.

I find it difficult to trust my baby's natural appetite and food preferences.

Many adults had their own self-regulated food preferences interfered with when they were little. If this is your experience, you may not always know when you are really hungry, and you may eat at regular mealtimes just because it is the convenient thing to do. Not being accustomed to trusting your own natural appetite, you will probably find it difficult to trust your baby's. Perhaps you will worry about whether she is eating enough of the right kinds of foods, and think that you should encourage or coerce her to eat.

Here is what a mother said to me about her toddler's eating habits, her own eating habits, her childhood, and her feelings:

> I've tried to stop asking her if she's hungry, and just assume that she's going to let me know. And I've begun to realize that her mealtimes might not be the same as mine. Sometimes I get real concerned, like when four hours have passed since she woke up, and she's not hungry yet. I've realized that when I wait until she tells me she's hungry, then she knows exactly what she wants to eat. When she doesn't eat something I've prepared for her, I feel like telling her what my childhood was like. I was told frequently that we were very fortunate to have this food, and didn't I know that the people in China were starving? And then my parents would bring out the food bills and tell us how much this meal just cost us. Another feeling I have when she leaves food on her plate is that I'm going to get to eat it. So then I eat it, and I feel bad because I've just eaten so much! There's a lot of tension on my part about food. It amazes me the way she can just play with her food without eating it. It's fine with her just to say she's not hungry, or she's done and wants to go play. I think what makes it hard is that I used to be that way when I was young, but it was taken away from me. I was made to feel like it's real important that I eat, and that I couldn't go out to play until I did. So I'm probably feeling some jealousy too.

In order to begin trusting your baby's natural appetite, it may be beneficial for you to become aware of ways in which you yourself were mistrusted, and to express the feelings surrounding these memories. This could help you become more relaxed about your baby's eating habits and give you the confidence to let her become self-regulated.

Another common feeling is anger. It can be frustrating and discouraging when your toddler refuses to eat something that you prepared with love and care. In fact, it can even feel like a form of rejection. Here is what a mother said:

> Last night I made some bean soup. Even before he tasted it he pushed it away. So I put it in the blender so it would be smoother,

and decorated it with croutons on the top. I thought he might like that. He took one sip and pushed it away. I'm fed up with all the nonsense running around making special things for him, and last night I was just furious. I felt like saying: You eat your soup, or else!

If you can remember to keep food and love separate in your mind, it will be easier to remain calm and objective when your baby refuses to eat a food that you have prepared. This does not mean that your baby is rejecting you. When your child is older and has her adolescent growth spurt, you will be rewarded with someone who will probably appreciate your cooking much more, and your grocery bills will increase considerably!

Sometimes deeper, traumatic experiences can interfere with parents' ability to trust their babies to eat what they need. Here is an example:

In one of my workshops in France, a woman mentioned that she felt chronically anxious that her ten-month-old baby was not eating enough. She feared that he would fail to thrive unless she frequently coaxed him to eat more. Her baby was present at the workshop, a strong, husky, happy baby boy who did not appear to be at all undernourished. I encouraged the mother to explore the origin of her feelings by asking if her baby reminded her of anyone else. She then realized that he reminded her of her own mother. As an adolescent, she had cared for her ill mother, and had prepared meals for her, continually coaxing her to eat. Unfortunately, her mother had become thinner and weaker, and had finally died. This woman cried hard for about 15 minutes while re-experiencing the anxiety and helplessness she had felt as an adolescent. Afterwards, she realized that her baby was quite different from her mother. He was healthy and thriving, and she understood that she did not need to coax him to eat more than he wanted.

This example illustrates how our past experiences can greatly influence our behavior as parents. It is important to look for these connections and keep the past separate from the present. By talking and crying about your own past hurts, you can become more aware of your baby's true needs.

EXERCISES

Explore your childhood.

1. Do you remember times when you were coaxed or forced to eat, denied a food that you wanted, or praised, rewarded, reprimanded, or punished for eating or not eating? How did it make you feel? Was there enough food (or too much food) in your home? Did you ever see food being wasted or saved? How did this make you feel?
2. Were there ways in which food was equated with love when you were growing up? Describe.
3. Were you ever overweight or underweight as a child or adolescent? Did you have any eating disorders? How did you feel about that?

Express your feelings about your baby.

1. How do you feel when you nurse your baby (or give a bottle)?
2. Do you feel that your baby nurses (or wants a bottle) too frequently or not frequently enough? Are you anxious about your baby's weight? Has anyone ever commented on your baby's weight? How did it make you feel? How do you feel about your ability to tell when your baby is hungry?
3. (If your baby is eating solid foods): How do you feel about trusting your baby's natural food preferences and self-regulation? Do you feel that your baby is eating enough of the right kinds of foods? How do you feel when your baby refuses to eat something that you have prepared?

Nurture yourself.

1. Sometimes parents are so involved with their babies that they forget about their own nutritional needs. Spend an entire day eating only what you really want to eat, at the times when you are really hungry, regardless of your baby's or other family members' diets and meal schedules.
2. The next time you feel the urge to eat when you are sad, angry, anxious, or lonely, call a friend on the phone instead.
3. If you are overweight, join a support group that addresses not only the nutritional aspect of weight reduction but also the psychological aspect.

CHAPTER 4

SLEEP: LETTING YOUR BABY REST

Should I let my baby sleep with me?

The young of all land mammals sleep in close proximity to their mothers. During the millions of years of prehistoric times, human infants probably slept with their mothers. In traditional tribal cultures today, the practice of sleeping with infants is still quite common. However, in the technologically advanced cultures of North America and Europe, this practice has been largely abandoned in favor of cradles and cribs. In most homes, the infant does not even sleep in the same room as the parents.

When and why did the natural practice of sleeping with infants become lost in Western cultures? During the 13th century in Europe, the Catholic priests first began recommending that mothers stop sleeping with their infants.[1] Although the primary reason for this advice was probably the rise of patriarchy and the fear of too much feminine influence on infants (especially male infants), the reason *given* for this advice was the fear of smothering the infants, commonly known as "overlaying." It is now believed that most of the cases of infant deaths during the Middle Ages were caused by illness or infanticide. When accidental smothering occurred, it was probably caused by parents who were under the influence of alcohol.

By the 14th and 15th centuries, the advice not to sleep with infants began to take effect, and cradles were commonplace items of furniture in most European homes with children.[2] The age at which infants were put to sleep in cradles for the night, rather than in their mothers' arms, became gradually younger. After the industrial revolution in the 18th century, the notion of "spoiling" became widespread in industrialized countries, and mothers were warned not to hold their infants too much for fear of creating demanding monsters.

During the twentieth century, infants in technological societies became more separated from their mothers than ever before in the history of our species. More and more births took place in hospitals, and the hospital central nursery was invented to protect the infants from infections. From day one, babies were expected to sleep alone, away from their mothers. The decline in breastfeeding, promoted by companies producing breast milk substitutes, further contributed to this separation of mothers from infants. During breastfeeding, mothers normally produce hormones (such as oxytocin and prolactin), which help create a strong desire to be physically close to their babies. Bottle-feeding deprives mothers of the hormones and eliminates the need for the biological mother's physical presence. The result of all these influences is that, by 1950, very few babies in Western, industrialized nations slept with their mothers.

It is little wonder that parents began seeking advice for a whole new array of problems. Experts in the field of child rearing found themselves searching for remedies for the babies who would not go to sleep at night, for those who banged their heads, for toddlers who climbed out of their cribs and kept coming into their parents' bed, and for the young children who wet their beds, or had nightmares and fears of the dark. Many of these sleep-related problems could be the result of forcing babies to sleep alone.

Could it be that the increasing prevalence of teen sexuality and pregnancy reflects a need to be held more than a desire for sex? The expression "to sleep with someone," implies to have sex. Perhaps this expression reflects a universal, unfilled childhood need to sleep next to one's parents and to be held during the night.

Fortunately, the practice of sleeping with infants and young children is becoming more widely recommended and accepted in Western, industrialized nations, as parents begin to trust their natural inclinations to share their beds with their infants. Starting in the 1970's a few books began to recommend that parents sleep with their babies. There are now many books that recommend bed sharing, commonly known as "co-sleeping."[3]

Babies have strong attachment needs that researchers are just beginning to understand. The need for close physical contact, both during the day and at night, is a vital and legitimate need during the first few years. Anna Freud, the daughter of Sigmund Freud, recognized this when she wrote: "It is a primitive need of the child to have close and warm contact with another person's body while falling asleep.... The infant's biological need for the caretaking adult's *constant presence* is disregarded in our Western culture, and children are exposed to long hours of solitude owing to the misconception that it is healthy for the young to sleep ... alone."[4]

Some child-rearing specialists state that babies will never want to leave once they have been taken into their parents' bed. This may be true during the first few years when children need the closeness and security. However, we do not need to force children to become independent. This occurs of its own accord when children outgrow their early needs.

The strong desire of human babies to sleep near their mothers may have its basis in our evolutionary history. During the hunter-gatherer stage of our species' existence babies would have been extremely vulnerable to predators and cold weather, especially at night. Infants who feared the dark and who refused to sleep alone had a much better chance of surviving than those infants who did not complain when put down. So there was strong selective pressure in favor of such fears.[5] Although predators are no longer a threat, and we have heated homes, modern human infants' reflexes, instincts, and needs are still geared to the hunter-gatherer way of life. Cultural changes have occurred much too rapidly to have any major impact on the genetic makeup of our species since that time.

I asked a father to share his feelings about sharing his bed with his infant son. Here is what he said:

I love it. Even with all the disturbances and inconveniences, it's still really fun to have him there. Sometimes when we wake up in the morning, we play together in bed. I cherish that. It's great to be all together as a family in bed. There's something really special about it.

Researchers have studied the sleep patterns and brain waves of infants who share a bed with their mothers, compared with those of infants who sleep alone. Infants who sleep with their mothers have more brief awakenings, and also spend less time in deep sleep than solitary-sleeping infants. This is probably because of the mother's sounds and movements during her own sleep.[6]

This nighttime stimulation has been proposed as a possible protection against sudden infant death syndrome (SIDS). One theory of SIDS is that the infants are sleeping so soundly that they are unable to arouse themselves and continue breathing during a long breath-holding episode (apnea).[7] Cross-cultural studies have shown that, in cultures where infants are held regularly and where mothers sleep with their infants, SIDS rates are low compared to those cultures where these practices are not followed.[8] The researchers do not claim that sleeping alone *causes* SIDS, but they do suggest that letting infants sleep with their mothers could be a protective factor for those infants who are at risk for dying of SIDS.

Sleeping with your baby may require time to adapt, but with a little perseverance, bed sharing can become enjoyable for everybody. However, if it does not work well for you to share your bed with your baby, then at least you can provide physical closeness until your baby falls asleep, and you can respond promptly when he awakens during the night.

What precautions should I take so my baby will not smother or fall out of bed?

Some parents worry about smothering their baby. This is a valid concern, because there have been reported cases in modern times of parents lying on top of infants and smothering them ("overlaying"), particularly with infants under three months of age.[9] However, this is highly unlikely if you use common sense precautions. Do not take your baby to bed with you if you are an extremely deep sleeper or if you are under the effects of drugs that affect your sleep, such as alcohol, tranquilizers, or antidepressants. This also applies to any other person who shares your bed. Mothers with young infants do not sleep very deeply unless they are under the effects of drugs. The slightest whimper of an infant usually awakens the mother. It is also dangerous to sleep with your infant if you are obese.

Another possible danger is that babies can become wedged in a crevice between the mattress and the wall. This is most likely to occur between three and seven months of age, when babies can move around, but may not have the strength to get themselves out of a tight place.[10] It is important to make sure that there is a tight fit between your mattress and the wall, and to use a bumper pad (as in a crib) to prevent your infant from falling into the crevice.

BED SHARING SAFETY TIPS

- Do not take any drugs that can affect your sleep.

- Never smoke in the room where your infant sleeps.

- Use a firm mattress and avoid down comforters.

- Take precautions so your infant will not fall out.

- Avoid crevices between your bed and the wall.

- Never place your infant on a pillow.

- Always lay your infant on its back to sleep.

- Do not sleep with your baby if you are obese.

- Tie your hair back if it is very long.

- Do not let your infant share a bed with another child.

- Do not place your infant near dangling strings.

- Never leave your infant alone in an adult bed.

Additional precautions are: do not sleep with your infant on a soft mattress, or on a water bed, bean bag chair, or couch; keep your baby near the top, not so far down in the bed that the blankets cover her head; never place your infant on a pillow. Also, it is much safer to place your infant on her back to sleep, rather than on her stomach. These guidelines should also be followed if your infant sleeps in a crib.

Another worry is the possibility of the baby falling out of bed. There are several different arrangements that can prevent this. The baby can sleep between the two parents, or be placed next to a wall (with a bumper pad against the wall). Another solution is to move a piece of furniture against one side of the bed, or to build a railing. If you do this, be sure there is a tight fit with the mattress, and the spaces between the railing slats are small enough so your infant's head or body cannot pass through them. Some families sleep on a large mattress on the floor, so if the baby should roll off, she would not hurt herself. Another solution is the "side-car" arrangement: a crib-like infant bed that attaches securely right next to an adult bed, with no barrier between the two. This allows the infant to have her own safe place, but to be within arm's reach.

Does bed sharing encourage incest?

Many people immediately think of incest when they hear about parents who bring their baby to bed with them. They worry that parents as well as children will become sexually aroused by each other's presence in bed and that, either incest will occur, or else the family members will have to make special efforts to restrain themselves.

These worries are ill founded. Incest has much more to do with the perpetrator's own abuse history than where the child sleeps. Parents who have incestuous tendencies are almost always victims of sexual abuse. This is the major factor predicting the likelihood of incest. It makes no difference whether the child sleeps separately or not.

If you feel the urge to stimulate your baby in a sexual way or use your baby's body for your own sexual gratification, you must not act on those feelings. To do so would be very harmful. You were probably sexually abused yourself, and you will benefit from therapy. Babies should never be forced to fill other people's needs, sexual or otherwise. Sexual abuse can cause such confusion in a baby or toddler that it can adversely influence almost everything in her life. Many adults remember being sexually abused as small children. The effects on their lives have been devastating. Once they begin to heal through therapy, whole areas of their lives start to improve.

What about children becoming attracted to their parents? Sigmund Freud believed that children from about three to six years of age develop sexual desires for the parent of the opposite sex. He named this incestuous tendency the "Oedipus complex," and believed that it caused considerable tension and conflict during the preschool years, which must be resolved before development could proceed normally. Freud considered this stage to be normal and inevitable. It is important to remember, however, that Freud lived at a time when bed sharing between parents and children was not common in Europe, and parents did not hold or cuddle their children very much. He built his entire theory on observations of children and adults who were deprived of early physical contact, and therefore starved for affection.

Another, more likely, theory is that incestuous feelings in young children are not normal or inevitable, but rather the result of unfilled needs. Children would not develop such longings for their parents' bodies if they had experienced sufficient touching and closeness during infancy. Dr. Arthur Janov describes how an unfilled need for closeness may become distorted and sexual in nature: "If a child is neglected and needs warmth desperately, he may eroticize that need if he cannot fulfill himself in a direct and straight way with his parent. The love need and sex then become confused and incestuous feelings can arise when the need for love does."[11]

If you give your baby sufficient holding and cuddling, both during the day and at night, you will meet her legitimate need for physical closeness, and there will be very few conflicts, tensions, jealousies, or guilt feelings during the preschool years. My prediction is that psychoanalysts will not see any evidence of the Oedipus complex in children who are raised with sufficient physical contact during the first few years.

What about my sex life?

Sleeping with your baby will probably require some readjustments in your sexual activities. It is generally believed in our culture that babies or children should not witness their parents engaging in sexual intercourse, because the children don't understand what is going on and may become frightened. Furthermore, people in our culture usually seek privacy for sexual relations.

Traditionally, the parents' bed is the place in which to have sex, but once it has been turned into the family bed, this becomes more difficult. Our culture has many rigid ideas about when, where, and how often to have sex. When parents begin sleeping with their children, the parents become more flexible, and sexual intercourse simply occurs when and where it is convenient. One solution is to put the baby to sleep in another room and then bring her into the family bed when the parents are ready to fall asleep.

After the birth of your baby, your sexual relationship will probably change anyway, whether or not you choose to sleep with your baby. Many breastfeeding women discover that they have a loss of interest and responsiveness to sex. This can last until ovulation resumes, or, in some women, as long as breastfeeding continues. One explanation is that nursing fills the need for physical contact and sensuality. Suckling causes pleasurable uterine contractions in some women, similar to (although milder than) those occurring during orgasm. Both sexual intercourse and breastfeeding are biological processes that insure reproduction and survival of offspring. If these two processes were not pleasurable, our species would not have survived. From a biological perspective, sexual intercourse is not necessary when there is a baby to nurse. In fact, having babies too close together in age would jeopardize the survival of both of them. It is therefore quite natural for a woman to have little or no interest in sex during the postpartum year when her physiology is geared for breastfeeding. Another reason why a mother may have a diminished interest in sex is that much of her energy and attention go towards caring for the baby, especially if she has little help from other people. However, there are large individual differences, and some women do not experience any loss of interest in sex.

It is interesting that in some cultures there is a postpartum sexual taboo, sometimes lasting as long as two years.[12] This maximizes the chances for survival of the infant by preventing another pregnancy. But this taboo also protects the man's self-confidence at a time when many women have diminished interest in sex. In Western cultures, there is no sexual taboo, and couples are led to believe that their sex life can resume normally after six weeks postpartum. Many men are deeply disappointed and resentful when this does not occur, and many marriages could be saved if the couples were forewarned that a woman's loss of interest in sex after the birth of a baby is normal and temporary.

In the following interview, a mother told me about the change in her sex life following the birth of her baby.

> Since Noel was born, our sex life has changed *radically*. To begin with it just hurt so much. And then I was afraid of getting pregnant again. Also, I was just plain tired, really tired. I didn't want to have anything to do with sex for months. Also I developed a lot of feelings of resentment against my husband, especially in the nighttime. I was the one who had to deal with Noel's waking up, and my husband would just turn over and go to sleep. Once we tried making love, but no sooner had we started than Noel woke up and wanted to nurse. We just ended up laughing about it. Often when I was nursing, to be quite honest, I had quite sexual feelings. It would often turn me on to nurse him. That was just from the manipulation of my nipples. But as well as that, he would touch me all over my breasts, just so gently. That's how I wanted to be touched. Anything else turned me *completely* off. To have a big man's hands on me just didn't do it. They were too rough, too hard, and too insensitive. And this soft little touch from Noel was just great. I loved it. I don't think I ever had an actual orgasm, but I was certainly aroused while nursing. It was just lovely!

Some men feel threatened by sexual rejection. These feelings probably come from early unmet needs for being touched and held. A baby boy who receives sufficient physical contact from his mother, both day and night, will not have to depend on sex later on in order to feel worthwhile as a man. If you are a man feeling dismayed and resentful by your wife's loss of interest in sex, try not to pressure her to choose between your baby's needs and your own. This would put her in a very difficult situation. Realize that her loss of interest is temporary, and that she needs your love and support. The more you can support her in her role as mother, the better your relationship with her will be. She needs to know that you love and cherish her even without sex. Try to remember that, together, you are nurturing a child who will grow up with fewer emotional scars that you yourself have.

If you are a woman involved in mothering a baby, don't forget to nurture your relationship with your husband, even though you might not be interested in sex. There are other ways besides sex to show love. Your baby will benefit from having two parents who have a solid and caring relationship with each other.

Here is what a father said to me after his first child was born:

> After Scotty was born, Cathy wasn't interested in sex at all. I was confused, dismayed, and upset. There was such a contrast between then and when she was pregnant. It made me feel really left out, Scotty getting all the attention. It wasn't fair. What had I done? Had I ruined my life by bringing another one in? The feelings that came up were that there was something wrong with me. It was difficult to remember that I was really okay and that the change was elsewhere. I made the assumption that Cathy didn't want to have anything to do with me, so then I felt that I didn't want to have anything to do with her. I felt that if she were more attentive to me, then I would have more interest in her. It got to be a real difficult sort of situation, a sort of downward spiral.

Marital problems such as this one can be worked out. It helps considerably if both parents have someone else with whom they can talk, cry, and rage, before their feelings build up to a crisis. Obtaining occasional help with childcare also relieves the pressures and allows the parents to have more time and attention for each other.

What can I do about bedtime problems?

Bedtime is often a time of difficulties in homes with a baby, especially during the second year. One study found that approximately 50% of babies between the ages of one and two regularly resist bedtime, causing problems for the parents.[13] However, bedtime can be without problems once the needs of babies are recognized. There are several possible reasons why your baby may not fall asleep when you would like her to: 1) your baby is not sleepy, 2) there is too much stimulation, 3) your baby needs physical closeness, 4) your baby needs to cry, 5) you are tense, or 6) your baby resents being told what to do. Each of these reasons will be discussed separately.

POSSIBLE REASONS WHY BABIES WON'T FALL ASLEEP

- Baby is not sleepy
- Too much stimulation
- Baby needs physical closeness
- Baby needs to release stress by crying (while being held)
- Parents are tense or anxious
- Baby resents being told what to do (more likely after 12 months of age)

Your baby is not sleepy.

Some parents feel that their baby should go to sleep at exactly the same time each night and take regular naps during the day. But adults rarely go to sleep at the same time two evenings in a row, because they are more tired on some days than on others. There is no reason to assume that babies are any different. Although it is convenient for parents when their babies are regular in their sleep habits, some babies' systems just do not work that way. It is often the parents who "need" the baby to sleep so they can get some sleep themselves, or time alone or with each other. It is important for you to be aware of your own needs, and to try to fill them, but not at the expense of your baby. Only your baby knows how much sleep she needs on any given day. Some babies need more sleep than others, and babies may need different amounts of sleep on different days, depending on such factors as age, amount of exercise, fresh air and sun, state of health, rate of growth, and amount of time spent crying.

Babies need less sleep than is usually believed or recommended, and the more they release tensions by crying, the less sleep they seem to need. Some evidence for this comes from institutionalized babies who cry very little and are known to sleep excessively. In a follow-up study of several institutionalized babies who were adopted into families, it was found that one response to improved nurturing care was a reduction in the number of hours of sleep. Furthermore, the adopted babies often had episodes of crying with unknown causes.[14]

Parents who allow their babies to cry as much as they need to (while being held) discover that their babies don't need much sleep. My son slept for about 13 hours a day at six months, 12½ hours at 12 months, and about 11½ hours at 18 months (including naps). By two years of age, he slept about 11 hours at night and no longer took any naps. My daughter followed a similar pattern.

On the other hand, some babies, who have been unable to sleep well because of emotional stress, begin to sleep longer and more deeply after a good cry. Once these babies catch up on their sleep, however, they will probably need less sleep than babies who have not cried enough. So babies who cry enough generally sleep soundly, but do not sleep excessively.

The implication of this is that you cannot assume that your baby will go to sleep when you think she should. If you look carefully for indications of sleepiness before putting her to bed, the process will be much easier. Indications of sleep readiness can include drooping eyes, rubbing her eyes, lying on the floor, or clinging to you.

Different cultures have vastly different bedtimes for babies. For example, in Southern Europe, where many people take an afternoon nap, it is common to see babies and young children still awake at ten or eleven o'clock at night. In England the tradition is to put babies and children to bed at six or seven o'clock before the adults have had their evening meal. There is no right or wrong way, and you can ease your baby's sleep schedule into one that fits your needs and lifestyle.

Rather than try to make your baby go to sleep when she is not ready, a better way to adjust your baby's sleep rhythm to an earlier bedtime would be to discourage a nap late in the afternoon. As your baby grows older and switches to only one nap a day, you can encourage this to be around midday or early in the afternoon. Be aware, however, that an earlier bedtime may mean that your baby will wake up earlier in the morning. On the other hand, if you want your baby to stay up later in the evening, then you can encourage a late afternoon nap.

There is too much stimulation.

Most tiny infants can fall asleep just about anywhere. But as babies grow older, people and objects become more and more interesting, social relationships become richer, and new communication and motor skills bring new excitement. Toddlers often prefer to play or interact socially rather than sleep. They may become so intensely involved in their activities that their sleepiness is masked. At times like this, you can look for signs of sleepiness in your baby or toddler, and then try to reduce the amount of stimulation. A dark, quiet room is obviously more conducive to sleep than a bright, noisy one.

Your baby needs physical closeness.

Even though your baby is sleepy and you have reduced the stimulation to a minimum, she may still resist being put down to fall asleep alone. As already mentioned, babies need physical closeness when falling asleep. I therefore recommend holding your baby or lying down with her until she falls asleep.

It is unusual for a baby to fall asleep alone without any control patterns. A survey of 126 healthy infants revealed that those who had an adult present as they fell asleep were less likely to use an attachment object or suck their thumbs.[15] Those who fall asleep alone must learn to repress their need for closeness, and also their need to protest and cry. They do this by clutching a favorite object or sucking their thumb or a pacifier.

Your baby needs to cry.

Sometimes it is hard to distinguish sleepiness from a need to cry. True sleepiness in a baby is characterized by a tired, relaxed look. A baby who is really ready to fall asleep will do so immediately and spontaneously once all distractions and stimulation have been reduced. She will not be fussy, whiny, fidgety, or hyperactive.

Some parents think that whining and fussiness are indications of sleepiness. One often hears parents say, "Oh, he's getting fussy. He must be ready for his nap." Whining and fussing are indications of a need to cry, not a need to sleep. Babies who fuss may be feeling sleepy, but they are not yet ready to go to sleep as long as they are fussing. Fussiness often occurs at the end of a day, but this is only because tiredness makes it more difficult for babies to repress their emotions. When a baby does not have much energy, therefore, she is more likely to allow her feelings to come to the surface and cry. But she will not be truly ready for sleep until *after* she has cried.

Fussy babies who have not cried as needed are unlikely to fall asleep without a control pattern to help them repress their emotions. (See Chapter 2.) This could be holding a special blanket, sucking a pacifier or a thumb, nursing, or being rocked. These control patterns put babies in a sort of temporary trance that helps them relax and fall asleep. However, if you regularly rely on rocking, walking, nursing, or other bedtime routines to calm your baby down and put her to sleep, there are some difficulties that can arise. You may be discouraged to find your baby waking up and crying as soon as you put her down. Perhaps you then begin rocking, walking, or nursing your baby again in order to put her back to sleep. But, once again, she refuses to be put down. This can continue for hours.

Some experts recommend putting the baby in her crib and walking out of the room. They claim that babies will cry for 20 to 30 minutes the first night, and for about 10 minutes the second night. By the third night they will fall asleep without crying. Others recommend a more gradual approach, starting with a few minutes of letting babies cry alone. Eventually, these babies learn to "soothe" themselves by using a control pattern such as thumb sucking.

I do *not* recommend any of these methods, for several reasons. Ignoring your crying baby can diminish the sense of trust that she has in you. She will learn that she cannot count on you to be available for her when she is upset. It can also foster feelings of helplessness, powerlessness, and fear. These possible effects can lead to later problems .

If you have rocked or nursed your baby to sleep and she wakes up and cries soon after you put her down, it is likely that she needs to cry. The rocking or nursing may have prevented her from releasing pent-up stress. You can solve this problem by holding your baby and paying attention to her, but *without* rocking or nursing her. She will then have an opportunity to cry without distractions. When she has finished crying, she will probably fall into a deep sleep, and it will then be quite possible to put her down without waking her up. The crying in this method is not out of fear or a need for your presence, because you are right there with your baby. It is the release of tensions that she needed to do before you tried to put her to sleep by rocking or nursing. Note that babies normally pass through a short phase of light sleep before going into deep sleep. So even after a good cry in your arms, you may still have to wait for ten to fifteen minutes after your baby has fallen asleep before putting her down. If you try to put her down too soon, she is likely to awaken.

Regular bedtime routines can be beneficial, especially for toddlers, who thrive on predictability. An evening routine could be, for example, a bath followed by teeth brushing and a story. However, when bedtime rituals (such as rocking or nursing) repress your baby's crying, they can become control patterns and lead to sleep problems. Toddlers often need to cry before falling asleep. If you allow your toddler to cry while you stay with her, she will sleep soundly and awaken bright and cheerful. So be sure to schedule in some listening time in your bedtime routine. (Later on, when your child is older, she will use this time, not only for crying, but also for talking about the upsets of her day.)

You are tense.

Some babies are very sensitive to other people's moods and cannot drift peacefully off to sleep if their parent is tense. If you are holding your baby and thinking: "He's got to go to sleep *right now*," chances are your baby will not fall asleep! Or if you are feeling stressed, anxious, impatient, or angry while holding your baby at bedtime, she may have a hard time relaxing because of this. Anything you can do to help yourself relax will probably also help your baby relax. If your own needs for sleep or time alone are not being met, try to find ways to meet your needs. When you are feeling less rushed or stressed, you will have more patience and be able to enjoy a more flexible bedtime routine with your baby, who will probably respond by falling asleep more easily.

Your baby resents being told what to do.

During the second year, toddlers enter a stage of development in which they yearn to be fully in charge of their own lives as much as possible. They deeply resent and resist being told what to do. This stage is healthy and normal, and is discussed in greater detail in Chapter 6. This desire for autonomy may be one of the causes for difficulties at bedtime during the second year. If you suddenly announce that it's time for bed, your toddler may strongly resist, even though she is sleepy. If you are more flexible and attuned to your child's signs of readiness, you will encounter less resistance, and may even be surprised to see your toddler willingly take the initiative about going to bed. Here is what one mother reported to me:

> We used to have a lot of problems about bedtime, but it's getting better. I think the problem was that Gloria didn't like being told she had to go to bed, and she would resist. And I think it made sense that she resisted. She was feeling that she wasn't ready yet. When we waited for her to indicate when she was sleepy, she did eventually tell us that she was sleepy and wanted to go to bed.

If your toddler feels that going to bed is less exciting than playing, you can make bedtime routines playful. For example, you can entice your toddler to take a bath by suggesting an enjoyable activity to do in the bathtub. When toddlers feel that activities are fun, they are usually quite willing to cooperate. Also, when bedtime implies a separation, it is normal for your child to resist. When you hold your child or lie down next to her until she falls asleep, bedtime will become a time of closeness that she will look forward to. (See Chapter 6 for more on eliciting cooperation in toddlers.)

How can I help my baby sleep through the night?

Waking up at night is a common problem, and many babies continue to do so until they are over two years of age. One study found that 35% of 12-month olds woke up at least once during the night.[16]

During the first several months, it is normal for infants to wake up one or more times during the night out of hunger. They are not able to go for very long stretches between feedings. By six months of age, most healthy babies should be able to sleep through the night, although some might still need one night feeding. If your older baby (over six months of age) awakens more than once at night, this is not likely to be from hunger. Other possible reasons to consider are illness, pain, a startling noise, or simply a need for closeness.

POSSIBLE REASONS FOR NIGHT AWAKENINGS

- Hunger (more likely before 6 months)
- Sickness, pain, discomfort
- Need for physical closeness
- Nightmare or fright
- Need to release stress by crying (while being held)

However, the most likely cause for night awakenings in older babies is a need to release accumulated stress by crying (while being held). Perhaps your baby does not have sufficient opportunities to cry during the day and at bedtime. As described in Chapter 2, babies learn to repress their crying by means of repetitive behaviors called control patterns, such as nursing for "comfort" or thumb sucking. If you regularly use a control pattern to calm your baby during the day or to put him to sleep, he may not be crying enough, and the accumulated tensions may prevent him from sleeping soundly.

Waking up and crying frequently at night is much more likely to occur if your baby's control pattern is associated with your body, such as rocking or nursing. If your baby's control patterns involve you in some way, he will seem to "need" you to do those activities with him every time his feelings come to the surface during the night. This is a different kind of neediness from a legitimate need for closeness at night.

Babies who have control patterns separate from their parents' bodies, such as pacifiers, thumb sucking, special blankets, or stuffed animals, are less likely to cry out for their parents during the night. These babies may wake up frequently, but the parents will not be aware of it, especially if the baby is sleeping alone in another room. Such babies will simply suck or clutch their beloved objects and fall back to sleep. If your baby does not regularly awaken at night, therefore, this does not necessarily imply that he is doing all the crying he needs to do. It may be that he has a control pattern present with him at night that he uses to repress his crying.

It is quite common for breastfed babies to awaken frequently at night well past the age of six months. Researchers have found that breastfed babies awaken more frequently at night during the second year than babies of a similar age who have been weaned.[17] The babies who awaken at night do not need such frequent milk intake any more, yet they seem to want to nurse every few hours around the clock. For these babies, nursing is almost certainly a control pattern that causes them to repress their feelings.

Breastfeeding for several years is a wonderful way to meet your baby's needs for nutrition and physical closeness. However, this does not necessarily imply frequent feedings at night. If you are suffering from lack of sleep because of this, you may wish to develop more of a listening relationship with your baby, in addition to your nursing relationship. If you stop nursing your baby for "comfort," but only for genuine hunger or thirst, you will both sleep better. But be prepared for some long crying sessions at first.

The first thing to do is to stop using control patterns at bedtime (such as nursing or rocking) in an effort to get your baby to sleep. Instead, hold him without distracting him, and allow him to cry if he needs to. Here is my own experience:

To my great delight, my son began going without night feedings at three months of age, and started sleeping straight through the night. But my delight was short-lived, because at six months of age he began waking up from two to six times every night. I recall that I purposely began nursing him at bedtime when he was about six months old, because it was an easy and convenient way of "putting" him to sleep. I failed to make any connection between nursing at bedtime and waking up in the night, and he continued to wake up *every* night. I would dutifully nurse him back to sleep, cuddle him with his head on my chest, or pay attention to him while he cried. I could not figure out why he kept waking up at night. Not until he was 23 months old did it occur to me that the bedtime nursing was preventing him from crying before going to sleep. So I held him one evening at bedtime without nursing him. He cried for quite a while, but he slept better that night. Within a few days, he was regularly sleeping through the night, and doing his crying in the evening before going to sleep (while I held him). With great relief I began to get enough sleep at night for the first time in two years! I never nursed him to sleep again after that, but he continued to nurse at other times during the day until he weaned himself at two-and-a-half years of age.

Bottles can be a control pattern as well, and some babies who are bottle-fed wake up at night demanding a bottle, even though they are well past the age of needing milk at night. The cure for this problem is the same as the cure for breastfed babies who wake up frequently: stop giving a bottle at bedtime and during the night, and allow your baby to cry if he needs to, while holding him and giving him loving attention.

After trying this, if your baby (over six months of age) or toddler continues to awaken frequently at night, and you suspect a nursing or bottle control pattern, you can offer him your loving arms and a cup of milk, juice, or water, rather than your breast or a bottle, when he awakens during the night. That way you will know that he is not crying from hunger, thirst, or a need for closeness. If he accepts the drink and goes peacefully back to sleep, then you know that he was simply thirsty or hungry. However, if he rejects it and cries or rages, then you know that he probably needs to release pent-up stress (assuming he is not ill or in pain).

In addition to these suggestions, you can also look for other methods (besides frequent nursing) that you might be using inadvertently to distract your baby from crying during the day. Perhaps you frequently entertain him when he fusses, not realizing that there is some underlying tension that he needs to release through a good cry. If you can allow your baby to cry as needed during the day (with your attention), this will reduce his need to cry during the night.

You can also strive to reduce stress in your baby's life. Is there too much stimulation or a stressful home environment? If your baby's life is calm and predictable, he will probably sleep better.

If you have tried these suggestions and your baby continues to awaken frequently at night, you can encourage him to cry the first time he awakens at night. If he has a good cry in your arms at that time, he is more likely to sleep through the rest of the night. It may take a few nights before you notice any results.

As mentioned in Chapter 2, a traumatic birth can cause a baby to awaken frequently at night and cry. All babies have several periods of deep sleep during the night, punctuated by brief intervals of semi-consciousness or even arousal. Perhaps those babies who cry out at such times are remembering being born and don't fall back to sleep as readily. Waking up is somewhat similar to emerging from the womb. Some parents notice that their babies have crying spells at the same time of day as their birth. If the birth occurred during the night, this will be their baby's fussy time. Such babies need to do their crying at night when the memories are triggered.

Waking up at night did not become a serious problem for parents until separate sleeping arrangements were adopted. It is extremely disagreeable and exhausting to get out of a warm bed several times in the middle of the night, turn on lights, put on bathrobe and slippers, go into another room, and lift a crying baby out of a crib. If you let your baby sleep in your bed, you will be near by when he needs you, and you won't have to get out of bed. This is a definite advantage of sharing your bed with your baby.

When the baby sleeps in a separate room it is very tempting to ignore him when he awakens and cries at night. In fact, some parents even convince themselves that their baby does not really need them at all. They come to believe that he has simply developed a bad habit that is easily cured. It is all too easy for them to follow the advice of some experts, whose cure for this is similar to the cure for the bedtime problem. They advise parents to ignore their baby so that he will learn that there is nothing to be gained by waking and crying.

I do not recommend this method. To ignore a crying baby at any time can be very harmful because it may lead to feelings of distrust, powerlessness, or anxiety. Babies need closeness, not only while falling asleep at bedtime, but also when they wake up at night. Your baby has no way of knowing that you are nearby if he cannot see, hear, smell, or feel you. Being left alone to cry is terrifying for him.

I am ashamed to say that I once tried ignoring my son when he cried at night. This was during the period before I learned how to help him sleep through the night. Here is what happened:

> When my son was ten months old, he slept in a crib in a separate room. He woke up regularly from two to six times every night. A friend convinced me that it was merely a bad habit and that I could cure him of it by ignoring him when he cried at night; so I tried it. He cried a long time (about 45 minutes) the first night, a little less the next two nights, and by the fourth night he no longer cried. However, a few nights later, I heard him whimpering several times during the night. I waited a while after he whimpered and then went quietly into his room. To my surprise, he was lying there wide awake with his eyes open. As soon as he saw me, he burst into tears, so I picked him up and he clung to me like a little monkey. I stayed with him and he cried continuously and heavily for *two solid hours*. Both he and I did quite a lot of crying during the following days. I realized that the experience of being left alone like that had been very traumatic for him. The next day, we moved his crib mattress into our bedroom (next to our big mattress, which was on the floor), and I let him sleep next to me from then on. (When he was three-and-a-half years old, his grandmother came to live with us, and he was quite happy to move into a room with her).

If your baby sleeps in a separate room, you should go to him every time he cries. Check to see if he is hungry, cold, wet, or sick. If he needs to cry, stay with him, hold him, and pay attention to him until he has finished crying. Even if you cannot figure out what he needs, or if you do the wrong thing, it is far better than ignoring him.

Should I give my baby drugs to get her to sleep?

Parents have been giving babies drugs to sleep since ancient times. The most popular drugs have been opium and alcohol. During the second century BC, the Greek physician Galen prescribed opium to calm fussy babies, and this practice has persisted throughout the ages. In Europe, the mothers and wet-nurses traditionally smeared their nipples with a lotion containing opium before suckling the babies, who would absorb some opium while nursing, and then go right to sleep. Popular preparations containing opium could be easily obtained from pharmacists. In the late nineteenth and early twentieth century, a popular colic remedy for babies containing opium called "Winslow's Soothing Syrup" was available in the United States without a prescription.[18] In Europe, another practice was to give babies a small bag of linen to suck on, filled with ground poppy seeds (a source of opium) and sugar. Another teething and sleep remedy was a piece of cloth soaked in fermented (alcoholic) cider. In Austria, these early pacifiers used by the farm women were called "Most-Zutz" meaning "cider-tit."[19]

Nowadays, doctors sometimes prescribe tranquilizers or sedatives for fussy and wakeful babies. In a survey in England, 25% of babies had been given sedatives by the time they were 18 months old.[20] Drugs can help babies fall asleep and sleep through the night, but this only masks the underlying problem of unreleased stress. Your baby will still have the tensions in her body that originally caused the wakefulness, and she will still need to cry. The drugs will only postpone the crying, and the tensions will remain until she has an opportunity to cry. Furthermore, unreleased stress can cause later negative side effects such as reducing resistance to infection, and lead to aggressive behavior, hyperactivity, and distractibility.

Another reason to avoid giving such drugs to babies is that the drugs can be addictive and can set the stage for later drug abuse. In Chapter 2, 1 explained how anything that is done to a baby when she needs to cry becomes part of an automatic behavior pattern, which is then re-enacted every time she feels upset. If you frequently put your baby to sleep with a drug instead of allowing her to use the natural relaxation process of crying, the drug may become a control pattern for her. Later on, her body might remember this early chemical addiction, causing her to seek chemical relief from painful emotions.

Western medicine relies heavily on the treatment of symptoms with drugs, but this can be deceptive. Doctors and patients need to start relying more on the body's natural healing mechanisms and trust the human body to overcome tensions. In order for the body's healing processes to operate, it is necessary to begin feeling some emotional pain. The processes of emotional release, such as crying and raging, are time-consuming, noisy, and messy. However, they are the outward indications that a person is feeling and dealing with painful emotions in a healthy way. By helping your baby relax and go to sleep in this way, with your loving attention, you will also be helping her to become an emotionally healthy person.

What about my own needs for sleep?

Having your sleep interrupted night after night can be extremely exhausting. Even if your baby sleeps with you and you don't have to get out of bed to tend to his needs, it is still hard to be awakened from your sleep. The suggestions in this book are no guarantee that your baby will always sleep through the night after six months of age. All babies have occasional wakeful nights during illness or teething, times of increased stress, or developmental changes.

There are several ways that you can fill your own needs for sleep. One way is to trade off with your partner tending to your baby's nighttime needs. The biological mother is obviously needed for breastfeeding, but another person of either sex can help out with your baby's other nighttime needs. You can also try to take a nap during the day when your baby sleeps. If your baby takes short or unpredictable naps (or no naps), then perhaps you can find another person to take care of him for a few hours a day while you rest. Loss of sleep may be especially hard for you if you must work at a job away from home, with no opportunity to rest during the day. Many parents find themselves going to bed earlier in the evening than they normally would. If your baby keeps you awake at night, you need and deserve all the help you can get.

Some parents ignore their crying babies at night with the justification that they need to sleep themselves so they can function as good parents during the day. But no amount of good daytime parenting can undo the loss of trust, or the fear, frustration, and powerlessness that a baby feels when nobody responds to his cries. If you regularly ignore your crying baby at night, this may make the job of parenting more difficult in the years ahead. You may have to deal with your child's later bedtime problems, fears, nightmares, bed-wetting, or overly strong separation anxiety. A few years of attentive parenting at the start can accomplish much toward the prevention of later problems. Babies have needs 24 hours a day, and the job of parenting does not end at 8 P.M. I think of the early years of parenting as a very worthwhile investment of time and energy. The more you invest in your child, the more emotionally healthy he will grow up to be.

However, it is important not to sacrifice your own needs to the point of building up resentment and anger towards your baby. If this occurs, you will benefit, not only from finding help during the day, but also from releasing your own painful emotions (preferably away from your baby). Here is what one mother did whose baby woke up frequently at night:

> I felt like I would just go crazy. I couldn't figure out what was wrong, what was the problem. And I would get so furious! It was hard to imagine that I could get that mad at him. Yet during the day, when I wasn't that tired, I really loved him a lot. But at night, when it went on and on and on, I would just get furious at him and feel like shouting at him or shaking him. My sweet little baby, I just felt like bashing him around so that he'd shut up and go to sleep. At that point I would cry out of sheer fatigue and frustration that I couldn't get him to sleep. My husband was there, but sometimes I'd be mad at him too because he would just sleep on through! That was hard. I never did hurt my baby. I never did anything to him. Somehow I was always able to stop myself.

The fact that this mother allowed herself to cry probably helped prevent her from harming her baby. If you have felt something similar to this mother, realize that you are not alone. It is only natural to feel angry when you are deprived of sleep. Try to allow yourself to cry as needed, ask for help, and remember that these difficult nights will pass. Don't give up on the suggestions in this chapter to help your baby sleep through the night. Understanding your baby's need to cry (while being held) can lead to considerable improvement in his sleeping habits.

EXERCISES

Explore your childhood.

1. What were bedtimes and nap times like for you as a child?
2. Were you ever allowed to sleep close to your parents or another person? What was it like?
3. Have you ever been afraid of the dark or afraid to be alone? Did you ever wake up in the night because of a nightmare or other reason and cry for help? What happened?

Express your feelings about your baby.

1. Have you ever slept with your baby, or do you regularly do so? If not, give it a try for one night and be sure to take the recommended safety precautions. How do you feel about letting your baby sleep with you?
2. How do you feel about your baby's sleep schedule? Do you wish your baby would sleep more or less than he/she does?
3. Do you have a bedtime or night waking problem with your baby? Talk about the feelings this brings up in you (anger, resentment, powerlessness, etc.).

Nurture yourself.

1. Have you been getting enough sleep since your baby was born? If not, how do you feel about that? Try to think of a way you can fill your own needs for sleep without compromising your baby's needs for attention.

2. Has your sex life changed in any way since the birth of your baby? How do you feel about your present sex life (or lack of it)?

3. If you feel an urge to engage in sexual activities with your baby, you were probably sexually abused as a child. Resist the temptation to act on your feelings, and realize that you need help. Think of this as an excellent opportunity to heal from your own abuse. Try to find a competent therapist who is knowledgeable about sexual abuse and who supports emotional release. (Note that feeling sexually aroused while nursing a baby is normal and is not an indication of sexual perversion.)

CHAPTER 5

PLAY: LETTING YOUR BABY LEARN

How important are the early years for the development of intelligence?

Psychologists used to think that genetic inheritance determined intelligence, and that this could not be altered very much by environmental conditions. Researchers have determined that our level of intelligence is determined by both hereditary and environmental factors. However, heredity accounts for less than 50% of the variability, while environmental factors (including the maternal womb environment) account for over 50%.[1] We now know that experience and stimulation, especially early in life, are important factors that help develop intellectual abilities.

The maternal womb environment was ignored in most studies until the 1990's, when researchers became increasingly aware of its importance. Studies have found that prenatal nicotine, alcohol, or cocaine exposure correlates with lower IQ and academic performance in the children.[2] Even in the absence of drugs, the fetus is affected by the mother's anxiety or depression. Researchers have found that infants born to depressed mothers tend to show more abnormalities in their behavior, physiology, and biochemistry, probably caused by maternal stress hormones during pregnancy.[3]

There is evidence that maternal stress hormones can affect a fetus's response to stimulation even before birth. Fetuses whose mothers had high levels of stress hormones showed a reduction in the ability to habituate to repeated stimuli such as a tone on the mother's abdomen. This indicates that the fetuses of the stressed mothers were not able to learn at an optimal level.[4] It is possible that the maternal womb environment can also activate specific genes in the fetus, while inhibiting others, thereby increasing certain behavioral characteristics such as impulsivity.[5] From a biological point of view, it makes sense for a baby to be impulsive and highly reactive to stimuli if the mother is stressed. This is nature's way of insuring that he will survive in a hostile or threatening environment. With so much energy being used for protection and survival, however, the development of cognitive skills is likely to be hampered.

Appropriate prenatal stimulation can enhance your child's cognitive development. As mentioned in Chapter 1, prenatal enrichment activities involving music, movement, talking to your fetus, and responding to its movements, can have long-term, positive effects.

After birth, experiences continue to have a large impact on later abilities. Research with animals has shown that early experience can change the actual structure of the brain, thereby limiting or enhancing adult abilities. In one study, young rats were placed for a few weeks in enriched environments (containing shelves to climb on, wheels to run in, objects to investigate, and other rats to interact with). These rats subsequently had larger brain cells than those who had lived alone in plain cages.[6] It is probable that similar changes occur in human babies' brains when they are raised in "enriched" environments. Research on sensitive periods for certain forms of stimulation in human beings provides further evidence for the importance of the first few years.[7] For example, we are especially receptive to learning languages when we are young. Later on in life this is much more difficult.

From conception to two years of age, a baby acquires a basic attitude towards learning, which will influence all subsequent learning. The famous educator, Maria Montessori, observed that by three years of age many children had already lost their desire to learn and their ability to concentrate. She established her school to counteract this apathy and put children back on the right path of learning.[8]

We do not know whether the effects of prenatal drug exposure, stress, or lack of stimulation are permanent. However, even when the physiology of the brain has been altered, we should not rule out the possibility of recovery because the brain can repair itself to a certain extent. Nevertheless, there is no doubt that life will be much easier for a baby if he has a healthy, drug-free, and stress-free environment from conception on.

Parents are therefore responsible for the most important learning experiences their child will ever have: those that he is exposed to before birth and during the first two years after birth. Fortunately, most families have the resources needed in order to do a fine job. A good learning environment for a baby does not require very much money or knowledge of developmental psychology. In fact, you do not even have to teach your baby, in the usual sense of the word. All you will need are a few household objects, a lot of attention and patience, and the ability to respond appropriately.

What guidelines can I use to select appropriate stimulation?

Appropriate stimulation is important because a lack of it can slow down your baby's development. The more infants are held, rocked, or touched during the first six months, the better their intellectual achievements will be, including spatial abilities, memory, verbal proficiency, and IQ scores.[9] Once babies begin to manipulate objects, researchers have found that the availability of a variety of play materials in the home also enhances the development of cognitive skills.[10]

The responsibility for selecting appropriate toys may seem an overwhelming task to you. But it is really quite simple and requires no knowledge of child development, because the best approach is to let your baby indicate what she is interested in doing. All you need to do is observe your baby carefully, because she will show you what she is ready to do. If there is nothing she can learn from a particular toy, she will ignore it. But if she is ready for a certain toy and able to learn something from it appropriate to her stage of development, it will be hard to keep her from playing with it. The same applies to games or activities. The need for stimulation is very much like physical hunger and, as with food, babies seem to know what toys or activities are best at any moment. Therefore, the only dependable guide to stimulation is your baby.

There is an important principle of learning that you can use in selecting appropriate stimulation for your baby: *meaningful learning occurs when people can relate new information to something with which they are already familiar.* The Swiss psychologist, Jean Piaget, described in great detail this process, which he called "assimilation."[11]

Suppose your baby already knows how to shake a rattle, and you give her a small container with some dry beans inside. When she shakes it and hears the rattling sound, she will realize that the new toy is similar to her old rattle because it also makes a sound when she shakes it. This will please her because she is able to "understand" and relate to the new object: "Here is something I can understand. It makes sense. I know what to do with it." The baby will learn that her old rattle is not the only object in the world that makes a noise, and she will learn that different objects make different noises. Her knowledge of the world will thus increase by a few small increments.

In practice, then, the guideline based on this learning principle involves observing carefully what your baby is already doing, and then giving her new toys (or activities) that are just slightly different from the old ones but based on the same theme. When your baby develops a new skill, look for the principle behind your baby's behavior and provide more objects (or activities), so she can become more proficient, For example, if your newborn stares intently at her father's striped shirt, give her more designs and patterns to look at. If your ten-month-old drops a rock in a wading pool and watches it sink, give him some bath toys that sink and others that float.

There must obviously be some stimulation to begin with so that your baby can develop new abilities. Routine care in an average household contains all the stimulation required to start developing most aspects of practical intelligence during the first two years, provided you allow your baby access to a variety of objects and experiences. New abilities emerge quite spontaneously through maturation of the nervous system, trial and error, and imitation.

When you buy toys for your baby, try to be aware of any possible sexist attitudes you may have. I recommend selecting a wide variety of toys for your baby, without worrying whether they are more appropriate for a boy or a girl. Don't be afraid to give dolls and stuffed animals to children of both sexes, as well as construction toys and sports equipment. Be aware of color stereotypes as well. There is no harm in giving boys clothing, room decorations, or toys that are pink or have a floral design.

Studies have shown that people perceive babies differently depending on their assumption of the baby's sex.[12] I noticed that when I dressed my infant son in pink pants or put a frilly sun hat on him, strangers thought he was a girl, and commented on how pretty he was. When I dressed him in blue or put a baseball cap on him, people assumed he was a boy and commented on his strength or alertness. This shows how we filter our perceptions of babies through our own sexist conditioning.

Studies have also shown that parents tend to treat their daughters differently from their sons, beginning at birth. Parents touch, cuddle, and talk to their infant daughters more than their sons. They also respond more promptly and sensitively to baby girls' expressions of pain or discomfort, while ignoring those of boys.[13] This could be one reason why girls tend to talk earlier than boys, and are generally more emotionally expressive. Little boys need just as much cuddling and social interaction as girls. This will not make them weak or overly dependent.

People who have difficulty accepting homosexuality fear that parenting boys in the same way as girls will turn them into homosexuals. There is no evidence that toys or parental behavior influences sexual orientation. However, non-sexist child rearing will probably produce less aggressive men who are sensitive and gentle. With a continuing rise in violent acts, committed mostly by males, this is certainly a goal worth striving for. Furthermore, both boys and girls will be free to consider a wider range of career options, unhampered by sexist stereotypes.

In addition to appropriate toys, intellectual competence develops better when babies have freedom of movement and opportunities to explore.[14] A baby's natural curiosity and tendency to explore will be discouraged and diminished if she is kept in a playpen. Some important concepts have their roots in a baby's own spontaneous movements. These include concepts of distance, speed, time, and spatial concepts such as the use of alternate routes to reach a goal.[15]

Babies who can crawl around freely in a large area can experiment with more varied perceptual stimulation, such as listening to the changing sound of a radio as they move away from it, or looking at a table from different perspectives. In this manner, they will learn more about the physical world than babies who are kept in playpens.

I recommend baby-proofing one or several rooms in your home, and letting your baby explore freely in those safe areas. Put all small, dangerous, and breakable objects out of reach, affix large pieces of furniture (such as book cases or TV's) to the wall so they will not topple over if your baby should climb on them, and protect all electrical sockets with baby-proof plugs. You can use gates or baby-proof doorknobs to prevent your baby from going into other rooms, and you can put baby-proof latches on drawers or cabinet doors.

Because infants and toddlers learn best through hands-on activities and movement, television and videos are inappropriate forms of stimulation. These not only promote passivity and take away valuable time from real learning, but can also lead to fears and contribute to violence. It is difficult to find a non-violent film for children. An analysis of animated feature-length films in the U.S. released between 1937 and 1999 found that *every* film contained at least one act of violence, and many of them involved serious bodily harm or even murder.[16] These films had been rated appropriate for all ages, but in my opinion they are not. Babies as young as 14 months of age tend to imitate actions they have observed on a TV screen, so it important to select wisely the models to which you expose your child.[17] But babies have much better things to do than watch TV. Although it may be tempting to keep your baby quiet by placing her in front of a TV, this is not likely to enhance either her cognitive or emotional development.

With the freedom to learn and explore, and the presence of developmentally appropriate toys and activities, your baby can acquire the skills and knowledge that will provide her with a basic foundation for all subsequent learning. Your selection of appropriate stimulation during the first few years can therefore greatly enhance your baby's development.

How can I tell whether my baby is understimulated or over-stimulated?

Overstimulation can cause confusion and anxiety and lead to a greater need to cry. It occurs when the environment contains many new objects, sights, or sounds that the baby cannot yet understand, but to which he is paying attention. If your baby is sleeping or ignoring the stimulation, he will probably not be affected. For overstimulation to occur, it is necessary for your baby to be taking in new sensory information and attempting to understand it.

You can expect your baby to cry following overstimulating experiences, because it is frustrating and confusing to be exposed to information that is not meaningful. The crying allows the distress and confusion to dissipate, and leaves the baby open and receptive for new learning experiences. Babies need the loving attention of another person while they are crying. Continuing to stimulate your baby or trying to divert his attention will not help, as it will only postpone the crying and perhaps even provide more overstimulation for him to cry about. Here is an example of overstimulation:

> When my son was seven weeks old I took him to a folk dance festival. For two full hours (except for a brief nursing episode), he was awake and alert, looking intently at all the activity. Then he began to cry and continued to do so vigorously for about a half hour, after which he fell asleep.

When a baby can relate a new sight or sound to something already in his memory, the reception of such information will probably be pleasurable rather than painful. The following example illustrates meaningful information intake:

> While shopping with my son when he was five-and-a-half months old, he suddenly began to coo and smile and reach out to the cartons of yogurt as we passed the dairy section. He had recently eaten yogurt from similar containers, and also played with an empty yogurt container at home. He was definitely delighted at recognizing something familiar in a place where most of the sights and sounds were still totally meaningless to him.

It is also possible to understimulate babies. Understimulation occurs when the environment is very familiar, and lacks enough new experiences or toys to which the baby can relate. A baby in such a boring environment will be intellectually starved and will probably cry until new stimulation arrives. By crying, he is expressing the great need he has for stimulation.

If babies cry because of both understimulation and overstimulation, how can you differentiate the two? When should you offer more stimulation and when should you stop trying to stimulate your baby? This is not an easy question to answer, but a useful guideline is your baby's own cues.

Babies indicate clearly when stimulation overwhelms them. When babies enjoy a form of stimulation, such as a mother singing, they will maintain a relaxed body state, look intently at her, perhaps reach their arm towards her, and coo. When babies are disturbed by some kind of stimulation, they may stiffen their body, turn their head away, flex their limbs, or cry. Some babies are more sensitive to stimulation than others, and they startle easily when a sound, light, or sudden movement disturbs them. Researchers have found that about 20% of all babies are highly reactive to stimuli.[18] This heightened sensitivity can be an inborn character trait, or it can be caused by prenatal drug exposure, a stressful prenatal environment, a premature birth, or other birth trauma. Whatever the cause, these hypersensitive babies need gentle handling with a minimum of stimulation.

If your baby is highly sensitive by nature, you will probably see this character trait continue as he grows older. He is likely to be cautious, conscientious, fearful, sensitive to other people's moods, and easily overwhelmed by new experiences. You will need to be aware of his tolerance level for stimulation, and let him adapt to changes at his own pace. With your love and support, your sensitive baby can grow into a highly intuitive, thoughtful, creative, and gifted child. Remember, however, that your sensitive baby may need to cry about things that do not distress other babies at all, and this greater need to cry will probably continue as he grows older.

Another guideline for appropriate stimulation is the age of your baby. Newborns are particularly easy to overstimulate, even those who are healthy and born at term, because everything is new and

incomprehensible (except for the sounds of a human body and movement). They have enough stimulation to cope with from ordinary
routine care, especially if they are carried or held much of the time
(as suggested in Chapter 1). They must adapt to lights and colors,
sounds, changes in temperature, hardness and softness, wetness and
dryness, stillness and motion. They receive a considerable amount
of stimulation from being caressed, diapered, washed, clothed, carried, spoken to, and rocked. They must adjust to the new sensations
of breathing, nursing, digesting, urinating, defecating, burping, smell-
ing, and crying. This takes some time because everything is so different from their experiences in the womb. Much of the crying that
occurs in the early months may be due to overstimulation. As a general guideline, the younger the baby, the easier he is to overstimulate.

Touching or holding your newborn will not overstimulate him,
because the need for physical contact is so great. Instead, it is wise to
protect your newborn from too much new visual or auditory stimulation during the early weeks. Parents of fretful newborns often think
that their infant is bored, so they take him for rides and excursions.
Such experiences are meaningless to young infants and only contribute to overstimulation and confusion. Until two or three months of
age, babies don't like novelty, and tend to prefer looking at pictures
with which they are familiar. Nothing seems to bore them.[19]

When your infant reaches two or three months or age, his need
for new stimulation will increase, and he will begin to look longer at
new pictures than at old, familiar ones. However, the type of stimulation three-month-olds most prefer is that which is only moderately
different from familiar experiences.[20] It is your role to fill this new
hunger for stimulation, because your baby cannot do it for himself.
Later, when your baby learns to crawl, he will be able to create his
own change in stimulation. But until that time, your baby is fairly
helpless, and you may find him quite demanding in a new way after
three months of age, because his need for stimulation increases. You
can fill this need by frequently carrying your baby around with you,
and by interacting with him. When you put your baby down, be sure
that he has objects within reach, colorful things to look at, and music
to listen to.

Once your baby learns to crawl, he is less likely to cry from boredom, provided there are enough appropriate toys and activities corresponding to his current interests, and provided he has a large area in which to move.

The possibility of overstimulation remains all throughout babyhood. Babies who are continually overstimulated may become chronically anxious or confused, and have little self-confidence in their ability to learn or understand new things. This could adversely affect their later intellectual achievements. Overstimulated babies also tend to have trouble sleeping. However, if they are allowed to cry to release the tensions of overstimulation (with love and attention, while being held), these negative effects are less likely to occur.

It is helpful to select outings for babies according to their ability to relate to the experiences involved. A trip to the zoo may be overstimulating for a baby who has never seen a live animal, but quite appropriate for a baby who is already familiar with dogs and cats. If you do need to take your baby to a place that is overstimulating, such as a party, you can lessen the negative impact by holding him close to your own body, with its familiar sounds and smell.

By carefully reading your baby's cues and not overstimulating him, you will keep his stress to a manageable level and help him learn about the world at a pace that is right for him.

My baby demands constant attention and always wants to be entertained. What can I do about this?

Until babies learn to crawl, they are fairly demanding, because they cannot yet get around on their own to provide their own stimulation. They are therefore very dependent on their parents to provide them with stimulation. It is important to offer your baby objects to play with, carry her around with you, sing and talk to her, and play simple games with her. Although your baby will become less dependent on you after she learns to crawl, she will probably still continue to request your attention frequently, and this is normal and healthy.

However, it is important to read your baby's cues very carefully. Some parents think their baby is bored when, in fact, she simply needs to release stress by crying. If your response to your crying baby is *always* to offer some form of entertainment, such as a song or a game, she will not have a chance to complete the crying she may need to do that is caused by a build-up of stress. There are times when your baby will need to be held lovingly and calmly without any additional stimulation, so she can cry freely with you as an empathic listener.

If you repeatedly distract your baby by trying to offer stimulation when she needs to cry, this can turn into a control pattern, that is, a habit your baby uses to repress emotions. Instead of crying, your baby will demand to be entertained every time she feels upset. Babies with this control pattern are often described as "spoiled." However, they have not been given too much attention, but rather the wrong kind of attention when they needed to cry. Living with babies who have this control pattern can be very irritating. Here is what one mother said:

> When he constantly demands attention, I get really impatient. I go crazy. I feel like pushing him away and getting rid of him. I wish somebody would take him away or get him out of my sight. It's just too much. I can't handle it. I try to figure out some way to get him to leave me alone.

It is not always clear when stimulation is distracting a baby from a general need to cry. Babies differ in their tendency to be distracted from their crying. One might cry even though you are rocking her, while another might temporarily postpone her crying. When babies become distracted, it is easy to assume (perhaps incorrectly) that the form of stimulation was a real need at that moment. On the other hand, you don't want to overlook your baby's genuine needs by assuming that she "just needs to cry."

When repeated attempts at providing stimulation do not work, and your baby is still fussy, you can assume that she probably needs to have a good cry (provided all other immediate needs have been met). Sometimes boredom seems to disappear magically without changing the environment once the baby has been allowed to cry. If nothing seems to make your baby happy for very long, you can hold her but refrain from distracting her, and see what happens. Speak gently to her and let her know that you are willing to listen. If she needs to cry, she will then do so. If not, she will probably find a way to entertain herself while being held. Your baby is unlikely to become bored when she is in your loving arms, so you don't need to worry that your baby is crying out of boredom when you hold her. After she has cried, she may be ready for stimulation, and you can then play with her in whatever manner she requests. Many parents find, however, that babies who have cried enough do not demand any further attention after crying, and are able to entertain themselves for longer stretches of time.

To correctly read your baby's cues and decide about her need for stimulation, you will find it helpful to take into account her past experiences. The following two examples from my own children both involve visual stimulation. In the first case, the stimulation acted as a distraction that prevented crying, while in the second case it was a genuine need.

At three days of age, because of an elevated bilirubin level, my daughter had to be placed in an incubator under blue lights for three days. I was able to take her out periodically to nurse her. Each time she was put back in the incubator she was required to wear a blindfold to protect her eyes. She was a very alert infant, and the blindfold was invariably placed over her eyes when she was busy looking around. She would cry and squirm and thrash her arms around in an attempt to remove it. Not only was it uncomfortable, but it was also preventing her from seeing, and it became associated with a loss of my closeness. After we had been home for a week, I noticed that she cried when I turned the light off one evening, even though I was holding her in my arms. When I turned it on again, she stopped crying, but started again as soon as I turned it off. It occurred to me that the sudden darkness might be reminding her of her blindfold experience, and that she needed to do some more crying about the incubator experience. So I left the light off and held her while she cried. This occurred on several more occasions. By eight weeks of age, darkness no longer triggered crying, and she was perfectly happy to be held in the dark.

Compare that to this next example:

> When my son was seven weeks old, we acquired a crib with a bright, yellow bumper pad with pictures of animals. When I put him in the crib for the first time, he stared at the bumper pad while making delighted cooing sounds. I then turned off the light in hopes that he would settle down and go to sleep. He immediately cried. As soon as I turned the light on again, he started his happy cooing sounds while staring at the bumper pad. It was clear that he needed more time to investigate it, so I left the light on for him.

You can also note *how* your baby asks for attention. If she indicates calmly and delightedly that she wants you to play with her, she probably does not need to cry. But if she demands attention in a whiny or frantic tone of voice, this is a possible indication of a need to cry. She needs your attention, but playing with her in this case will only distract her and postpone the crying.

Babies who cry as much as they need to often play happily alone, and that is a great relief to many parents. However the decision as to when and for how long babies entertain themselves is best left up to them. Babies do have a genuine need for attention, and only they know when they need it and when they do not. They are unable to postpone this need. Later on they will be able to wait for your attention, but this is too much to expect of a child under two years of age.

Therefore, I recommend that you try to be available when you are with your baby, because responding to genuine requests for attention will not spoil her. It is only when these demands become excessive, and when your baby can *never* entertain herself that you can suspect a need to cry to release pent-up emotions and stress.

As a parent, you have a vital role to play in controlling and moderating the amount and kind of stimulation your baby receives. It is important to be aware of your baby's need for stimulation, but also to not assume that every whimper implies that you must entertain your baby. Sometimes an appropriate response is to hold your baby without distractions and listen to her. You will probably make some mistakes when interpreting your baby's signals, but even if the removal of stimulation inadvertently causes a new hurt for your baby, this is not a major trauma, and she can easily heal from this.

How directive should I be?

You do not need to tell your baby what to play with or how to play, as too much direction can interfere with the learning process. Instead of saying: "Let's build a tower now, " or "Let's read this book now," you can try saying, "What would you like to do?" If given a chance and some aware attention, babies will spontaneously take the initiative and indicate what they would like to do. You can trust them to select meaningful stimulation for themselves, but what they choose to do may not be what you had in mind. Some parents find in dismay that their baby much prefers playing with a box than with the new toy that was in it!

If you continually suggest activities, your baby may become dependent on this, and lose his spontaneity and initiative. This will lead to boredom when nobody is available to make suggestions or entertain him. He may even demand constant attention, and you may begin to feel that you have "spoiled" him. However, if you give him non-directive attention, these problems will not be as likely to arise. If your baby learns to take the initiative when you play with him, he will continue to do so when playing alone.

In a long-term study of the effects of experience on later intellectual competence, researchers found that the parents of highly competent preschool children had interacted with their children in certain characteristic ways. They had not directed their babies' activities, but had made themselves available and had responded promptly and appropriately when the babies initiated interaction or requested something.[21]

There are times, of course, when you will want to initiate an activity such as a new game. But after you have done so, it is wise to hold back and observe your baby carefully to see whether he wants to continue. What begins as a picture book session at your suggestion may turn into a romp on the bed at your baby's instigation. You need to be ready to give up an activity if your baby loses interest, even though you yourself may be enjoying it!

It is a mistaken notion that children will never learn anything unless adults teach them. Unbidden teaching can interfere with the natural learning process by denying babies opportunities to think, discover, and experiment in their own way, or by introducing concepts for which they are not ready. Therefore, I do not recommend that you attempt to teach your baby in any structured way. A more helpful approach is to think of yourself as a facilitator of learning and to offer a variety of objects, and then observe. Meaningful learning occurs when a baby is actively involved in some activity of his own choosing. Babies *create* learning out of their experiences.[22]

Some parents worry when their baby is not developing according to the norms, as did this mother of three children:

> I used to worry a lot, especially with my first baby, because he did everything later than babies are supposed to. He didn't walk until after 18 months, and he didn't begin to talk until he was over two years old. But he's six years old now and doing fine in school. He can read very well. Both of my other babies were also late in learning things, but I haven't worried so much about them. I figure that's just the way our family is. They'll catch up. My husband didn't walk until he was two years old, and he's perfectly normal.

Try to refrain from pushing your baby to learn skills or concepts before he is ready, because you will probably fail, and both of you will become frustrated. This can damage your baby's self-esteem and attitude towards learning, and it can also create tensions in your relationship with each other. Instead, trust that your baby will learn skills in his own time. However, if you have genuine concerns about your baby's development, then do not delay in finding a competent doctor to diagnose any possible developmental disorders or physiological problems. If there is a problem, early intervention programs can be extremely beneficial.

The mother of another toddler described to me the strong urge she had to interfere while her son was playing, even though she was aware of the harm in doing so:

> I feel like I interfere too much in play-type situations because I tend to want to see him do things *the right way* (laughter). I know that's not right, I know I shouldn't, but it bothers me to see him struggling with something or maybe not knowing how to do it. So I always think I have to demonstrate it or show him how. But some-

times when I show him, then he still doesn't do it that way because he has to figure it out himself. Later, when he figures it out himself, he's able to do it. But it's hard for me to keep from showing him how to do it. I keep saying, "This is the way you do it. You stack them this way," or "You take it apart that way," or whatever. It's hard to let him make his own mistakes and do it his own way.

Some parents do not recognize the importance of movement and actions during the early years and become impatient for their child to get on to "real learning," such as reading or mathematics. However, the brain will not be able to learn academic subjects and use symbols unless it has been adequately prepared in certain ways. Piaget's detailed analysis of the development of sensori-motor intelligence during the first two years has shown how a baby's spontaneous actions with objects and with his own body lay the foundation for all subsequent learning.[23] For example, abstract mathematical concepts grow out of early experiences of crawling around, grasping and dropping objects, putting them into containers, comparing, grouping, sorting, and building. Babies know very well how to prepare their brain for higher learning, and they do it spontaneously and joyously. It is therefore inappropriate and unnecessary to teach babies to read or count.

Although structured teaching is unnecessary, there are two kinds of useful didactic experiences that will enhance your baby's development by helping him frame his experiences within a meaningful context. The first is to encourage your infant to attend to objects or events in his environment. (You can say, for example, "Do you hear the music?" while humming along with the tune to draw your baby's attention to music.) The second is to comment on your baby's spontaneous activities and interests of the moment. On a nice day in a park, as your baby reaches for a butterfly, you could say, "Are you trying to catch the butterfly? Oh dear, it flew away." Studies have shown that talking to a baby in this manner enhances language skills and cognitive development.[24]

Be careful not to interrupt your baby needlessly when he is concentrating on an activity. Babies also need times when they are not expected to listen or interact with someone else. If you observe your baby silently at times, you will notice that he concentrates very intensely as he experiments with new skills or practices old ones. A good guideline is to be sensitive to your baby's mood and current interest, and adapt your interventions accordingly. An interesting study showed that children whose mothers were highly intrusive, frequently interrupting their activities when they were six months old, were more likely to be diagnosed as hyperactive at six to eight years of age.[25] If you do need to interrupt your baby (for example, because it is time to go somewhere), give him plenty of warning, and, if possible, let him take a toy with him.

If you remember to view your baby's play as fundamental to his learning process, you will find it easier to be sensitively attuned to his needs. Babies often attempt to learn in ways and at times that are inconvenient for parents. They refuse to get out of the bathtub because they are busy exploring the properties of water, or they persist in dropping food on the floor to study the laws of gravity. If you recognize these activities as attempts at learning, rather than as misbehavior, you will find it easier to deal creatively with these conflicts in ways that satisfy everybody's needs. (See Chapter 6.)

Although you may have a strong desire to teach and share your wealth of knowledge with your baby, it is important to understand that babies learn best through their own, self-initiated experiences. Imposed, structured teaching is usually not helpful. Instead, give your baby lots of love and attention, have patience, and trust that your baby will acquire the skills he needs to become a competent person.

Are rewards and praise helpful?

Some psychologists believe that babies learn only when there is an external reward, such as a piece of food or verbal praise. These theories of learning (called behaviorist theories) were derived primarily from studies of rats and pigeons. But researchers such as Piaget, who studied human infants in depth, believe that such explanations do not adequately account for the majority of learning that takes place. They suggest instead that human beings are born with a natural, spontaneous tendency to interact with the environment in as many ways as they can, thereby developing new skills and acquiring knowledge.

In other words, babies do not need to be taught, nor do they need to be rewarded. They simply need to have access to a variety of experiences and objects and allowed to play. It is through spontaneous free play that they acquire the foundations of practical intelligence that will be the building blocks of all subsequent learning.

The following example, involving the systematic practice of hand-eye coordination, illustrates how self-motivated babies can be:

> At four-and-a-half months of age my son was lying next to me, and slowly brought his right hand from his side to touch one of the large blue buttons of my sweater. He fingered it a little while, and then quickly swung his arm back to his side. He repeated this same action sequence *over fifty times,* touching the same button with intense concentration.

External rewards are not only unnecessary, but they also have hidden pitfalls. Researchers have found in hundreds of experiments that when children are rewarded for doing something, they tend to lose interest in the activity that was rewarded.[26] One experiment demonstrated that preschool children who received an expected reward after doing a drawing activity subsequently lost interest in the activity when the reward was removed. On the other hand, children who were never rewarded in the first place did not lose interest.[27] It seems that when rewards are given, children begin to perform in order to obtain the reward, and lose touch with their original interests and desire to learn. Psychologists call this "loss of intrinsic motivation". Therefore, it is not a good idea to reward your baby's accomplishments with external reinforcers, although it is quite appropriate to show encouragement and interest in her developing skills.

Many people feel that praising children is helpful and beneficial, but praise, like material rewards, can actually *reduce the* desire to learn rather than enhance it. Furthermore, because babies already enjoy learning new skills, praise is unnecessary. Babies do not care whether their accomplishments are "good" or not. Such value judgments can be confusing because the word "good" implies the possibility that they could have been bad. This could lead to anxiety later on about whether or not their accomplishments are "good" enough. The learning process operates much better without value judgments.

When your baby accomplishes something new, try to give non-judgmental feedback or encouragement. Here are some examples: "You did it! You rolled over all by yourself!" "Now you can put your shirt on. It's fun to dress yourself, isn't it?" "You worked a long time on that. It's the highest tower you've ever built!" Notice in these examples that there are no value judgments, but only factual feedback and a comparison of the child's performance with her own past performance, rather than with a theoretical model of perfection.

HOW TO ENHANCE YOUR BABY'S INTELLECTUAL COMPETENCE

- Provide a stress-free environment with plenty of physical contact. Avoid all forms of punishment.

- Provide an enriched environment with appropriate stimulation, but don't overstimulate.

- Allow freedom of movement with opportunities to discover and explore in a safe environment.

- Frequently interact with your baby (talking, singing, playful games).

- Be available to give attention as needed, but don't help too much. Let your baby struggle a little while learning new skills.

- Refrain from structured, imposed teaching.

- Encourage new skills and show delight with your baby's accomplishments, but avoid rewards or praise with value judgments.

- Show empathy with your baby's frustrations, and accept crying and temper tantrums.

How much should I help my baby when he has trouble doing something?

It is tempting to help babies accomplish tasks that appear too difficult, but this can interfere with the learning process. Maria Montessori wrote: "The child's first instinct is to carry out his actions by himself, without anyone helping him, and his first conscious bid for independence is made when he defends himself against those who try to do the action for him."[28]

Frustration and failure are important aspects of the learning process. Every time you do something for your baby that he could do by himself, you are denying him the opportunity to feel a sense of accomplishment from mastering a difficult task. He may even start to feel incompetent, which is not the message you want to convey. For example, if your baby is trying to build a tower with blocks, it does little good for you to build one for him. His pleasure and sense of accomplishment will arise from struggling to build one himself and finally succeeding, not from seeing you build one.

When babies and toddlers become frustrated while attempting a difficult task, they sometimes cry or even have a temper tantrum. The most helpful response is to allow the crying and be an empathic listener. You can let your baby know that you understand how he feels by saying, for example, "You're really mad because you can't get that cover off the box." After a good cry, when he has calmed down, he may suddenly be able to do what he could not do before! But even if he can't, at least he will have vented his frustration. To help a frustrated baby not only denies him an opportunity to learn, but may also prevent him from releasing the feelings of frustration that have *already* occurred. These will cause tensions until he is allowed to release them.

Babies become frustrated when the world does not work according to their expectations, for instance, when a round peg does not fit into a square hole, or when they are pushing a toy truck sideways and it won't roll that way. At such times they also need to cry and rage. They will, of course, never be able to do what they are trying to do, but once they have cried, they will be better able to accept and understand these new pieces of information about the world.

Sometimes it does make sense to help babies. If you see that your baby is becoming so frustrated that he gives up altogether, or if he is clearly *asking* for help, then it is quite appropriate to respond promptly and help your baby overcome his difficulty. If you pay close attention to your baby's cues, you will learn to tell when he needs help, when he does not, and how much help is appropriate.

If you think that your baby has a legitimate need for assistance, you should do only the minimum necessary so your baby still has an opportunity to learn something and to feel a sense of accomplishment. Perhaps you can slightly modify the task to make it easier, or give a hint. The following example illustrates this:

> At 21 months of age, my son was playing with a small ball in the living room. After a while the ball rolled under a chair. He put his hand between the chair and the couch and was able to grab the ball, but as he attempted to pull it out it kept getting stuck. It was obviously too big to fit through that space, but he attempted the same thing several times and began to show definite signs of frustration. His arms were not long enough to reach the ball from any other angle. My first thought was to get the ball for him, but it occurred to me that I would be depriving him of a learning experience, so I refrained. There happened to be a pinwheel on a long stick nearby, and I knew that he had, on previous occasions, retrieved toys using a long object as a tool. Instead of getting the ball for him, I suggested that he use the pinwheel. He immediately picked it up and began swiping at the ball with it. He was able to move the ball to a place where he could easily reach it with his hand and pull it out. He was quite proud of himself.

The fact that babies show signs of frustration indicates that they are very motivated to accomplish the task. It would be a shame not to make use of these high levels of motivation when they occur, because that is when meaningful learning can take place.

Some babies become very frustrated for several weeks before they finally master a developmental milestone, such as rolling over or crawling. I call these "developmental frustrations," and there is not much you can do other than offer your empathy. I remember when my daughter was trying to crawl forward to reach a toy. In spite of her efforts, she could only manage to go backwards! It did little good to bring the toy to her, because she would just become frustrated the next time she tried to crawl. These frustrations typically build up and are released in crying spells before falling asleep. (If you distract your baby from crying, he is likely to awaken several times at night crying.) After he has mastered a new skill, you will probably notice a period of relative peacefulness with less crying, at least until a new developmental frustration comes along.

Sometimes doing less for our babies actually helps them acquire self-confidence. Frustrations are an inevitable part of the learning process. Letting babies vent their emotions allows them to be well prepared for later learning because they will not have a backlog of frustrations. They will approach new educational experiences without tension or anxiety, and have confidence in their ability to master new skills, even those that appear at first to be very difficult and frustrating.

1 find it difficult to give appropriate attention to my baby.

Many of us still suffer, as adults, from the effects of learning-related hurts, and this makes it hard for us to give good, non-interfering attention to our babies. These hurts include being examined, praised, graded, compared, criticized, ridiculed, and punished; having one's curiosity and urge to explore stifled; being told what, where, when, and how to learn; suffering from boredom or forced sitting for lengthy periods of time; not being allowed to struggle and make mistakes; not being encouraged to ask questions and make our own discoveries; and being interrupted while concentrating. There is a strong pull to re-enact what we experienced. If your own parents continually pointed out your mistakes, you will probably find yourself frequently correcting your baby before you are aware of what you are doing. It can be very helpful to talk (and maybe also cry and rage) about the hurtful ways in which you were taught as a child. (See the exercises at the end of this chapter.)

There is another aspect to this whole problem. Many parents resent having to pay attention to their children because our culture belittles and degrades the important work of parenting. People have traditionally considered this to be "mere" women's work that requires no special skills. It is little wonder that so many mothers are anxious to get out of the home to where they feel the real "action" is. If you are a woman feeling bored playing with your baby, much of your feeling may actually have its roots in these cultural attitudes. You may begin to pity yourself for being stuck with such "demeaning" work. If cultural attitudes were to change overnight, and child rearing were considered to be an important, challenging, and interesting job, and if parents were given both financial and emotional support to be responsible for their baby's care and education, there might be fewer bored parents. If it were a well-paid job, it would probably be in great demand, because what could be more exciting than the opportunity to observe a new human being discover and learn? The unfolding of a child's intelligence is, in fact, where some of the real "action" is.

However, even with the most favorable cultural attitudes, child rearing is nevertheless extremely demanding, and no single person can be expected to meet a baby's needs for social interaction, day after day. The job is too difficult to do alone. The mother of a toddler told me how hard it was for her to be alone with her daughter for three full days with no help:

> I was all alone with Judy for three full days once. The first day I felt pretty good, but the second day was the "down" day for me. I guess I was realizing that I was sort of stuck. When I woke up in the morning, I felt as if I didn't have anything else to give. I just didn't want to be with her that day. I resented having to be the sole caretaker for those three days, and not being able to share my parenting responsibilities with somebody. I had no recourse but to deal with the situation the best way I could by myself. So I cried in front of her, and I was rather bitchy. She was very demanding, asking me to do this and do that. I did them and sat there crying while I did them. Then I decided that I had to have a feeling of accomplishment, so I started cleaning the house like crazy. I just put all of this energy into cleaning the house. When I know what I want to do I can stop and give her attention, knowing that I'll get back to what I'm going to do.

Parents do need help. Our species did not evolve in isolated nuclear families with one parent alone at home with the children. Instead, we evolved in large clans, and there were always other people to help and interact with the children. In an ideal society, no single person would have to give attention or be responsible for a baby for more than a few hours at a time. Another mother I interviewed said this:

> I can give him attention for bits of time, but not for a long stretch. It never feels like I'm playing enough with him, or that I'm really giving him attention. It never feels like I have enough time for myself, and the tension really builds up. But if I can have just three hours to myself, I come back and I have a *lot* more attention for him and the rest of my family.

Although babies do need a lot of attention, it is important to keep a balance between child-centered and adult-centered activities. In fact, babies are sometimes happier and less demanding when their parents are involved in adult activities, rather than always observing or entering into the babies' world of play. Babies learn from observing adults do meaningful work, imitating when they are old enough, and participating when they can. So there is no need to feel guilty if part of your time is spent doing adult activities or chores. You can still be available for your baby if she should need you. If you become too child-centered, your baby will not learn about the other important work you do. So let your baby watch you doing household chores and pursuing your own interests such as reading, playing a musical instrument, gardening, or working at a home computer. By the time she is a year old, she will probably start to imitate you, and she will become aware of meaningful skills to learn.

Giving aware, relaxed attention to babies is important, but not always easy. However, don't forget that your baby also needs opportunities to observe your activities so she can learn by imitation and find a meaningful framework in which to acquire new skills.

What games can I play with my baby?

The preceding sections focus primarily on play with objects. There is another kind of play that involves people rather than objects or toys. This includes all the silly little games that parents play with their babies, the spontaneous person-to-person interactions that form the very basis for healthy attachment.[29] When parents are sensitively attuned to their babies, these daily reciprocal exchanges help babies acquire self-confidence, a sense of trust, security, reciprocity, humor, and joy. These games also help babies acquire cognitive and interpersonal skills. Babies need these kinds of interactions, therefore, not only for optimal emotional development, but also for intellectual development to proceed normally.

Laughter is very important in fostering healthy attachment and also in helping babies release tensions. After about five months of age, babies begin to laugh, and this is an important form of tension-release (just like crying). While crying is a release of grief, frustration, or terror, laughter seems to provide a healthy release of lighter fears and anxieties.

In a study of the development of laughter during the first year of life, the most powerful laughter-producing stimulus was a situation in which the mother said "I'm gonna get you," while leaning towards the baby and grabbing him around the waist.[30] Another powerful laughter-producing stimulus was the mother wearing a mask. Both of these situations probably caused mild fright in the babies. However, if the fear becomes too strong, babies cry rather than laugh. When a stranger wore the mask, the babies *cried* instead, showing how close crying is to laughter.

Laughter-producing games are beneficial when they provide babies opportunities to release fears that they *already have*. The games must not cause any new fears, and the baby must judge the situation to be of no real threat. When past traumatic experiences or chronic anxiety are brought up in a safe play situation, it can be beneficial for babies because they do not feel threatened. You are therefore setting up therapeutic situations when you help your baby laugh by playing such games.

There are many enjoyable and beneficial games to play with babies. In this section I discuss some that are particularly important for healthy psychological development. Many of these involve laughter.

Contingency play

As soon as your baby is old enough to coo or reach out and touch your face, you can begin to play games involving cause and effect. When your baby initiates an action, you can respond in an amusing way. For example, if your baby touches your nose, you can say, "peep" in a high-pitched voice, and repeat this if he touches your nose again. Babies enjoy these games very much, and will soon learn to repeat the action that brought the amusing response from you. You can also imitate your baby's movements or sounds. This kind of interaction allows babies to learn about cause and effect, and it introduces them to the concept of a dialog in which partners take turns. It also helps them develop a feeling of powerfulness because your response is contingent on their behavior. This must feel very gratifying when everybody is bigger than they are and most of their daily life is unpredictable and confusing.

Nonsense play

I call nonsense play the kind of games that babies invent spontaneously when they purposely do something wrong. I noticed that both of my children purposely did things wrong (while laughing) after they had mastered specific skills, whether it was putting a puzzle together or reciting a nursery rhyme. One day, when my son was twenty months old, he pretended to blow his nose in his shirt and laughed. Another time, he put his pajama pants on his head and laughed. He thought this was very funny, and repeated this behavior for several days. Rather than assume that toddlers are just "fooling around" or "wasting time," I prefer to think of these games as self-initiated therapy. My son knew how to blow his nose in a tissue and also how to put his pajamas on, but he had only learned to do so recently. Purposely doing these things wrong allowed him to release tensions through laughter resulting from his previous frustrations.

This kind of play fosters the development of creativity and humor. In fact, many good comedians (such as Charlie Chaplin) elicit laughter in their audience by making mistakes. This allows people to release tensions about their own anxiety, embarrassment, and feelings of incompetence. So comedy is actually a therapeutic art. If you allow your baby the freedom to be "silly" at times, he will become skilled at creating humorous situations, and this will be therapeutic.

Separation games

Separation games can be very therapeutic in helping babies overcome anxieties about separation, and in establishing a healthy attachment to their caretakers. Peek-a-boo is an important separation game played by parents and babies all over the world. In this game there is a disruption of visual contact between you and your baby. You cover your face or hide behind something, and then suddenly reappear, saying "peek-a-boo!" This will probably cause your baby to laugh. You can vary the game by using a piece of cloth or your baby's own hands or feet to hide her face.

The fear involved in the game of peek-a-boo is that of separation anxiety and perhaps also birth trauma. (Re-establishing visual connection between parent and child after an interruption simulates the birth experience when the infant first opened her eyes.) It is interesting that the words "peek-a-boo" stem from old English and originally signified "alive or dead." It is as if you are asking your baby the chilling question, "Am I alive or dead?" or "Are you alive or dead?" Separation from the mother, to a baby, does signify possible death, so this game touches on deep emotional issues.

Your baby will enjoy playing peek-a-boo as long as she realizes that you have not really disappeared. If you stay hidden too long, she will probably cry. Most babies go through a stage of intense attachment to their parents that is strongest between six and 18 months of age (see Chapter 7), and the game of peek-a-boo elicits the most laughter with babies in that age range. It is interesting that babies living in institutions do not respond well to this game.[31] This is probably because they have not had the opportunity to form strong attachments to anybody, and therefore have no separation anxiety.

When your baby can crawl, a variation of peek-a-boo is to put a sheet over her and then pretend that you cannot find her (while touching her through the sheet to reassure her, if necessary). You can then create a tunnel with the sheet through which your baby can crawl to reach you. This is a birth simulation game that can help your baby heal from birth trauma. You can also cover your baby with pillows and let her pop out when she wants to. Babies born by Cesarean section will probably especially enjoy that version.

Hide-and-go-seek is a separation game that you can play after your baby learns to walk. At first your toddler will probably hide in a very visible place, and be delighted if you pretend that you cannot see her. Later, she will learn to hide out of sight, and she will also enjoy looking for you. In addition to helping your child cope emotionally with a fear of separation or death, hide-and-go-seek will help her understand the world from someone else's point of view, which is an important cognitive skill.

Power-reversal games

Certain types of activities help babies release feelings of chronic powerlessness. The crucial element in these power-reversal games is that the adult pretends to be weak, incompetent, ignorant, or scared. A favorite one with most babies and toddlers is "Knock Me Over." If you let your baby "push" you over, and you then fall down dramatically, pretending to be overpowered, your baby will probably laugh heartily and want to repeat the game. Power-reversal games are similar to the simple cause and effect games mentioned above, because the baby initiates the action and acquires a sense of powerfulness.

Babies laugh during this kind of play because the games deal with issues of power and strength, yet are quite different from the usual, everyday experience of being overpowered by adults. Babies must live with the fact that they can be removed from any spot against their will, simply because they are small. When, for a change, they are given an opportunity to be powerful and to "knock" big people over, this allows them to feel safe enough to release their anxiety and powerlessness through the tension-release mechanism of laughter. As your toddler grows older, she may enjoy this same game in the form of a pillow fight in which you let her win. There is no need to worry that this kind of play will cause your child to become aggressive. On the contrary, the laughter will help to dissipate aggressive energy resulting from pent-up emotions.

There are many other power-reversal games. For example, when your toddler learns to run, she will probably enjoy playing tag if you pretend that it's hard to catch up with her, or if you run slowly enough to let her catch you.

Games of mock attack

Some people think that tickling is beneficial because it makes babies laugh. However, I do not recommend tickling because it is a form of attack that can cause babies to feel powerless. Some babies seem to enjoy being tickled, but only because it is the only form of touching they have ever experienced, aside from routine care. Being tickled is better than no physical contact at all with another person. These babies have a great need of being lovingly caressed. At first they may react to caresses or massages as they would to tickling (by laughing, squirming, or tensing their muscles), and it may take some time for them to develop confidence and relax while being touched.

Adults who feel the need to tickle babies or engage in rough or aggressive play (such as throwing them up in the air even though it frightens them) may be acting out of an unconscious desire for power and domination. Perhaps they feel the need to overpower someone helpless because they were made to feel helpless when they were little. Babies benefit much more from gentler forms of play with people who are careful not to frighten or overstimulate them.

Some examples of mock attack that babies seem to enjoy include blowing on your baby's tummy, gently nibbling his ears or toes, gently bumping heads while saying "boo!", or playfully saying "I'm gonna get you!" while grabbing your baby around the waist.

You can also use mock attack games to help a toddler cope with specific fears. If you bring up the fear in a playful, non-threatening way, your toddler will laugh and release tensions. The following example illustrates how a playful situation helped my son deal with a fear of dogs by releasing tensions through laughter.

> At 19 months of age, my son had a fear of barking dogs because he had been frightened on two occasions by a dog barking loudly and suddenly from the other side of a fence. An over-friendly puppy had also once pounced on him. One day I got down on my hands

and knees and began to bark at him while coming towards him. He laughed heartily and ran away, but returned again and again to be barked at some more. This went on for quite a while, and he loved it. He would laugh and point to me saying, "mama, mama" (perhaps to reassure himself that I really was his mother rather than a dog!). Later on his seven-year-old cousin, who had been watching, tried the same game with him, but this was too frightening for him and he came running to me crying.

Movement activities with body contact

Here are some examples of movement games with body contact that babies seem to enjoy:

- Hold your baby in your arms and rock or dance to music.

- While sitting in a chair, give your baby a ride on your feet.

- Bounce your baby on your knees, pretending to be a horse.

- Lie on your back with your knees up and let your baby slide down your legs to your abdomen.

- Lie on your back with your legs in the air. Place your baby on her tummy on your feet, hold her hands, and move your legs up and down.

- Give your baby piggyback rides.

- Say nursery rhymes that involve touch (such as "This Little Piggy" while wiggling each of your baby's toes in turn).

These activities can be combined with other types of play. For example, while giving your baby a piggyback ride, you can collapse once in a while, pretending that you are too weak to carry her (power-reversal play). Or you can play peek-a-boo (separation game) while your baby is lying on your feet up in the air.

You and your baby will probably invent many games together. These daily interactions will help your baby release tensions through laughter, and will also provide her with valuable cognitive skills as well as a sense of connection and emotional security.

EXERCISES

Explore your childhood.

1. Do you remember being rewarded in any way for learning or performing well (by praise, grades, privileges, money, etc.)? How did it make you feel? Do you remember times when you were criticized or punished for not learning or performing well? How did it make you feel? Were you pressured to excel?
2. Can you remember times when you were given or denied a toy that you really wanted? How did you feel? Did you have enough (or too many) toys? What were your favorite toys? What feelings do you have connected with them?
3. Recall times when your parents played with you. Do you wish they had played with you more? What were some of your favorite games?

Express your feelings about your baby.

1. Do you worry about your baby's development? Do you have educational or career goals for your baby? Does this cause you to pressure your baby to learn or perform?
2. How do you feel when your baby a) makes a mistake, b) struggles to do something difficult, c) refuses a toy that you offer? What do you feel like doing at those times? (This is not necessarily what you *should do!*)
3. Give your baby your complete, undivided, and non-directive attention for one hour without interfering, and let your baby take the initiative. Is this easy or hard for you? How does it make you feel?

Nurture yourself.

1. Take the time to learn something that you did not have a chance to learn as a child.
2. Spend an evening playing a game with another adult (or with a group of adults).
3. Watch a funny film or go to a play that makes you laugh.

CHAPTER 6

CONFLICTS: LETTING YOUR BABY FEEL RESPECTED

Should I use punishments or rewards?

All punishment produces emotional pain, and corporal punishment produces physical pain as well. When a parent inflicts pain on a baby in the form of punishment, this can destroy the baby's sense of trust and security. Babies need to know that they are loved, deeply and unconditionally, no matter what they are doing. There is no possible way that punishment can communicate love. You will need to set limits on your baby's behavior at times, but you can do this without using any punishments whatsoever.

There is considerable research on the negative effects of punishment. Studies have shown that corporal punishment of children (spanking) correlates with insecure attachment during childhood.[1] Other studies have shown that it correlates with later anxiety, depression, suicide, and other psychiatric disorders.[2]

The use of punishment can also adversely affect intellectual development. Researchers found that eleven-month-old babies whose parents used frequent punishment with them had lower IQ's than babies whose parents punished them less often.[3] A possible explanation for this is that the use of punishment inhibited the babies' intellectual development. There is also a correlation between the use of corporal punishment and school performance. Children whose parents use harsh discipline do not do as well in school.[4]

If you slap your baby after he drops a piece of food on the floor from his high chair, he is not likely to understand what he is being punished for. Does it mean not to let go of objects? Never to drop anything on the floor? To stop wondering about the laws of gravity? The trouble with punishment is that babies learn to inhibit *all of the behaviors and intentions* that preceded a punishment, rather than only the specific one the parents had in mind. Curiosity and exploration are inseparable components of most of babies' behaviors. The consequence of too many spankings may therefore be a diminished desire to explore and learn. This could help explain why the use of punishment correlates with lower IQ and school performance.

Another negative side-effect of punishment is that it may result in an avoidance of the situation altogether.[5] One example of this is constipation resulting from the use of punishment during toilet training. From the baby's point of view, it is better not to defecate at all, rather than to risk defecating in the wrong place.

Still another negative consequence of punishment is that it can lead to aggression, but sometimes the effects do not appear until later in life. Studies have found that children whose parents use corporal punishment (spanking or hitting) are more likely to show antisocial and violent behaviors later on.[6]

In addition to these negative side-effects of punishment, there is considerable evidence that it is not even very effective. Studies have shown that the use of punishment does not enhance a child's moral development, nor does it result in improved behavior or a more obedient child.[7]

The very concept of punishment implies that babies misbehave. *Babies do not misbehave.* They always act in ways that will best get their needs met. These needs include food, attention, meaningful connection to others, and the acquisition of new information and skills. Unfortunately their behavior is sometimes dangerous for themselves or conflicts with other people's needs. This occurs because they lack information, or they have pent-up, painful emotions that need to be released. To speak of "misbehavior" is to miss the point.

It will never be possible to eliminate all painful situations. For example, a baby feels pain each time he falls down and bumps himself on a hard floor while learning to walk, or when he touches a hot radiator or stove. These painful, natural consequences of certain behaviors, however, do not appear to have any of the disagreeable side effects that parental punishment produces.[8]

There are times when such "discipline" by the physical world can be even more effective (and less damaging in the long run) than scolding or spanking. If your baby insists on approaching a hot stove to touch it, you will not help him learn very effectively by yelling "no" or slapping him each time. Another solution is to warn him by explaining that it is very hot, but then, if he still wants to touch it, supervise him carefully while letting him touch it once briefly to find out for himself what the word "hot" means. He will probably not touch it again because he now has the information he needs.

This approach is unlikely to make your child feel unloved, insecure, anxious, or aggressive. His exploratory urge will not be dampened because it will be very clear to him exactly what behavior to avoid in the future. His relationship with you will remain intact and loving. You are treating him with respect and expecting him to take responsibility for his own actions. Before using this approach, however, it is better to baby proof your home as much as possible and keep your baby in safe areas so he will not encounter any harmful objects or situations.

The following example illustrates how this "punishment" by the physical world (natural consequence) can be an effective teaching tool when it is not possible to remove the source of danger:

As a toddler my son began to open and close the closet doors, which folded out as they opened. I worried that he might pinch himself in the crack between two folding sections while closing them. So I tried several methods to prevent him from opening them, but nothing seemed to work. Then I tried to teach him how to close them so that he would not get pinched, but he saw no sense in doing it that way. Finally, in exasperation, I gave up and decided to risk letting him close them in his own way. Just as I had feared, one day he pinched his hand quite badly while closing the closet doors. After paying attention to him while he cried for about 15 minutes, I again showed him how to close the doors without getting pinched (by placing one hand on each side of the crack). He paid very close attention to my instructions, and was always extremely careful after that incident to close the doors in that manner. He never pinched himself again.

If your baby hurts himself during his experimenting and exploration, it is important to allow him to cry while paying attention to him. Once he has vented his feelings about getting hurt, he will be ready to understand what happened and to learn something from the experience. There are, of course, many situations that are too dangerous, and you will need to find other methods to protect your baby from harm. Another section discusses ways of setting limits without using punishments.

Rewards appear to be much kinder than punishments, but in reality they have many hidden pitfalls. (See Chapter 5 for a discussion of the pitfalls of rewards and praise in regard to the learning process.) Studies have shown that even very young infants can learn to modify their own behavior in order to obtain something that is rewarding to them.[9] But the fact that rewards can have an effect does not imply that parents should use them as disciplinary methods.

The use of rewards is actually quite similar to the use of punishments because the absence of a reward is equivalent to a punishment. Babies who frequently receive rewards for "good" behavior may therefore become insecure or anxious in much the same way as those who are punished.

Some parents use special treats, such as candy or cookies, to reward their babies. The problem with this is that it can create an artificial desire for the treats. It is especially risky to use sweets to get babies to stop crying, as this can lead to a sugar addiction and compulsive overeating, in addition to a repression of emotions (as discussed in Chapter 2).

The use of rewards may successfully get your baby to do what you want him to do, but it will probably not solve the underlying problem or instill any values. If you reward your toddler with a special treat only on the condition that he put his toys away, he may indeed learn to do so. But he will probably not learn to value orderliness for its own sake. Furthermore, if you frequently control your child's behavior with rewards, he may continue his "good" behavior only as long as you keep giving rewards. Will he continue to put his toys away when you stop offering the special treat?

Another problem with the use of rewards is that it teaches children to do whatever brings immediate gratification. When better rewards come along, as they inevitably will, the children may turn to those instead of parental rewards. What if a drug dealer or an unethical leader offers more interesting rewards than yours? The goal of parenting should be to help children learn to recognize and avoid people's efforts to manipulate or control them. When parents themselves become the agents of manipulation, children are not free to learn to think before acting.

Research has shown that the use of rewards can actually backfire because it causes people to lose interest in the behavior that was rewarded (by destroying "intrinsic motivation," as mentioned in Chapter 5). Numerous studies have shown that children come to *dislike* whatever they must do to obtain a reward.[10] In other words, an effective way to get your toddler to dislike putting toys away is to offer him an enticing reward for doing so!

Because of your greater strength, knowledge, and access to resources, you are much more powerful than your baby. But the misuse of this power can have damaging consequences on your child's development and your relationship with him. Although rewards and punishments may sometimes succeed, in the short term, in changing your child's behavior, this does not justify their use.

Should I train my baby to be obedient?

Until the second half of the twentieth century, few people questioned the value of obedience training. It was prevalent among the ancient Babylonians, Greeks, Hebrews, Romans, and Europeans, as well as most traditional African and Asian cultures.

During the Middle Ages in Europe, people thought that children who were disobedient, stubborn, willful, or who cried a lot were possessed by a demon. One remedy was to bring such a child to a priest and have the demon exorcised through a religious ritual. If that didn't work, parents tried to "beat the devil out of them," an expression that still remains with us today. A variety of torture instruments have been used throughout the ages to instill obedience in children, such as a rod called a "discipline," a whip called a "cat-o-nine tails" and a knife called a "goad" that was used to prick children.

By the 17th century, most people had abandoned the idea of demonic possession, but attributed children's misbehaviors and disobedience to an inherent sinful nature. The goal of discipline was to break the child's will and instill unquestioning obedience. In addition to the usual beatings and whippings, other methods were to lock children in dark closets, tie them to their beds, or deprive them of food. Parents routinely brought young children to witness public executions, and showed them graphic pictures of hell.

There is still a widespread belief that babies are born with an evil nature. Even today, some people still describe babies as little tyrants, and warn parents to show their baby "who is the boss" right from the start, so their baby will not get control over them. However, human infants are extremely helpless and vulnerable, and do not have the cognitive ability to understand the concepts of power and control. All they know is that they have needs. This distorted, absurd notion that babies will control the parents if the parents don't control them probably stems from people's own feelings of powerlessness and anxiety resulting from an oppressive, punitive childhood.

Perhaps it was the Second World War that caused some people to question the virtues of obedience training. Even though many people consider Hitler to have been a psychopath, the reality is that he had millions of followers who were ordinary, seemingly decent citizens. In fact, they acted just as many modern parents want their children to behave. They did not question his orders or ideas, believing that they were for their own good and the good of the country. Those people had lost the ability to question authority, think for themselves, and take full responsibility for their own actions. They had acquired a distorted morality that justified, in their minds, obeying his orders and killing innocent people. According to Alice Miller, the root of the problem was that Germany has a tradition of punitive authoritarianism for raising children, and most German people who participated in the war had suffered considerable pain through harsh punishment as they were growing up. Furthermore, they had not been allowed to express their emotions and were taught that it was "for their own good."[11]

Was it a peculiarity of the German people that made them obey mindlessly and destroy millions of innocent lives in the gas chambers? A psychology experiment with average American adults of various occupations indicates that it was not. Volunteers were told to administer electric shocks to a man each time he made an error in a learning task. The man was actually a stooge, and his efforts in the learning task were faked. He did not really receive any shocks, but participants in the experiment were led to believe that he was experiencing painful shocks. With each additional "error" the volunteer was told to increase the intensity of the shock, up to 450 volts on a shock generator. The stooge complained bitterly and screamed for the experiment to stop, but the experimenter kept telling the person to continue giving him shocks. Although many of the participants dissented and felt that it was wrong, *most did not disobey.* In fact, almost two-thirds of the people continued to give shocks up to 450 volts![12]

This frightening experiment demonstrates that people are willing to obey authority figures even though the command goes against the people's own best judgment and values. Anyone who has been subjected to harsh obedience training as a child will be susceptible to this as an adult. Parents, certainly, do not want their children to grow up unable to do what is right in the face of opposition, yet many parents give their children the very upbringing that promotes this blind obedience to authority figures.

Some parents think that, without obedience training, children will not spontaneously cooperate at all. The reality is that babies have an inherent tendency to cooperate because it is part of their human nature to do so. A team of psychologists observed infants from birth to twelve months of age, and found that the most cooperative nine- to-twelve-month-olds were those whose mothers were sensitive to their signals, accepted most of their behavior, and avoided imposing their will on the infants. These babies complied with their mothers' simple commands and prohibitions more than those whose mothers were insensitive, rejecting, or interfering. Mothers who used disciplinary measures, such as slapping their infants or dragging them away from forbidden areas, had infants who were not any more cooperative as the result of such "training." Obedience training had no effect on the infants' behavior, whereas the quality of the mother-infant relationship did.[13]

If you wish to foster a tendency towards cooperation in your baby, you can start at birth by responding promptly and appropriately to her signals, accepting as many aspects of her behavior as possible, and avoiding interrupting, controlling, or imposing your will, except if absolutely necessary. When your baby reaches the crawling stage, there will be no need for obedience training. If your baby feels confident in your love, she will *want* to comply with your wishes. However, this cooperative attitude will come about only if these wishes are reasonable, within her ability to understand, and do not deprive her of any real need.

When all of these conditions are filled, the first signs of cooperation start to emerge during the second half of the first year, at about the same time that most babies start crawling. It is probably not pure coincidence that the ability and tendency to cooperate occur at approximately the same age as the ability to crawl. This inborn tendency to comply probably had important survival value during the evolution of the human species. Crawling infants who readily heeded parental commands and prohibitions in a hazardous environment had a much greater chance of surviving.

Although researchers found no visible results of obedience training by the end of the first year, the continued use of punishments and rewards does eventually succeed in subduing some children into obedience. This type of obedience is not the spontaneous, joyful type seen in unpunished children who are eager to cooperate, but rather an automatic, unthinking type of obedience based on fear. This is the dangerous type of obedience, which leaders like Hitler can easily take advantage of for their own purposes. Compliance itself is not bad. It is the blind, submissive obedience to authority figures, rooted in fear of punishment, that can be dangerous.

Most babies go through a period of negativism beginning during the second year, and lasting well into the third year. During this period, a strong urge to be autonomous may seem to overshadow any natural cooperative inclinations. However, if you treat your toddler with tact, patience, and respect during this period, she will continue to show cooperation. This is discussed more fully in a later section.

The goal of discipline should be to nurture your baby in such a way that her natural tendency to cooperate can flourish. This implies no punishments, rewards, or obedience "training." This approach will not produce a selfish, demanding child, as many people fear, but one who is compassionate, cooperative, and altruistic. An added benefit is that you will enjoy a close, mutually respectful relationship with your child, and will have fewer discipline problems and power struggles with her as she grows older.

How permissive should I be?

An overly permissive approach can also have negative consequences. If you allow your baby to do destructive or unacceptable things, or sacrifice your own needs, you are not doing him a favor, and you may both suffer in several ways.

Here is an example of permissiveness: a mother lets her baby crawl on her stomach even though it is uncomfortable for her. She fails to say "no" and take care of her own needs for fear of frustrating her baby and discouraging his desire for physical contact. In such a situation, a baby is receiving two conflicting messages: permission to crawl on his mother's stomach, and a look of pain on his mother's face. The problem is that the baby will probably sense his mother's discomfort, even though she does nothing to stop him. If this type of confusing situation is repeated often, the baby may eventually begin to mistrust his own perceptions and therefore learn to disregard the subtle, nonverbal cues that would allow him to be sensitive to other people's feelings and needs.

Another problem with permissiveness is that your baby may learn that his needs are more important than other people's needs and that he can do anything he wants, even if it hurts others in the process. As he grows older, he may become selfish and demanding with very little consideration for other people's needs and feelings. This is certainly not a desirable outcome.

A more subtle, but major, problem with permissiveness is that, when parents sacrifice their own needs, they often build up resentments and anger towards their children. This resentment can cause the children to feel insecure and anxious, and to become overly demanding or clingy in an effort to reassure themselves of their parent's love. It is somewhat paradoxical that, the more you sacrifice your-self for your children, the more insecure they will probably feel.

There are several possible causes for permissiveness. Some par-ents over-react to the oppressive, punitive methods that were used with them as children. In an understandable effort not to hurt their own children in the same way, they are afraid to set any limits or do anything against their baby's will. A mother, who once consulted with me, never drove anywhere in her car with her baby because he cried whenever she put him in his car seat. She was afraid of being too authoritarian, as her own parents had been. But this was severely limiting the places she could go with him, and she was beginning to feel resentful.

Feelings of guilt can also cause a parent to be overly permissive. If a mother feels guilty because she had considered an abortion, she may become self-sacrificing in an unconscious effort to prove to her baby that she loves him. Some parents are afraid to say "no" because they want their children to like them. If a father is divorced from his child's mother, he may feel the need to give in to all of his daughter's demands in an effort to make her like him better than her mother.

Some parents are overly permissive with a child who has a chronic illness or handicap, out of pity, anxiety, or a fear of frustrating the child, combined with a deep-seated terror that the child might die. But all children need reasonable boundaries, and no child will ben-efit in the long run from a parent who is too self-sacrificing or fails to give clear messages. Whatever its deeper cause, the result of permis-siveness is usually not beneficial for the child, the parent, or their relationship.

Actually, there are very few parents who are totally permissive all the time.[14] What usually happens is that permissive parents resort to authoritarian and punitive methods at times when their anger builds up and they can no longer tolerate their child's behavior. This may be even more confusing for a child than a consistently authoritarian parent. It has been shown that this pattern of discipline is often asso-ciated with serious behavior problems later on. The most aggressive five-year-olds in a sample of children studied were those whose par-ents were highly permissive but who occasionally used severe pun-ishment.[15]

To avoid the problems caused by permissiveness, it is best to be honest, and to communicate clearly and act decisively (but not punitively), as soon as your baby does something that you consider unacceptable. For example, you can say, "that hurts," while lifting your baby off your stomach and suggesting a piggyback ride instead. Rules and limits are not *in themselves* harmful, provided your baby's needs are met in other ways. Punishment is damaging, and unfilled needs are harmful, but mere limits are not. Your baby can be quite happy developing skills in ways you find acceptable. A problem arises only when your baby has a legitimate need that is not met in any way.

Both authoritarian and permissive approaches are harmful; in fact they are actually quite similar. As Thomas Gordon has pointed out in his book, *Parent Effectiveness Training*[16] both involve the concepts of winning and losing. When the parents are authoritarian, they are the winners of the conflicts and the children are the losers. When the parents are permissive, the children are the winners and the parents are the losers. Neither of these two situations is desirable.

How can I discipline my baby without punishments or rewards?

There is a third approach for solving conflicts, which is completely outside of the authoritarian/permissive continuum. I call it "democratic discipline," because it is an approach in which nobody wins the conflicts at the expense of anyone else. However, it is not a simple technique that can be described in one or two words, but rather a way of being with children in a mutually respectful relationship.

Preventing conflicts before they occur is an important part of democratic discipline. As soon as your baby becomes mobile, you will need to decide which objects are too dangerous or precious for her to play with. The best way to set limits is to baby-proof your home as much as possible. This will allow your baby to move and explore freely without any danger to herself or the environment. (See chapter 5 for more on baby-proofing your home.)

It is often easier to change the environment than your baby. The frequency with which you must modify your baby's behavior will reflect how well you have baby-proofed your home. The ideal environment would be one in which it is never necessary to say "no" to your baby. Scrutinize your home carefully to look for all possible hazards.

Another aspect of preventing conflicts is to keep special toys in various locations (such as near the telephone, in the kitchen, or in your car) so your baby will have something to play with when you are unable to give your undivided attention.

Even in an ideal environment, however, you will still have conflicts with your baby. These fall into two categories: 1) your baby does certain things that you do not want her to do (such as drawing on the walls or banging blocks against windows), and 2) your baby does *not* do the things that you want her to do (such as holding still to be changed or agreeing to leave a playground when it is time to go).

When you have a conflict with your baby, the first step is to figure out what everybody needs at the moment. You can begin by asking yourself two questions: "What does my baby need right now?" and, "What do I need right now?" The next step is to look for a solution that meets both of your needs. The solution must be acceptable to everybody. Here is an example:

> As a toddler, my son would sometimes tug at my legs when I was trying to cook dinner. He wanted me to carry him, and was perfectly happy when I did so, but it was impossible for me to cook dinner while holding him. What did he really need? To be near me and to see what I was doing. What were my needs? To be able to cook dinner. Solution: I pulled a chair over to the counter where I was working, and let him stand on it. He was near me and was able to watch me, yet I was able to get my cooking done. We were both happy with that arrangement.

It is not enough just to stop unacceptable behavior. Babies need to have alternative behaviors offered because they cannot easily turn off their exploratory urge, nor can they channel their behavior into acceptable outlets by themselves. They lack the information to do so. How are they to know that a window could break but a rug could not? Or that throwing a ball is acceptable but throwing a cup is not? How are they to understand why Mommy can hold them at certain times and not at others? It is always a good idea to offer one or several alternatives that are consistent with your baby's needs of the moment. It is important to explain your needs to your baby, even long before she can talk, because she will learn that other people have needs, and understand why there is a conflict.

Often the most difficult part of solving conflicts by the democratic approach is to discover exactly what everybody needs. If you are not sure of your baby's needs, you can try different solutions to see what satisfies your baby. But once you know the needs, it is almost always possible to find a solution acceptable to both of you. Keep in mind that your baby's needs will change as she grows. Here is an example:

> When my son was nine months old, he began refusing to have his diapers changed. This aggravated me considerably, and nothing seemed to work. (I had tried singing to him, giving him toys to play with, and changing his diapers in different places.) So I began forcefully holding him down on the floor, and every diaper change was torture for both of us. He would scream, and I would feel guilty and exhausted. I tried to figure out what exactly it was that he didn't like, and I discovered it was the fact that he had to lie down. He had recently learned to pull himself up to a standing position, and could not tolerate lying down even for one minute. I discovered that when I changed his diapers while he stood up, he cooperated beautifully and stood very still. So I learned to change his diapers while he stood up, hanging on to the side of the bathtub, and both of our needs were met.

If you frequently stop your baby's behavior without attempting to fill her underlying needs, she may rebel and cease to comply with any of your requests. It is therefore much better, and easier in the long run, to make the effort to meet her needs as well as yours.

Some parents feel that babies should learn that they can't always have their own way. They worry about "spoiling" their baby, and think that a few deprivations or frustrations will allow her to become an altruistic person. Nobody wants their child to grow up as a thoughtless or selfish person, but deprivations or frustrations will not help your baby become altruistic. In fact, they are likely to have an opposite effect. If you do not strive to recognize and meet your baby's needs, she may become frustrated, angry, and mistrustful. Later on she will find it difficult to be aware of other people's needs because nobody attended to hers.

Babies need to know that other people are "on their side" rather than against them. After a few years, once every legitimate need has been met, they will spontaneously become altruistic. But they need that indulgence during the first few years in order to have the confidence, trust, and security from which true empathy for others can arise. They also need time to develop the cognitive skills that will allow them to understand another person's point of view. If you use a democratic approach for solving conflicts, your baby will learn that other people have needs, because you do not sacrifice your own needs.

If you are afraid of losing control of your baby, or feel that you must always be the "boss," this probably has its origin in your own childhood when you frequently had *your* power taken away by authoritarian parents. You will understandably feel a strong urge to keep your child submissive and obedient in order to maintain a sense of security and control. If you wish to become less authoritarian, it will be helpful to talk about your childhood memories of being disciplined. Perhaps you have some repressed anger at your parents. If you can release this anger (into a pillow, or with an accepting listener or therapist), you will find it easier to move towards a more democratic approach to discipline. The exercises at the end of this chapter may be helpful in this regard.

Sometimes you may not be sure of your own needs, or feel unable to decide whether or not you are justified in setting a limit. Conflict-resolution will obviously be easier when you know what your own needs are. Life with a baby is a continual decision-making process, because you are faced with situations with which you have never dealt before, especially if this is your first child. You will need to ask yourself repeatedly, "What do I really need right now? Does it really bother me that my baby is doing that? " It is important to be completely honest with yourself and your baby so that you do not give conflicting messages.

EXAMPLES OF THREE DIFFERENT
APPROACHES TO DISCIPLINE

• A 7-month-old bites mother's nipple while nursing.
  Authoritarian: Mother slaps baby.
  Permissive: Mother does not remove baby's mouth.
  Democratic: Mother gives baby a rubber toy to bite.

• A 10-month-old tears up magazines.
  Authoritarian: Father slaps baby, removes magazine.
  Permissive: Father lets baby destroy magazines.
  Democratic: Father gives baby an old magazine to
    tear up.

• A 15-month-old resists leaving when it is time to go.
  Authoritarian: Mother forcefully carries baby out.
  Permissive: Mother lets baby play, but is late for work.
  Democratic: Mother finds a toy that baby can bring.

• An 18-month-old does not to go to sleep before 11
  p.m. The parents have no time for themselves.
  Authoritarian: Parents put baby in crib at 8 p.m.
  Permissive: Parents spend evenings with their baby.
  Democratic: Parents hire an occasional evening
    babysitter.

• A 21-month-old eats standing up, causing a mess.
  Authoritarian: Mother withholds food until baby sits.
  Permissive: Mother lets baby eat standing up.
  Democratic: Mother lets baby stand on a chair and
    eat at a counter. The mess is confined to counter.

• A 24-month-old refuses to let father dress her, but
  takes a long time to dress herself.
  Authoritarian: Father forcefully dresses her.
  Permissive: Father lets her dress herself, but is late.
  Democratic: Father finds one or two articles of cloth-
    ing that she can put on easily by herself.

Here is what the mother of a toddler said about certain conflicts she had with her toddler:

> Our big problem is at dinnertime, when she wants to get down and we're still eating. It doesn't feel fair to keep her in her high chair, so we let her out, but then she hangs on me or wants to sit on my lap when I'm eating. I want to eat my dinner in peace and I just want to say, "No! It's my time to eat. You chose to get down. You can go play, but please don't hang on me." But sometimes I think that I wouldn't want to be excluded if I were she. It's hard to be consistent. Sometimes I have my arm about her and say, "Go!" at the same time! There's a lot of tension, not knowing quite what to do. Also, I want her to have clean hands before she gets out of her high chair. If I'm wishy-washy about it, there's no solution. It's a matter of knowing what I want and setting the limits and saying, "This is it, I can't live with it any other way." But so often I kind of vacillate, and begin to think that I *can* live with it. But I really can't live with her getting grease all over the furniture. So I kind of define my limits as I go. It's a self-awareness process. Once I know what my own feelings are, I'm able to cope with the situation a lot better.

One way for you to become aware of your own needs is to spend time talking with another adult about the feelings that arise during conflicts with your baby. Once you have expressed your feelings, your own needs will become clearer.

Sometimes it is helpful to look beyond your immediate need to figure out what your deeper need really is. For example, if you feel the need to have your baby go to sleep at exactly seven o'clock every evening, you will have a conflict when your baby screams and refuses to go to sleep. But what is your *real* need in this situation? Is it to have more time for yourself or with your partner? Or are you worried about what your mother-in-law will think if your baby stays up later? Once your real need is clear, it will be easier to find a solution that meets everybody's needs. If you need more time with your partner, perhaps you can find a babysitter to spend one or two evenings a week with your baby. This will meet your needs without abandoning your baby in her crib.

Many of our concepts of unacceptable behavior have their origin in our own oppressive childhood. Perhaps the idea of a rigid bedtime was instilled in you from the time you were a baby. It would be very difficult for you, in this case, to allow your baby the freedom to stay up later when you yourself were denied this privilege. If you are aware of these rigid ways you were brought up, and if you can remember how it felt, then you can change your concept of what constitutes acceptable behavior. It is especially helpful if you can release any painful emotions you have, perhaps pent-up anger at your own parents, or terror at being left to fall asleep alone at night.

What if I cannot find a solution that meets everybody's needs?

Sometimes it may seem impossible to find a satisfactory solution to a conflict with your baby. Perhaps you must go to the airport and your baby refuses to be dressed, or your toddler climbs onto the kitchen counter and reaches for the blender. Or perhaps your baby refuses to hold still so a doctor can examine his ears. The only reason such conflicts arise is that babies have less information than adults, and lack the mental ability to visualize consequences. Once children acquire more information about airline schedules, sources of danger, and medical procedures, such conflicts are much less likely to occur.

At times like these you still do not need to use punishment, but you *may* have to use your greater strength to restrain or move your baby, and your baby is likely to respond with frustration and anger. When you decide that an occasion requires the use of power, you can minimize the trauma for your baby by using the following four suggestions: 1) warn your baby ahead of time, 2) give explanations, 3) be firm but loving, and 4) allow your baby to protest and cry. Each of these four suggestions will be discussed separately.

The use of power can be less harmful if your baby knows ahead of time what to expect. For example, you can warn your baby that he may stack the blocks one more time, and after that it will be time to go. This is less traumatic than suddenly being whisked away with no previous warning. (There are many situations, of course, when there is no time for warnings, especially when the baby's immediate safety is at stake.)

It is best to use verbal explanations with babies right from the start. They need to be told that the airplane could leave without them, that the blender blades could cut them, and that the doctor needs to see what their ears look like in order to help them get better. Babies may not understand these explanations at first, but as they grow older and acquire more language skills, this will provide them with important information.

It is less confusing to your baby when you are firm and do what you say. If you vacillate or change your mind, your baby may feel that he has power to control the situation after all, only to find his power eventually taken away. So it's important to be decisive and to follow through with your behavior.

The fourth suggestion is very important. Babies need to be allowed to cry and rage when you do something against their will. If you must restrain your baby or pick him up against his will, you can empathize with him let him know that you understand how he is feeling. He may need to cry and rage, and you can allow him to do this in your arms. It is important to pay attention to him, but refrain from distracting him in any way (as described in Chapter 2).

I used these suggestions in the following medical situation:

> When my son was eleven months old I suspected an ear infection. I explained to him that we were going to see a doctor who might be able to help him get better. While we were in the waiting room, I told him what the doctor would do, and even demonstrated by looking in his ears. Once he was on the examination table, he screamed and wiggled, and it was necessary to hold him down forcefully. I calmly explained that I had to hold him there so the doctor could look into his ears. He screamed and cried during the whole procedure while I gave him my full attention. Afterwards I held him in my arms while he cried some more.

The crying that occurs in such situations may be the hardest type of crying to listen to because you will probably feel responsible for causing your baby's pain or frustration. However, it will not be helpful to deny your baby's feelings with statements such as, "It didn't hurt," "There, there, it wasn't scary," "It's all right," "Don't be angry," and so forth. Babies have very strong feelings that must be

acknowledged, accepted, and listened to. Medical professionals sometimes feel that it is their job to keep babies quiet. When people tried
to stop my baby from crying, I would say, "It's important for him to
know that it's okay to cry here."

Conflicts frequently arise when babies reach for dangerous or
precious objects, and it is not always possible to completely baby
proof every environment your child will be in. Until about one year
of age it will be fairly easy to substitute one object for another, or
one activity for another when your baby does something inappropriate. After that age, however, it is usually more difficult to do this
because toddlers are very determined. It is wise to keep inappropriate objects entirely out of babies' field of vision, but this too will
become more difficult as your baby grows and learns to climb up on
furniture.

Sometimes you may need to remove your baby or an object for
reasons of safety. Your baby is likely to cry or rage whenever you set
limits like this, and it is important to allow him to do so. Here is an
example:

> At 16 months of age my daughter climbed onto the coffee table in
> the living room and began investigating the lamp switch near the
> light bulb of the lamp that was on the table. I was afraid she could
> get a shock or a burn, so I told her she could get hurt, and I demon-
> strated an acceptable substitute behavior: gently patting the base of
> the lamp. However, her exploratory urge and curiosity were greater
> than her tendency to comply, and she continued to reach for the
> lamp switch. I then gently but firmly lifted her away from the lamp,
> and held her in my arms while explaining again that it was danger-
> ous to touch the switch. She cried hard for about one minute while
> I paid attention to her. She then went over to the lamp, and I again
> showed her how to pat gently the base of the lamp, which she was
> happy to do. She did not try to touch the switch again. I had set a
> firm limit, but without inflicting any needless pain, confusion, or
> fear by spanking.

A spanking in the example above would only have added additional pain and frustration. My daughter had enough frustration to
deal with simply by having such a limit set (in this type of situation

with no available substitutes). However, there is no denying the fact that punishment can be effective, at least in the short term. A spanking causes fear, and this naturally leads to avoidance of the situation that caused it. This cycle of pain, fear, and avoidance is a very basic mechanism that is present in quite primitive animal species. Without this mechanism our own species would not have survived throughout the ages. However, the use of punishment causes so many negative side effects that it is always better to look for non-punitive ways of solving conflicts. Sometimes you may need to use your greater strength to control your baby's behavior and keep him safe, but this is quite different from the use of punishment.

When will my baby learn household rules, and what if she "tests" the limits?

When you guide your baby away from unacceptable behaviors towards acceptable ones while trying to meet everyone's needs (the democratic approach to discipline), you may be surprised to find her acting in the same unacceptable way the next day. Some parents assume that their babies are "asking" for firm limits at those times, and the parents then feel justified in using punishment. However, it is incorrect to assume that babies are simply asking for someone to take control. If you look deeper into the possible reasons for this behavior, you can deal with it in non-authoritarian ways.

There are several possible reasons why your baby may act in ways that look as if she is purposely provoking or "testing" you. A first important consideration is the age of your child. Until 18 months of age or so, babies do not have the ability to understand general rules governing their own behavior, rules that transcend the confines of time and space.[17] If you tell a 14-month-old toddler not to touch the stove, you will probably find yourself having to repeat this many times, as she approaches the stove. Every moment in time is entirely new for babies this age, and they cannot understand the concept of "never." They are unable to visualize the future, and have no way of knowing that what applied *then* also applies *now*. Until your toddler can understand the concept of a rule, therefore, you will need to handle each situation as an entirely new one, and gently guide her behavior. This is why it is so important to baby-proof your home as much as possible. You will both be less frustrated if the necessary limits are built into your toddler's environment.

POSSIBLE REASONS FOR "TESTING" BEHAVIOR

- The limit ignores the baby's legitimate needs.
- The baby is too young to understand rules.
- The baby is gathering information to formulate a rule.
- The baby needs attention.
- The baby wants a limit that is consistent with the parent's feelings (if the parent is self-sacrificing).
- The baby has built-up stress and needs a pretext to cry.
- The baby is compulsively re-enacting a previous situation to overcome fear caused by the parent's anger. (The baby will be laughing in this case.)

Between 18 months and two years of age, your toddler will acquire an ability to understand simple rules, and this will lead to a different kind of "testing" behavior that is, in reality, an attempt to obtain important information. Perhaps you will first notice her new rule-learning ability in her speech. Linguists have discovered that, when toddlers begin to combine two words, these simple phrases often occur in a certain fixed order that constitutes a simple grammatical rule.[18] You will also see this rule-learning ability emerge in your toddler's behavior, although it can look very much like obnoxious, provocative behavior. The following example illustrates this.

> At 21 months of age, my son was banging on the table with his spoon. I immediately told him not to do this because it could make dents in the table, and I suggested that he bang on his placemat instead. He then proceeded to hit everything within reach with his

spoon, each time looking at me for my reaction. He banged on a plate, a glass, another placemat, and another part of the table. I told him each time whether or not it was all right for him to hit the object. Finally, after having exhausted all the possibilities within reach, he happily banged his spoon on his own placemat and another placemat (the only two acceptable places). He seemed very pleased with himself at having figured out the "rule " for that particular behavior. He had proceeded very much as a scientist collecting data to test a hypothesis.

Aside from the developmental stages described above that can lead to two kinds of "testing" behavior, another reason for this kind of behavior is a need for attention. Your toddler's behavior may be a way of letting you know that her genuine needs are not being met, and she may do anything to be noticed. I observed this well-known phenomenon with my daughter.

One afternoon I was sitting on the couch, reading to my six-year-old son. My 15-month-old daughter kept toddling over to us wanting me to look at her books with her. I tried to get her involved in something on her own, but she kept demanding my attention. Finally, she picked up a small magazine I had given her, stood in front of me, and started tearing pieces off and putting them in her mouth. (She knew I didn't like her to do this.) I went over to her to take the paper out of her mouth, but she tried to get me to chase her by running away. This whole sequence of events was repeated a second time. I then realized that she was deliberately putting paper in her mouth to get my attention. (I had not given her any undivided attention all day.) So I held her on my lap while finishing the story I was reading to my son, and then spent some time with her.

Some parents claim that the child is "only trying to get attention," as if there were something bad about this. However, babies have a genuine need for attention, and they do not ask for more than they need. If they do not receive good quality attention, they will find ways of being noticed, even if their behavior makes the parents angry. From the child's point of view, any attention is better than none. In the above example, my daughter was feeling left out, and her provocative behavior was her way of letting me know this.

Parental over-permissiveness can also lead to "testing" behavior in toddlers. If you have not been authentic with your baby, sacrificing your own needs to avoid frustrating her, she will sense this ambiguity on your part and become anxious and confused because of it (as described in a previous section). This is especially likely to occur if you are beginning to feel resentful of your baby. Babies want things to make sense. If your actions do not correspond to your emotions, your baby will feel uncomfortable and do whatever it takes to reach consistency and clear communication in her relationship with you. She will probably provoke you until you give a clear, unambiguous message consistent with your own needs, and set a firm limit on her behavior. Even though it may cause her some frustration, this is what she wants and needs.

An example of this is when mothers continue nursing their toddlers even after the mothers no longer wish to breastfeed. It is wonderful to nurse your toddler for several years, but nursing should be mutually pleasurable. If you are beginning to resent it, but continue to do it out of a sense of duty, your toddler will be aware of your reluctance and feel insecure and anxious. She may become obnoxious and provocative, with frequent "testing" or aggressive behavior until you give clear messages consistent with your own desires. When mothers consult with me about this problem, I tell them that it is okay to stop nursing if they no longer enjoy it. When they follow my advice, their relationship with their child usually improves dramatically.

Another result of over-permissiveness can occur when parents attempt to satisfy every little whim, mistaking all crying as an indication of an immediate need when in fact it is an attempt to release stress. This behavior, although well intentioned, can deprive babies of opportunities to release stress by crying, and lead to a build-up of stress and tension. Babies will then look for opportunities to cry, and even *create* them, if necessary. Thus, some "testing" behavior may be an indication that babies are looking for a pretext to cry. If you firmly say "no" or lovingly restrain your baby, this limit on her behavior will provide the necessary pretext, and she will finally be able to have a good cry. Afterwards, her provocative behavior will probably disappear.

There is one additional possible reason for "testing" behavior. If, for example, you have reacted angrily when your baby dropped food from her high chair, your reaction will probably frighten her. This will lead to an urge to repeat the behavior in an attempt to understand what happened and to heal from her fright. Babies know intuitively that they must re-experience trauma, at least symbolically, in order to heal from it, so they tend to re-enact compulsively whatever brought a previous alarming reaction from their parents. When this is the cause of "testing" behavior, your baby will probably laugh while repeating the behavior. This indicates that she is releasing tensions and healing herself from the anxiety caused by your previous reaction. Unfortunately, it is easy to misinterpret this kind of "testing" behavior and to assume that your baby is purposely being obnoxious and provocative.

To avoid this situation, try to refrain from over-reacting to your baby's behavior, but calmly stop whatever behavior is unacceptable while finding other ways for your baby to meet her exploratory needs. If you have frightened your baby by your anger, you can help her heal (and avoid this kind of provocative behavior) by playing games of mock anger in which you *pretend* to be angry at something your baby does. She will probably love it and laugh a lot, assuming she is old enough to understand that you are only pretending. You can adapt the power-reversal games described in Chapter 5 for this purpose. When your child is in a swing, for example, you can pretend to be angry and playfully accuse her of "kicking" you every time the swing approaches you and her foot touches you. This will probably make her laugh and allow her to release tensions from the times in the past when you really were angry with her.

Some parents wonder whether they need to be consistent in setting limits. In all families there are some rules that do not change from day to day, and for these you will obviously want to set limits consistently. Such rules might be no water play outside the bathroom or no drawing on the walls. Toddlers will eventually be willing and able to follow these household rules without the use of punishment. In fact, once your toddler's ability to understand rules emerges, she may surprise you by insisting on rigidly adhering to routines. Two-year-olds are often described as compulsive because they typically

insist on having everything done "correctly," up to the smallest detail. Your child may refuse to eat without wearing a bib, or cross a
street without holding someone's hand, if those are the rules you
have taught her. Toddlers enjoy exercising their new mental ability
and they like having some structure in their lives. There is quite a
difference between a one-year-old's inability to understand any rules
and a two-year-old's rigid adherence to rules. So if you become impatient setting the same limits repeatedly with your 15-month-old,
you can console yourself with the knowledge that things will soon
change!

There will be many times, however, when you will want to change
your baby's behavior, but not teach her a general rule. For example,
if she is banging her spoon loudly on her high chair tray, it may
bother you if you are trying to carry on a conversation. In that case,
you can give your baby some pots and pans to hit in another room.
You do not want her to refrain forever from banging with a spoon,
but only at that particular moment in time. Thus, it is perfectly all
right to set different limits on different days, unless it is something
you *never* want your baby to do. So finding ways to meet everyone's
needs (the democratic approach to discipline) allows you to be flexible, as well as very human, with your baby. You do not have this
freedom with an authoritarian approach. In fact, parents who regularly rely on punishments or rewards find that they are forced to be
consistent in setting limits because inconsistency would greatly reduce their effectiveness. With a democratic approach, you do not
need to be consistent, and your baby receives realistic information
about human beings, whose needs change from day to day.

How can I handle my toddler's negativism?

The previous section discusses rule learning and limit "testing."
Eliciting cooperation can also have special challenges, especially
during the second year. "Negativism" is very common in toddlers
between 18 and 30 months of age. It can begin as early as 15 months
and last well past the age of three. Babies of this age are often described as obstinate, willful, disobedient, unmanageable, and prone

to tantrums. They typically resist any attempts to change or control their behavior, and their favorite word is "no!"

What is going on? If all has gone well during the first year, babies will develop a sense of powerfulness. They will realize that their needs will be met and they can play an active role in determining what happens to them. During the second year, toddlers begin to want some autonomy and to make their own decisions. Now that they have learned some basic motor skills and can understand a considerable amount of language, they feel that there should be no limits to what they can do. This is a healthy and normal stage occurring in toddlers who have a strong sense of their own worth, capabilities, and powerfulness. So try to resist imposing your decisions on your toddler or forcing him to do things against his will, unless it is absolutely necessary.

This period does not always run very smoothly. Even though toddlers yearn to be self sufficient, they are still acutely aware of their own limitations. They realize that there are many things they cannot yet do, and they are easily, and frequently, frustrated. This requires considerable patience from parents.

> At 22 months of age my son began trying to undress himself and would cry and rage if I did it for him, but he was not very adept at taking his clothes off. So after trying and failing to undress himself, he would invariably cry and rage out of pure frustration, and scream because I wasn't helping him!

Toddlers realize that they depend on others to supply food, love, and stimulation. The major decisions affecting their lives are still made by others (e.g., who takes care of them, where they live, and where they go each day), so they strive desperately to assert themselves when and where they can. One of the ways in which this desire for power and autonomy manifests itself is in their "no!" This one word says, "I am not going to let you run my life for me. I want to be treated as a separate person and have some say in what happens to me. I want to make my own decisions."

When your toddler says "no," it helps to think of this behavior as an indication that he is practicing important skills. While becoming a separate person from you, he must learn to figure out the logical opposites of words and actions, an important intellectual skill. For example, what is the opposite of approaching someone, or of getting dressed? Furthermore, he is learning the consequences of standing up for himself and following his own wishes. Although this resistance can be difficult to deal with at the time, try to imagine your child as an adolescent saying "no" to friends who tempt him with drugs or sex. If your child learns as a toddler that he will not lose your love for opposing your will, he will have the strength later on to say "no" to his peers without fearing loss of their friendship.

SUGGESTIONS FOR ELICITING COOPERATION IN TODDLERS

- Situations that are not very important (ex: which shirt to wear):

    - Give your toddler opportunities to say "no" and then give in delightedly.

- More important situations (ex: cleaning up, caretaking routines, leaving a playground):

    - Offer choices.
    - Be playful.
    - Give reasons for requests and prohibitions.
    - Don't phrase a command as a question (when there is no choice).

- Crucial situations when all else fails (ex: medical procedure, removing a dangerous object):

    - Warn your child ahead of time and give explanations (if you have time).
    - Be firm but loving.
    - Allow your toddler to protest and cry.

The democratic approach to discipline involves looking for non-authoritarian ways to elicit cooperation in toddlers. Giving choices can be very effective in helping your toddler feel autonomous. If he refuses to hold still when you dress him, one solution may be to let him try dressing himself, another, to let him decide what to wear (a red shirt or a blue shirt, for example), or where to be dressed (either the bedroom or the bathroom, perhaps). You can also let him know that you are ready to dress him and ask him to let you know when *he* is ready. Or you can let him decide what to play with while you are dressing him. It is necessary to allow plenty of time for caretaking routines such as dressing during the period of negativism. Be careful not to give too many choices, however. More than two alternatives can be confusing for toddlers.

Another way to elicit cooperation is to make the activity seem like a game instead of a duty. Instead of saying, "It's time to put the blocks away now," you can say, "Here's a little mousie going home," while making a block scurry into the box like a mouse. Toddlers will soon catch on to the game and want to join in the fun of bringing all the "mice" home. When it's time to brush teeth, you can suggest that you take turns brushing each other's teeth, or you can announce that it's time for the tooth brushing song, and sing a song while brushing your child's teeth.

A third approach for encouraging your toddler's cooperation is to let him know *why* you are making certain requests of him. Everybody deserves to know the reason for commands and prohibitions with which they are expected to comply, and babies are no exception. Here is an example from my experience with my son, which occurred before he was two years old:

> I wanted the door kept closed so that flies would not come into the house. One day, when my son came in from the back yard, I said, "Would you please close the door?" He refused, so I rephrased my request: "Please close the door so the flies won't come in the house." My son immediately jumped up and went to close the door! After a few more reminders during the next few days, he automatically remembered to close the door every time he came in or went out to the back yard.

This example also points out another important aspect of eliciting cooperation. When giving a command in a situation where there is no choice, it is better not to phrase it as a question, because your child will interpret this to mean that he has a choice. Some parents, in an effort to be polite and not sound too authoritarian, ask questions such as: "Would you please get dressed now?" or "Shall we go now?" This polite phrasing, although clear to adults, is not at all clear for toddlers, who understand the question literally and think they have a choice. If you really mean that it is bath time, it is better to say, "Now it's time for your bath." Once that is established, you can then give legitimate choices, such as "Which bath toys do you want to play with today?"

Sometimes the need for autonomy is so great that it seems to obscure any natural inclinations towards cooperation. But if you can help your toddler feel that you are on his side and do not force obedience, he will be more cooperative throughout this period. Be aware, however, that extreme rebelliousness may be an indication of pent-up stress and a need to release emotions. This is discussed in a further section.

A toddler's desire for autonomy can trigger a feeling of powerlessness and anger in adults. When you find yourself in a situation in which you cannot easily exert control (as with a strong and willful toddler), you may be reminded, perhaps unconsciously, of the powerlessness you yourself felt when you were small. Your toddler is not really the origin of your anger. He is an innocent little person trying to fill his own needs, and his behavior merely brings to the surface feelings of powerlessness in you that have perhaps been buried from your consciousness for many years.

A mother described how her feelings of powerlessness with her toddler brought up strong anger:

> When he won't let me dress him, I realize that there is no way I can force him to let me. He's too strong for me. At those times, I begin to feel completely helpless and powerless. It feels like there is absolutely nothing I can do to get him dressed. This makes me so angry that I just feel like hitting him good and hard and screaming at the top of my voice.

Some parents feel incompetent when they cannot control their willful children, as one mother reported to me:

> I realize that she's a person. What right have I to control her? And yet there's also this feeling (and I'm sure it has to do with the way I was raised) that parents are supposed to have control of their children. One thing that really bothers me is that she doesn't get by with anything with her babysitter. Her babysitter only has to say, "no" and that's it. That bothers me. I feel as if she thinks she can get by with me, and I feel I should have control.

It is helpful to express these feelings with another adult. Some of the exercises at the end of this chapter address these feelings.

Although this stage of autonomy in toddlers is sometimes very trying for parents, your sensitive, respectful parenting will have long-term positive effects. Your child will feel encouraged to continue taking charge of his own life and resist being oppressed later on. He will be better able to resist peer pressure and have the strength and self-confidence to say "no" to drugs or sex as a teenager. You will also build a good relationship with him and he will be less likely to rebel against you during adolescence.

What should I do when my toddler has a temper tantrum?

A temper tantrum is the natural, spontaneous release of anger and frustration. A toddler who is frustrated and angry will typically cry hard while thrashing her arms and legs. Some remain standing, while others throw themselves on the floor. Although loud and disagreeable, it is important to remember that temper tantrums are a healthy stress-release mechanism, and should never be considered "misbehavior." Some parents can accept sad crying, but not angry crying (temper tantrums). However, I recommend responding to tantrums in the same way as regular crying: with love and acceptance.

The release of angry feelings occurs from birth on when infants thrash and kick while crying. But most people do not describe this as a temper tantrum until the second year. One-year-old toddlers yearn to be autonomous, so they begin to encounter more frustrations, and this results in temper tantrums that often start between 12 to 15 months of age. Temper tantrums are more common in toddlers who were frequently distracted from crying during the first year. The tantrums are a healthy indication that they are attempting to "catch up" on their crying.

The active movements in a temper tantrum are necessary in order to discharge the energy that results from your child's physiological stress response. In prehistoric times, feelings of rage would probably have occurred primarily in association with actual physical threats to our survival. Our stress response prepared our body for flight or fight, which enhanced our survival. Nowadays, we still have this same primitive stress response that sends blood to our arms and legs, increases our heart rate, and mobilizes our reserves of sugars and fats. The problem is that most of our modern forms of stress and frustration are not physical threats to our survival, and we do not need to run away or fight. But our natural response to strong emotions is still to become physically active while crying hard. This is precisely what children do spontaneously during a temper tantrum. They go through the movements of flight or fight by actively flailing their arms and legs. This release of energy seems to convince the brain that the threat has been dealt with and overcome. This helps the child attain a state of true relaxation (homeostasis) after having experienced a strong emotion. The stress hormones excreted in tears may also contribute to this calming effect.

When a toddler actively kicks her legs, arches her back, and throws her head back during a temper tantrum, this could also be an indication that her current frustration has triggered a memory of her birth trauma. During birth, babies normally push with their legs to help propel themselves out, and they need to stretch out their body, arch their back, and tilt their head back in order to pass through the mother's pelvis. Their body remembers, and they may need to reenact the same movements while crying or raging, in order to heal from the terror or frustration they experienced while being born. Some parents notice these kinds of movements in their crying infants already during the first year.

If your toddler throws frequent tantrums, I recommend looking for sources of stress and frustration in her life. Is there a stressful daycare situation? Are her days too rushed or overstimulating? Has there been a recent change? Are there family tensions? Is there sibling rivalry? Has something frightening happened? Is she watching violent TV? Is someone being authoritarian and punitive with her? If you detect nothing unusually stressful, and if your child has no handicaps or medical problems, then this is probably a normal developmental stage in which she becomes easily frustrated. Remember that there is often increased crying and raging preceding the acquisition of new skills. Keep in mind also that some toddlers are easily overwhelmed by new experiences and deeply affected by everyday, minor upsets. Their intense emotional reactions are necessary in order to heal from the effects of these experiences. These highly sensitive toddlers are often the ones who will be labeled later on as "gifted" children.

Sometimes toddlers reach for something they know they cannot have, such as candy in a store. It is important to realize that you can say "no" to the candy while saying "yes" to the tantrum that often follows. There is no need to "give in" to your toddler's tantrum by changing your limits. Your child needs to release the frustration caused by not having what she wants. If you allow your toddler to cry and rage as much as she needs to, she will emerge from the tantrum quite calm and happy, with no trace of any anger, and may even act as if nothing has happened.

Insignificant events can trigger a full-blown tantrum, for example when you butter the "wrong" side of the bread, give your toddler the wrong kind of cereal, or offer a broken cookie. The temper tantrum usually has nothing to do with the event, and it looks as if the toddler is "over-reacting." But toddlers use these situations as pretexts to release accumulated stress. This has been referred to as the "broken cookie" phenomenon.[19] If you allow the tantrum to run its course, your toddler will probably be quite relaxed and cooperative afterwards. We adults have "broken cookie" days as well. Sometimes we burst into tears at some minor event if we are already feeling overwhelmed and stressed.

Some parents find it quite difficult to accept temper tantrums, especially those triggered by minor events, because they think their toddler is "spoiled" and just trying to "get her own way." A genuine tantrum can look like manipulation, but it usually is not. If there are real tears flowing, then it represents a genuine release of pent-up emotions, because it is impossible to fake tears. There is no need to "give in" to a tantrum if you suspect a "broken cookie" type of situation that does not reflect a genuine need. In fact, if you try too hard to satisfy your child's every little whim, you may inadvertently prevent her from releasing stress through a healthy temper tantrum. This can cause her to become overly demanding, because she will continue to look for another pretext about which to cry and rage. Only when you stop "giving in" will she be able to have a tantrum and release stress.

During temper tantrums, toddlers usually discharge their anger harmlessly, without attempting to hurt another person. However, there may be times when your toddler directs her anger at you and attempts to hit you. This is more likely to occur if she herself has been hit or spanked in the past, or if she has observed violence in others (in real life or on TV). There is no need to become overly concerned about this, but the hitting should be stopped. Violence and hurtful behavior towards others is not a healthy release, but rather a distorted expression of anger in toddlers who do not feel totally safe to have a genuine temper tantrum. (See the next section.) If your toddler hurts herself during a temper tantrum, you must step in and protect her from harm. Toddlers who have been allowed to cry freely from birth are unlikely to hurt themselves or anyone else during a temper tantrum.

If you send your angry toddler to another room or remove love and support in some other manner during a temper tantrum, this can trigger a fear of abandonment. Your toddler may learn to repress her anger in order to gain your love and acceptance, and this would not be a healthy thing for her to do. She needs continual reassurance that nothing she could ever do would cause you to reject her in any way. She needs love and acceptance more than ever when she is crying or raging.

I recommend staying near your toddler and paying attention to her during a temper tantrum, even though this can be quite difficult to do. You can offer to hold her if she lets you, but don't insist on this. She may need plenty of space and freedom to thrash around. It is important to act as a mirror of her emotions by reflecting back her feelings and saying, for example, "You are very angry." Let her know that it okay to show her anger, and that you love her even though she is angry. The tantrum will pass, and you will find a much relieved and relaxed little child who will probably want to snuggle in your arms.

If you find it difficult to accept your toddler's tantrums, perhaps it is because you yearn to release your own pent-up anger. It is quite difficult to let someone else have the freedom to release angry feelings when you were not allowed to do so yourself. Perhaps you were ignored, distracted, shamed, or punished when you attempted to release anger as a child. If your toddler's tantrums frequently trigger your own anger, I recommend exploring the origin of your feelings in your own childhood. (See the exercises at the end of this chapter and also of Chapter 2.) If you are afraid of becoming abusive, you should obtain all the help and support you can find.

If you worry that your toddler's temper tantrum in public might disturb other people, it is a good idea to take her to another location or distract her in some way. But as soon as possible, try to allow the temper tantrum to run its course. If you are in a place where noise is acceptable, there is no need to stop the tantrum or remove your child. You can calmly demonstrate to other people how to support an angry toddler through a temper tantrum, by showing acceptance and love.

Accepting temper tantrums in this manner has many benefits. It will allow your child to release frustrations and anger, thereby reducing the likelihood of hurtful behavior towards others. It will also enhance your child's health and serve to lessen the probability of depression and self-destructive behavior later on in life. You will create an atmosphere of emotional safety and acceptance, and your child will feel comfortable sharing her emotions with you as she grows older. Finally, it will help to increase your child's self-esteem, because she will feel unconditionally loved.

What should I do if my baby is destructive or violent?

Destructiveness and violence are distorted behaviors resulting from an accumulation of emotional stress (sadness, fear, frustration, etc.) combined with a suppression of healthy forms of emotional release, such as crying and temper tantrums. If you have repeatedly ignored, distracted, or punished your baby's attempts to cry or rage, he will learn that it is not safe to release his feelings. With so many pent-up emotions and tensions, he could become obnoxious, hyper-active, or violent. Perhaps you will find him throwing blocks at the cat, hitting or biting other children, throwing a breakable dish on the floor, or purposely making a mess of your piles of laundry.

Some parents feel that in such circumstances their child is "asking for a spanking," and they are tempted to use corporal punishment. Although the use of spanking is an oppressive method that I do not recommend, it does often serve the purpose of helping a child to start crying. After a good cry, he feels better and the violent behavior diminishes. However, it is not the spanking itself that causes children to behave better, but rather the fact that they have a chance to do some crying. The spanking provides the trigger that allows them to start crying, and this helps reduce their stress level.

It is possible to stop destructive or violent behavior without punishment. If your toddler is often aggressive, the first step is to allow him to cry whenever he spontaneously does so. If you give him loving attention at those times without interrupting the crying, both you and your child will build up trust in each other. He will learn that it is now safe to cry, and you will develop confidence in your ability to let him do so. This will probably help him become less violent.

A good time to begin encouraging your toddler to cry may be when he hurts himself physically, because most toddlers are able to cry quite spontaneously at such times. Sometimes children who have pent-up emotions cry for a long time after minor injuries, if allowed to do so, become they use the injury as a pretext to "catch up" on their crying. Some children seem to have more injuries than others. This accident proneness could be an unconscious attempt to find a pretext to cry in an environment where crying has been distracted or punished.

You can also look for ways in which you might inadvertently be stopping your toddler from crying. If you have repeatedly distracted your baby from his tears, this may be one of the reasons that he is now showing aggressive behavior. Do you interpret all fussiness as an indication of boredom and a need to be "entertained"? Do you frequently nurse your toddler for comfort instead of allowing him to have a good cry in your arms? Does he use a pacifier or a bottle to comfort himself? Violence in toddlers is a common result of control patterns such as these that suppress emotional release. Try to be aware of what you do when your toddler is obviously upset, and refrain from putting something in his mouth or distracting him in other ways at those times.

Another way that some parents inadvertently repress crying is when they rush over to "comfort" their toddler at the slightest whimper instead of letting their child come to them if he needs attention. This can cause him to stop crying before he has finished releasing pent-up stress. Before your baby could crawl, it was quite appropriate to pick him up when he cried. But once he can crawl or walk, you do not need to be in a hurry to hold him when he cries, unless he is badly injured. If you are in the same room, he will see and hear you, and come to you if he needs physical closeness. Meanwhile, you can empathize with him and allow him the freedom to have a good cry. Or you can approach him and put your hand on him, but let *him* indicate if he wants to be picked up before imposing this on him. He may surprise you by choosing to stay where he is while he cries.

If you begin to show more acceptance of his crying, this will allow him to release his painful emotions and tensions instead of keeping them bottled up inside. As you develop a deeper listening relationship with him, he will "catch up" on his crying, perhaps by finding little pretexts about which to cry or rage (as described in the previous section). This will allow him to reduce his pent-up frustrations, and you will see an improvement in his behavior, with less obnoxiousness, destructiveness, or violence.

If, after several weeks of your efforts to be more accepting of your child's crying, he still acts aggressively, you may have to step in more assertively. When he tries to hurt someone, you can bring him into a room where there are few distractions, hold him firmly but lovingly, and tell him that you cannot allow him to act that way. If you give him good, loving attention, and encourage him to cry, he will probably soon begin to do so. The safer and more loved he feels, the easier it will be for him to have a healthy emotional release. Don't be surprised if he struggles to get away, or asks for things he does not really need. This is a typical reaction at first, but he will probably soon accept being held and sob loudly within the safety of your arms.

> Some friends were visiting for a week with their two-year-old son. His mother nursed him frequently "for comfort," and he did not cry very much. He frequently bit his siblings and my own children for no apparent reason. One day, after he had bitten another child, his mother asked for my help. With her permission, I took him into a quiet room where I held him on my lap, explaining that I had to protect the other children, and that we were going to sit together for a while. He began to cry, and continued to cry hard for almost an hour. He then fell asleep peacefully and had a long nap. When he awakened later, he was happy and completely non-aggressive. He did not bite again during the rest of their stay. His mother was amazed that he had fallen asleep without nursing, and also surprized at how gentle he was during the following days. She had assumed that he had an impulsive, aggressive personality, and was relieved to learn that his behavior was simply the result of pent-up stress.

Babies who become violent may do so because their parents spank them, or because other children hit them, but violent behavior can occur even without this. The boy in the previous example had never been spanked or hit. His painful, pent-up feelings were simply accumulations of fear, frustration, or grief. Babies are so vulnerable that, even with the best of parenting, they experience some emotional pain and stress, and need to cry on a regular basis to reduce stress.

This way of "forcing" a violent toddler to cry by holding him, even though he may protest at first, may appear to go against one of the messages of this book, which is to trust one's baby. However, toddlers would never develop such aggressive behavior in the first place unless their natural, spontaneous tendency to cry had been stopped. If the mother had had correct information about the importance of crying, she would have interpreted his cues more accurately as an infant. Instead of nursing him frequently to calm him down, she would have allowed him to do all the crying he needed to do, while lovingly supporting him. It is also important to remember that babies who have not been allowed to cry enough have, to a certain extent, lost touch with what they really need. They may not be aware that, when they hit or bite, they really need to have a good cry. But they usually welcome the opportunity and will cry freely if people don't try to stop them.

If your toddler is acting aggressively and needs to be restrained in order to protect others and also to help him begin crying, it is important *not* to do so in the spirit of punishment or anger. If his behavior makes you feel very angry, take time to regain a sense of composure and self control before trying to give your baby the attention he needs. Otherwise, your anger may make him feel unsafe or unloved, and nothing will be accomplished.

If you lack the time or attention necessary to help your toddler release painful emotions, you can try to improve his mood with a game or a change of scene. Any destructive behavior must be stopped, or course, but you can modify activities so that your toddler is temporarily distracted from the situation that triggered his violent behavior. You can encourage him to release his pent-up feelings at a later time when you have more time and attention for him.

Children who have been allowed to release painful emotions from birth are gentle, loving, and cooperative. They do not hit or bite other children, and they are kind to animals. Aggression is not an inborn human trait, but rather an acquired behavior resulting from an accumulation of stress. These children *can* be helped, and with appropriate and loving interventions, it is usually not very long before their inherent gentle nature reveals itself.

How can I help my toddler learn to share?

Babies cannot put themselves in someone else's position or understand another person's point of view, and their actions are guided entirely by their own needs and wants. If a toddler sees a toy that looks interesting, she will take it from another toddler just as she would take it off a shelf; for her there is no difference. She will also hang on tightly to toys that others attempt to take away from her. Studies have shown that the most frequent types of interactions between one-year-olds in a playgroup setting are disputes over toys. The researchers claimed that this should not be considered aggression, but merely a result of the toddlers' desire to possess the toys.[20] This normal, self-centered behavior implies that babies do not grasp the concept of sharing, and no amount of preaching will make them understand.

When toddlers fight over toys, parents often wonder whether to intervene. When two babies play together frequently, and if one of them always overpowers the other, it may be helpful for parents to intervene. This situation arises frequently when two siblings are close together in age. It is not good for the younger one to have her toys taken away all the time because it could cause her to give up defending her own rights. Her self-image will be one of someone who is weak, defenseless, and powerless, and this attitude may be quite difficult for her to overcome. She needs someone to defend her rights. She would also benefit by spending less time with her older sibling and more time with other babies her own age or even younger, if possible. Likewise, the older sibling could benefit by playing with other toddlers her own age or older. That way both would have the occasion to experience a different type of interaction with others, and their view of themselves and of the world would become more realistic. Sibling rivalry is less likely when children are at least three years apart.

In Western, industrialized cultures, the concept of ownership is very strong, and we unconsciously teach this to our children every time we give them a present and make it clear that it belongs to them. Because of this, they learn to value their possessions, and we should not be surprised when they hold on to their toys tightly. If you force your toddler to share her toys, this may only make her more possessive and resistant. The most helpful thing you can do is to respect her possessiveness, but let her know how the other child is feeling. To avoid disputes, some parents keep a supply of special "sharing toys" and bring them out when another child visits. When your child is old enough, another solution is to discuss with her ahead of time which toys she will be willing to share with a friend who is coming to play with her.

In general, there is no need to intervene immediately when two toddlers fight over a toy. However, if the dispute continues for very long, if they are physically hurting each other, or if they ask for help, you can act as a mediator and reflect back each child's feelings, while allowing them to release their anger and frustration by crying. This will help them learn to understand each other's feelings. Here is an example:

> Sammy had a small toy zebra. Betty grabbed it out of his hand. Sammy began to cry and went to his mother. She held him and said, "It makes you sad and angry when Betty takes a toy away, doesn't it?" Sammy looked at the zebra in Betty's hand and cried some more. His mother said, "Betty wants to play with it too. You both want the zebra." The she said to Betty, "Sammy is crying because you took the zebra from him. He wants to play with it." Betty looked at Sammy and clutched the zebra tighter, saying, "Betty want zeba." The mother said, "Yes, you want to play with the zebra. You both want it. Will you let Sammy know when you are done playing with the zebra?" After a while, Betty saw another toy and dropped the zebra. Sammy picked it up.

In this example, the mother did not solve the problem for the toddlers or preach about the virtues of sharing. Instead, she acted as a sounding board, reflecting back each child's feelings. Although this does not appear to accomplish anything immediately, if you use this approach, your child will gradually begin to develop her own strategies for getting along with other children. She will also learn empathy at an early age because a toddler who has fully experienced what it feels like to have a toy taken away will eventually begin to understand what another child feels in a similar situation.

My son went through several stages while learning to share. He played with another toddler several times a week, and we adults handled each dispute through mediation, by reflecting back each child's feelings and needs. We also tried to be good role models for polite, sharing behavior. When the two boys were between the ages of one and two years, they tried different strategies. First, they simply held on to toys tightly and turned away from the other. Then they began to say "no" to each other. Eventually they learned to offer each other toys in attempts to trade. Finally, they began to ask each other verbally for toys, rather than grab them.

By the time these boys were two-and-a-half years old their disputes had decreased considerably. They began to share spontaneously and to take turns, even saying "please" and "thank you" to each other! It is unlikely that such mature interpersonal behavior would have emerged so early if someone else had always imposed a solution on them. Because they were not interfered with and allowed to release their anger during conflicts, they were able to become aware of their own and each other's feelings. As a result, they learned to understand another person's point of view and the concept of sharing at an early age. With this kind of support, we can trust babies to become thoughtful and altruistic of their own accord.

It may be shocking or embarrassing to see your well-loved toddler grab toys away from others or refuse to share, but this behavior does not imply that you have done anything wrong. If it really upsets you, it may be useful to explore memories of your own childhood peer relationships. Perhaps you have some guilt feelings for having mistreated your own siblings, or anger at siblings or other children who bullied you. These feelings may interfere with your ability to remain an objective mediator during your child's conflicts with other toddlers. You may benefit from talking with another adult about these childhood memories, and releasing the anger or guilt.

Babies are not born knowing how other people feel. Instead, altruism and the concept of sharing arise naturally out of a child's interactions with other people. If you show compassion and act as an objective mediator when your toddler has disputes with other children, she will eventually learn more mature ways of interacting. This approach is much more effective, in the long run, than lectures, adult-imposed solutions to disputes, or any kind of artificial consequence or punishment. The reward for your patience and tactful interventions will be a child who is kind and considerate of others.

What is the best way to toilet train my baby?

Most babies are not ready to be toilet trained until they are at least two years old, so if you wait until your toddler is past his second birthday, the whole process of toilet training may last only a few weeks. I recommend a child-oriented, gradual approach that takes into account your child's signs of readiness.[21]

There are physical, cognitive, and emotional requirements that indicate readiness for toilet training. Your child must be able to control the muscles involved in urinating and defecating, and his bladder must have reached a certain size so that he does not feel the urge to urinate more frequently than every few hours. It helps considerably if he has the ability to imitate, understand a certain amount of language, and follow rules. In addition to these, an important emotional requirement is that he must be willing to take on the big responsibility of being aware of his body in the ways that toilet training requires. Sometimes toddlers are busy perfecting other skills, or their attention is preoccupied by stress. So they may not be emotionally ready for toilet training even though they are physically and mentally mature enough. Specific signs of readiness could include your child's comments about urinating and defecating, an indication of discomfort with a wet or soiled diaper, attempts to imitate parents or siblings using a toilet, or doll play that involves urinating or defecating.

The best approach for toilet training is to purchase a child-sized potty, demonstrate to your toddler what it involves, and then let him take the initiative. It is quite helpful to let him watch you or his older siblings use the toilet, because toddlers are natural imitators. You can also give your toddler a doll that wears underpants and wets, and engage him in doll play with a potty. Children who are ready for toilet training are likely to be fascinated with such doll play. By this time, your toddler will probably attempt to sit on the potty. Even if he hasn't shown any interest, you can give him a pair of underpants and ask him if he would like to wear them. You can explain that underpants are supposed to stay clean and dry, and that the way to keep them that way is to pull them down and to urinate and defecate on the potty. Some children remember to go to the potty better if they are not wearing anything from the waist down. Because of this, some parents wait for warm weather and begin toilet training outdoors in a yard, dressing their toddler in only a shirt. This also reduces the amount of cleaning up work.

After your toddler understands the implication of wearing underpants, you can let him decide each day whether he wants to wear underpants or diapers. Don't force him to go without diapers, because on some days he may feel less sure of himself or have other things on his mind and prefer to wear diapers. You can encourage him to wear underpants, while still letting him have the final decision as to what to wear. Don't rush him.

When your toddler chooses to wear underpants, you can continue to let him take full charge of the situation. There is no need to bring him to the potty or to keep asking him if he has to go to the potty. He will learn much more quickly if you do *not* remind him, because he will soon discover that he must use his own resources for remembering. You can help your toddler be fully responsible for his own toilet training by dressing him in clothes that are easy to remove on the days that he chooses to wear underpants. It may be helpful if the underpants are one or two sizes too big at the beginning so that he can easily pull them down and up again.

There are many advantages to this approach. First, when toddlers are allowed to decide for themselves whether or not to wear underpants, there are likely to be very few accidents, and this is easier on the parents. Secondly, this approach is not likely to lead to any toilet training problems because the toddler is allowed to be in charge of himself. Problems of resistance can arise when parents force or bribe toddlers to sit on the potty before they are ready. The third advantage of this approach is that the child is allowed to maintain his sense of powerfulness, autonomy, and human dignity.

Although the use of rewards (and sometimes even punishments) can result in a toilet-trained child, I do not recommend that approach. Methods of toilet training based on the use of rewards have been quite popular at times, and parents have resorted to these with the hopes of quick and easy results. Researchers have discovered, however, that parents who attempt to put such methods into practice often run into difficulties because of the toddler's temper tantrums.[22]

This indicates that the toddler is being frustrated and denied an important opportunity to be in charge of his own life. Such methods appear to be humane because of the treats used as rewards, but the drawback is that they do not allow the child to take the initiative and be fully autonomous. When parents give commands to sit on a potty and then reward their toddler for obedience to their authority, they are communicating to him that they have no faith in his ability to learn and grow. A child-oriented approach without the use of external rewards may take longer, but your child will feel that it is truly his own accomplishment.

A child-oriented approach requires patience and trust. You may begin to worry that your child will never want to wear underpants. But all babies yearn to do things in grown-up ways. When they are ready to sit on a potty, they will do so, although this may occur closer to the age of three than the age of two. Trust your child to grow up in his own way and at his own pace. The less you push him, the quicker he will do it, and the better he will feel about himself. When toddlers have the secure knowledge that they can return to carefree babyhood and diapers whenever they want to, they will then have the courage to venture forth and try this new way of doing things.

You do not need to become overly concerned about occasional setbacks, which are quite common. Don't be surprised if your toddler wears underpants for several weeks, using the potty successfully during that time, but then one day wants to wear diapers again. This could be an indication of stress, but it does not imply that all is lost. If you grant his wishes, he will soon be requesting underpants again. Some toddlers become bowel trained before they are bladder trained. For others the reverse is true. Boys tend to take longer than girls to become fully toilet-trained.

The following example illustrates how my son took charge of his nighttime toileting:

> At two years and 11 months of age my son wore underpants during the daytime but still wanted diapers on at night. One evening he asked if he could wear underpants to bed. I said he could. That night he wet the bed, but the following evening he wanted to try wearing underpants again. He woke up during the night and said he had to go to the bathroom. There were no more accidents, and he

continued to request underpants at bedtime. Then one evening, a week later, he announced that he wanted to wear diapers to bed. I did not understand why, but granted his wish and put diapers on him. During the night he developed a fever, which lasted most of the next day. By the following evening he was feeling better and once again requested underpants at bedtime.

You can expect setbacks to occur during periods of stress, such as an illness, a trip, a move to a new home, the birth of a sibling, or parental divorce. Because of this, it is wise to postpone efforts to toilet train your child if a major change is about to occur. If your child does show some regression in toilet habits after having been toilet trained, look for sources of stress and try to minimize these. Just put diapers on your child and don't pressure him to wear underpants or use a potty. Instead, try to help him release stress, as described elsewhere in this book. Your child will spontaneously begin using a potty again when he feels more secure and relaxed.

Developmental fears can sometimes interfere with toilet training. After two-and-a-half years of age, children become aware of death and their own vulnerability. This can cause a fear of defecating because it represents a loss of a product of their own body, especially when they watch their bowel movement disappear down the toilet. Some sensitive toddlers begin to hold back and become constipated at this age. Until your child has overcome this fear, it is best to flush the toilet when he is not looking.

Sometimes constipation begins following a single incident such as a toilet overflowing, an angry remark by a babysitter, or a painful bowel movement. Once you have ruled out medical causes for constipation, you can assume that fear (rather than stubbornness) is the most likely cause. Don't pressure your child to use the potty. Instead, you can help him overcome his fears through play therapy. Give your child some brown play-dough (to represent feces), a doll, and a small potty, and encourage free play while you pay attention and observe. You can also contribute to the play by pretending that the doll is afraid of the potty. If you can get your child to laugh, this will allow him to release his anxiety and tension. Children can work out many of their fears through laughter and symbolic play with appropriate materials.

There is no need to make a big issue of toilet training. Too much praise or pressure may adversely affect a sensitive child and lead to self-consciousness, resistance, and constipation. The best approach is one that is relaxed, fun, non-judgmental, and matter-of-fact. There is no need to dwell on successes or failures. Learning to use a potty is only one of the many steps that babies take towards adulthood, and certainly not the most important one.

Should I allow my toddler to masturbate?

Some babies discover their genitals during the second half of the first year, and proceed to engage in genital play when their diapers are off. This self-stimulation increases during the second year.[23] Babies do this because the genitals are a very sensitive part of the body and genital stimulation is pleasurable at any age. Some toddlers use an object, such as a ball or a stuffed animal, and press it against their genital area.

Psychologists have observed two stages of self-stimulation.[24] The first, lasting until the age of two-and-a-half or three, is characterized by exploratory genital play. Babies without diapers on will typically handle their genitals in a casual manner. This self-stimulation seems to be pleasurable to them, but not really purposeful. The second stage, beginning around two-and-a-half or three is characterized by a more rhythmical, determined type of masturbation, accompanied by more arousal and excitement than the genital play of the previous stage.

Genital play and occasional masturbation are indications of normal, healthy development. An interesting study revealed that genital play is more common when there is a good mother-child relationship. In cases where the relationship is problematic or lacking altogether (as in institutionalized infants), genital play is less common. Normal sexual development, beginning with genital play during the first year, requires a good relationship with a loving mother figure.[25]

Excessive masturbation, however, can be an indication of sexual abuse. If a child has been fondled inappropriately, she will naturally tend to reproduce the stimulation in an attempt to understand and cope with the confusion and tension arising from the abuse. I therefore recommend that you check into the possibility of sexual abuse if your toddler masturbates excessively.

Not all children who masturbate frequently have been sexually abused. If you have ruled out the possibility of sexual abuse, you can consider excessive masturbation to be your child's way of coping with stress, just as some toddlers suck their thumb. In fact, I do not consider it any more of a problem than thumb sucking. You toddler may have acquired the habit of masturbating when she was feeling stressed or anxious, but not safe enough to have a good cry. So excessive masturbation in this case can be considered a control pattern, a self-soothing behavior that helps your child repress emotions. If your toddler masturbates frequently, it will not be helpful to comment on this behavior, just as it is not helpful to comment on thumb sucking. Instead, try to reduce sources of stress or anxiety in her life, and help her release pent-up feelings by crying and raging (as described in Chapter 2).

Whether or not your child's masturbation is an indication of other problems, reprimands and punishments are never helpful. Toddlers who are punished for touching their genitals may grow up with a compulsive craving for sex, while others may turn off all feeling and repress all thoughts of sex.[26] Harsh punishment is especially harmful. Sexual perversions are often the result of distressing experiences occurring early in life at the same time that innocent exploration of the body was taking place. For example, a possible consequence of being spanked for masturbating may be a sado-masochistic association of sexual pleasure with pain. This is because anything that occurs during a hurtful experience tends to become re-enacted when the experience is triggered (assuming the person was not allowed to release emotions at the time of the original hurt). Be aware, however, that sexual perversions can also result from sexual abuse.

It may be embarrassing for you to allow your toddler to touch her genitals. Perhaps you were led to believe that masturbation was bad, and were distracted, reprimanded, or punished for touching your own body. You may benefit from exploring your childhood memories so you will have a more accepting attitude towards your own children than your parents had with you.

How can I prevent myself from harming my baby when I'm angry?

Many parents are unable to control themselves at times, and hit their baby out of anger. Some seriously abuse their babies. Studies have shown that most parents who seriously abuse their babies were abused themselves when they were children (either physically or sexually).[27] Most parents feel shame and remorse when they realize that they have harmed their child, but they don't know how to stop this cycle of abuse.

Abusive parents yearn for the love they never received, but may be unable to reach out to other adults. Feeling alienated, they turn to their own babies as a source of love and comfort. Because they see their baby as a source for filling their own needs, they have trouble understanding and meeting their baby's needs. Furthermore, they expect comprehension and obedience from their babies at an unrealistically early age, just as was expected of them. When the babies fail to live up to their expectations, as they inevitably will, the parents feel rejected and unloved. Having been brought up in an authoritarian and punitive atmosphere, their immediate reaction is to strike out and hurt their babies physically. Such babies are more likely to become abusing parents when they grow up, and the tragic cycle repeats itself from generation to generation.

It is not surprising that child abuse occurs so frequently in cultures that condone punishment and obedience to authority. Once parents accept such standards, differences in the severity of punishment are merely a matter of degree. Some corporal punishment leads to hospitalization of the infant while some does not, but every case of slapping, hitting, spanking, punching, or shaking is an instance of child abuse.

Researchers have discovered that the major triggering factor for child abuse in babies under 12 months of age is inconsolable crying, while in babies over 12 months of age, most child abuse occurs in situations involving diaper changes or toilet training.[28] In a survey of battered infants, 80% of the parents reported that excessive crying by their infant had triggered the abuse.[29] If your baby's crying triggers your anger, read Chapter 2 of this book and do the exercises at the end of the chapter. Also try to find other people to help you with childcare, especially if your baby keeps you awake at night. If diaper changing, toilet training, or anything else is a source of conflict and anger for you, take the time to explore your feelings with another adult. Remember that it is normal and healthy for toddlers to have a strong will of their own, even though they are sometimes difficult to deal with because of this.

Don't be too hard on yourself if you have slapped your baby once or twice in anger. If you allow your baby to cry and express her fear and anger, she can heal from that experience. Try to apologize and figure out why you lost control, and strive to avoid a similar situation in the future.

However, if you find yourself frequently hurting your baby (or wanting to do so), you should realize that you have a problem, but that you can be helped. Most large cities have child abuse hotlines that you can call up at any time of the day or night. There is nothing shameful in seeking help when you need it. Perhaps you would benefit from a support group or therapist help you heal from your own past abuse and find ways to maintain control of yourself when you are with your child. You can also try to reduce stress in your life, and get some time away from your child. If you are overwhelmed with work, emotional, or financial problems, this will only make the job of parenting more difficult for you. So be sure to take care of your own needs and get all the help you can find. Most importantly, *don't isolate yourself.* Try to find supportive people to give you companionship and help. Don't believe the myth that parenting is easy and that you should be able to cope alone. You need at least as much nurturing as you give to your child.

Even with sufficient support, however, all parents feel like hurting their children at times. It helps if you can allow yourself to release your anger without directing it at your child, perhaps by screaming into a pillow or calling a friend. Here is my own experience with anger:

> There were times that I became so angry with my toddler that I felt like hitting him and really hurting him. This usually occurred in the bathroom when I was trying to brush his teeth. He simply would

not let me, no matter how enjoyable I tried to make it, and he did not do an adequate job by himself. Instead of hitting him, I would leave the bathroom to rage and cry into a pillow. I always had more patience afterwards, and I was glad that I had not actually hit him. I learned that, if I waited until he told me when *he* was ready, then he did eventually let me brush his teeth.

If you feel guilty about something hurtful you have done to your child in the past, remember that guilt is a combination of remorse and anger directed towards yourself. In order to overcome the remorse, you may need to grieve deeply about having hurt your child. By doing so, you will also be grieving for yourself as a former hurt child, and healing from your own childhood pain. As for the self-directed anger, it is never helpful to berate yourself, as this will only lead to depression and more guilt. Instead, try to redirect your anger towards its rightful target. Perhaps you need to express anger at your own parents who hurt you, at the "experts" who gave you harmful advice about raising children, or at the social or economic conditions that prevent you from being the kind of parent you would like to be. This will allow you to see your mistakes without being crushed by them, to forgive yourself, and to improve your parenting skills as you learn and grow with your child.

Although most abusers were abused themselves as children, a reassuring fact is that not all abused children grow up to be abusers. In fact, most do not. So if you were abused as a child, this does not imply that you will automatically abuse your own child. There are many other factors that contribute to child abuse, including alcoholism and drug addiction, illness, poverty, high family stress levels, lack of information about normal child development, spousal abuse, and lack of extended family or community support. I have known many parents who were severely abused themselves as children, yet who have never harmed their own children. Some of these parents have had therapy, while others have surrounded themselves with a supportive network of people. One mother told me that she decided never to hit her child, and she sits on her own hands, if necessary, to prevent herself from doing so. It *is* possible to stop the cycle of abuse.

EXERCISES

Explore your childhood.

1. What style of discipline did your parents generally use with you (authoritarian violent, authoritarian non-violent, permissive, or democratic)? Were you expected to be obedient? How do you feel about this?
2. Recall specific occasions when you were punished or rewarded as a child, and describe how you felt.
3. Did you have temper tantrums? How did your parents respond? (distract, ignore, punish you, send you to your room, or give in to your demands?) How did you feel about this?

Express your feelings about your baby.

1. Think of a conflict you have with your baby and talk about how you feel in that situation. What do you *feel* like doing? (This is not necessarily what you *should* do!) Have you had a similar feeling before? Does it remind you of anything from your own childhood?
2. Describe a situation in which you are unsure of your baby's needs or your own needs, and are not sure whether to set a limit? Explore your feelings.
3. How does it make you feel when you must do something against your baby's will and your baby protests (for example, put your baby in a car seat)? Are you reluctant to be firm when necessary? What makes this hard for you?

Nurture yourself.

1. Join a support group with other parents, in which you can openly share feelings and discuss conflicts you have with your child. If you had an abusive childhood, it will be helpful to join a group of child abuse survivors who are struggling to break the cycle of abuse with their children.
2. Find a way to take at least two hours of time for yourself every week, doing something fun or relaxing, such as jogging, swimming, watching a movie, going out to dinner, or getting a massage. If you take your baby with you, make sure that the activity is for *you*.
3. With your partner, take turns listening to each other at the end of each day, even if it is only for ten minutes each. Or call a friend and take turns listening to each other.

CHAPTER 7

ATTACHMENT: LETTING YOUR BABY FEEL SAFE

When will my baby become attached to me and how will he show his attachment?

In the first chapter of this book, I discussed parent-infant bonding, the process by which parents fall in love with their infant. The present chapter deals with the infant's love for its parents, which is normally referred to as "attachment."

Normal, healthy babies who are treated with love and sensitivity become very much attached to their parents (or primary caretakers). This is not very noticeable during the first few months, because newborns usually do not mind being held by strangers, and they do not generally become distressed when their parents leave them with a substitute caretaker for short periods of time. Once babies begin to smile, they will smile generously at any face, whether it is a familiar one or a strange one.[1] However, definite signs of attachment and preference for their primary caretakers gradually become more apparent as babies grow older.

By the time babies learn to crawl, they show their attachment to their parents by following them and actively seeking to maintain contact with them. If the parents stay in one spot, babies typically use them as a secure base from which to explore, periodically returning for reassuring contacts.[2]

The two aspects of attachment that have received the most attention by psychologists are fear of strangers and a resistance to separation from the parents. The official terms for these fears are "stranger anxiety" and "separation anxiety." A mother describes this:

The first signs appeared at exactly six months. Until that point, anybody could pick him up and hold him. I could leave him with someone and everything would be just dandy. When he was six months old I went to a workshop with him and some people were supposed to be taking care of him, but he cried and cried. So then I stopped leaving him with people when he cried, but it got worse and worse. Eventually somebody just had to touch him while I was holding him and he would cry. Or if a stranger just spoke to him, he would cry. It got to the point where I couldn't leave him for a second with anybody else. He would just cry all the time when I wasn't there.

Separation anxiety usually begins around six to eight months, peaks between 13 and 15 months, and starts to decline after 18 months of age. It is often still present after two years of age.[3] Psychologists used to think that babies became attached to only one person (usually their mothers), but studies show that multiple attachments are not only possible, but also quite common.

In an extensive study of the development of social attachments in infancy, the conclusion was that not all babies showed anxiety at being separated from their mothers. Some babies appeared to be more attached to their fathers or to grandparents. One-third of the babies in the study had separation anxiety with more than one person as soon as any separation anxiety occurred at all. Babies can become attached to anyone who pays attention to them, whether or not the person feeds or cares for them in any other way.[4] In the Efe Pygmy culture of Zaire, infants spend up to fifty percent of the time with adults other than their own mother, and they are even nursed by other lactating women. Consequently, they become attached to several adults.[5] In Western cultures, infants in two-parent families usually become attached to both parents.[6] Attachment to siblings becomes evident when infants are in a strange situation. They are usually less upset when an older sibling is present.[7]

Studies have shown an increase in saliva cortisol levels (indicating a physiological stress response) in nine-month-old babies who were separated briefly from their mothers and left with an unresponsive caretaker. However, this increase was not as great if the babies were left with a warm, responsive person.[8]

Stranger anxiety is the fear caused by a stranger's attempts to interact with a baby even though the baby may be sitting on his mother's lap. Studies show that most normal babies show some fear of strangers sometime during the first two years. It begins during the second half of the first year, just like separation anxiety, but does not usually last as long. It gradually declines during the second year and is usually entirely gone by two years of age. Babies who have stranger anxiety reserve their smiles for familiar caretakers. When a stranger approaches and attempts to interact, babies will typically stare soberly, frown, turn away, or even cry.[9]

Both separation anxiety and stranger anxiety have been found in babies of several different cultures, including Guatemala, Uganda, the Hopi Indians of North America, and Kibbutz-reared children in Israel. These fears are present in babies raised totally at home as well as those attending a daycare center.[10]

Not all babies follow this same pattern of separation and stranger anxiety, and the intensities of the two fears do not always coincide. But the majority of normal babies do show either separation anxiety or fear of strangers (or both) at some point during the first two years. It is important to be aware of this developmental stage and to act in ways that best support your baby's emotional growth, as described in the following sections of this chapter.

Why do babies develop separation anxiety and fear of strangers?

Attachment has been the subject of considerable research. There is ample evidence to suggest that both separation and stranger anxiety are normal phenomena that occur in healthy babies, and do not indicate deviance or pathology. Babies who are raised in insufficiently staffed institutions do not show either separation anxiety or fear of strangers, and act equally accepting of everybody. This is alarming to psychologists.[11]

In Mary Ainsworth's famous study of attachment and exploration of one-year-old babies in a strange place (the "Strange Situation" study), she found that there was a clear-cut relationship between the baby's attachment behavior and the quality of the mother-infant interaction during the first year of life.[12] Babies whose mothers had been sensitive to their signals, accessible to them, non-interfering, and accepting of them showed clear-cut, unambivalent attachment to their mothers in a strange place. They used her as a secure base from which to venture forth and explore. Most of them showed some distress and cried when she left the room for a few minutes (even though another adult was in the room), and they clung to her strongly when she returned. These babies clearly wanted their mothers. The authors called these babies "securely attached," and concluded that this was normal, healthy behavior of twelve-month-old infants.

Babies in this study who had received less sensitive mothering deviated from this behavior in various ways, depending on how their mothers usually treated them. Babies whose mothers tended to ignore and reject them showed little or no tendency to seek proximity or contact with their mothers. When their mother picked them up they did not cling or resist being released. They showed no distress when their mother left them with a stranger, and upon her return they avoided or ignored her. These babies were labeled "anxious/avoidant," and Ainsworth considered this to be a form of insecure attachment, even though the babies appeared to be independent and self-sufficient.

Another group of babies, labeled "anxious/resistant" appeared to be very anxious and clingy and did not explore the new environment very much. They cried extensively when the mother left, but seemed inconsolable when she returned, showing anger towards her while at the same time clinging to her. These babies' mothers had been inconsistent in responding to their needs during the first year.

Researchers have generally interpreted this study to mean that the quality of the mother-infant interaction affects a baby's attachment behavior. Strong, healthy attachment occurs in babies who have a deep and rewarding relationship with a sensitive mother figure who responds promptly to their needs. More recent research has shown that infants of depressed mothers do not become as securely attached as do those of non-depressed mothers, probably because depressed mothers are inconsistent in meeting their babies' needs.[13]

Longitudinal studies have found that babies' behavior in the Strange Situation at twelve months of age predicts later social and emotional adjustment. In a study of over 200 children whose attachment histories were known, those who had been labeled "securely attached" in the Strange Situation as infants differed greatly at four to five years of age from those who had been labeled "anxiously attached."[14] The securely attached children were more curious, confident, independent, socially competent, self-reliant, showed more empathy, were more likely to be leaders, and had more friends. They also engaged in more fantasy play. Of particular concern to the researchers were the infants labeled "anxious/avoidant" in the Strange Situation. When they were four to five years old, these children were sullen or oppositional, sought attention in inappropriate ways, but did not usually seek help when injured or disappointed. Furthermore, they often victimized other children, and their victims were often other anxiously attached children. These striking differences persisted as the children grew older. Eleven-year-old children who had been securely attached as infants had more friends than those who had been anxiously attached.[15]

This study indicates that a strong attachment to the mother and a dependency on her during infancy is a good sign for later development, while an avoidant or resistant infant is a cause for concern. It is unfortunate that many Western cultures place such great importance on independence and self-reliance, the very traits shown by "avoidant" infants in the Strange Situation. These are the infants who develop the most serious behavior problems later on, and who, ironically, do not become independent and self-reliant preschoolers.

The whole issue of separation anxiety and fear of strangers can be considered from an evolutionary point of view. The British psychoanalyst, John Bowlby, was the first person to use the term "attachment" to refer to a baby's bond to its mother, and he felt that this was biologically adaptive to insure survival. He considered babies' behaviors such as clinging, smiling, following, and protesting during separations to be genetically programmed "attachment behaviors" designed to guarantee proximity to the mother. Babies with strong attachment behaviors received more warmth, protection, nourishment, and attention, and therefore survived better than those with weak attachment behaviors. Because closeness to the mother is necessary for survival, Bowlby claimed that it brings feelings of security and joy in babies. Conversely, separation from the mother can lead to anxiety, grief, and depression.[16]

It is probably not pure coincidence that separation anxiety begins around the same time that infants learn to crawl, during the second half of the first year. In a species with many predators, such as our prehistoric human ancestors, it would have been very dangerous for the young to wander off alone. A strong attachment to the mother, with an accompanying fear of being separated, would have evolved because of its survival value. Although the likelihood of predators on human babies has lessened considerably, our species is nevertheless the product of its evolutionary past, and we are genetically programmed to expect a hunter-gatherer lifestyle. What once had survival value is experienced by present day babies as real needs. Perhaps this is why even a brief separation from the mother signals danger to babies today and triggers a physiological stress response.

Another explanation for stranger and separation anxiety is the communication theory.[17] Babies and parents develop rich patterns of communication with each other, many of which are nonverbal. You learn to tell when your baby is hungry, tired, or upset; you recognize her look of discomfort with a soiled diaper, or her facial expression when she is concentrating. You know what she means when she points to the kitchen cupboard or attempts to repeat the game of hide-the-block that you played with her the day before. Once your baby has developed this intimate understanding with you, any stranger will appear to speak a different language. This must be very frustrating and frightening for babies. In fact, strangers usually do not frighten babies until they attempt to communicate with them in some way. Babies prefer to be with the people who know and understand them. If babies could talk and be easily understood by others, the dependency on familiar caretakers would not be as strong. This may be one reason why fear of strangers and separation anxiety both decrease after 18 months of age, which is when most babies begin to talk.

Added to all of this is the fact that, until approximately 18 months of age, babies lack the ability to understand that their parents will ever return, even though it is explained to them. They have no way of visualizing a future event, and they have little concept of time. The words "soon" or "in a few hours" mean nothing to them. All they know is that their parents are gone, and this is terrifying.

How can I help my baby become securely attached?

A basic requirement for the formation of a healthy attachment is that babies need to have a continuous and predictable relationship with at least one person. This first love relationship will be the basis for all future relationships. If a baby were to be cared for by a different person every day of her life, it would be very difficult for her to form stable, trusting relationships as an adult. Adults who were passed from one foster home to another as babies and young children have great difficulty forming lasting, loving, and trusting relationships. In the past they were labeled "affectionless."[18] Nowadays, psychologists say that these people are suffering from "attachment disorder."

Even short separations can be traumatic for babies, so try to avoid separating from your baby for more than a day, especially during the first two years. If you must be away from your baby, try to find other caretakers who are very familiar to her, and who are warm and responsive.

If you avoid too many separations, respond sensitively to your baby's cries, do your best to meet her needs, and follow the suggestions in this book, your baby will probably become securely attached.

Accepting your baby's emotions is an important factor in healthy attachment, because babies cannot feel truly accepted if their deepest emotions are continually ignored, denied, or repressed. Remember that not all crying indicates an immediate need. Symptoms of mild insecure attachment, such as anxious clinging, aggressive acts, or precocious independence, can occur when parents continually ignore babies' cries or distract them from crying when they need to. Not only will such babies suffer from accumulated tensions that need an outlet, but they will also begin to feel that a part of themselves has been rejected. They will eventually learn to repress their painful emotions in order to be loved and accepted.

In Western, industrialized cultures, parents are expected to foster independence in their children at an early age, and to discourage attachment and dependency. Parents are sometimes made to feel inadequate when their child is strongly attached to them, and proud once she shows more independence. People often comment admiringly, "Look how independent that baby is!" Unfortunately, I have never heard anyone say approvingly, "See what a healthy, strong attachment that baby has!" Independence is considered especially wonderful for little boys, to the great detriment to their emotional health. According to the research definition of secure attachment, over half of babies are securely attached at twelve months of age. However, the research does not distinguish between different degrees of secure attachment. In my observation, few children, especially boys, grow up with sufficient physical and emotional closeness. In fact, most children of both sexes are starved for affection, but they learn to repress this need. Children who are truly securely attached are comfortable hugging and cuddling with their parents *throughout adolescence.* They also feel comfortable crying with their parents if they need to, even after they are grown up, knowing that they will be accepted and listened to.

Interestingly, researchers have found that there is a correlation between a parent's own attachment history (based on an adult attachment interview) and the child's attachment status.[19] Parents who were themselves securely attached to their own parents tend to have babies who are securely attached to them, while those who were insecurely attached to their own parents tend to have babies who show similar patterns of insecure attachment with them. This makes sense because we tend to imitate our own role models when we become parents. These patterns of attachment can be changed from one generation to the next, but it requires adults to become aware of the ways in which they were hurt as children, and to work through the pain and anger instead of denying and repressing it. It is healthier to admit openly to yourself that your parents made mistakes and that they hurt you, rather than to claim that they were perfect.

It is normal for attachment behaviors to increase during stressful times. Don't be surprised if your baby resists separations more strongly when she is ill or in pain. A major change, such as a move to a new home or a family trip, can also cause a temporary increase in attachment behaviors.

Your own stress level can also affect your baby's attachment. Unfortunately, your baby will need increased contact and reassurance at the very times when you are least well equipped to provide this. Feelings of insecurity can occur because of this. In fact, researchers have found that a child's attachment status can become less secure if the family is going through a stressful time due to unemployment, poverty, illness, or conflict between the adults.[20] If you are under stress, try to obtain as much emotional support as you can from others, because this will allow you to be more attentive and responsive to your infant. This will help her feel securely attached in spite of your hardships.

FOSTERING SECURE ATTACHMENT

- Provide continuous care from the same people.

- Provide lots of physical closeness, including at night.

- Avoid separations of more than a day.

- During separations, be sure your baby is with a familiar, warm person.

- Fill your baby's needs promptly.

- Interact with your baby sensitively and lovingly.

- Never leave your baby to cry alone.

- Accept stress-release crying while holding your baby, empathizing, and listening.

- Never punish, hit, shake, or yell at your baby.

- If you are stressed, find support for yourself.

If your baby is insecurely attached, or if you adopt a baby who has not had the opportunity to form a healthy attachment, it is possible for your baby to become securely attached. However, simply loving your baby and responding to her needs will probably not be sufficient. You will also need to spend many hours accepting her crying, because insecurely attached children cannot fully love and trust until they have released emotional pain from the past with an empathic witness. Some parents, who adopt older babies or toddlers, report that the babies cry immediately, while others find that their babies go through a period of quiet, docile behavior, only to be followed by considerable crying and raging once they feel safe and loved.

How can I help my baby feel comfortable with a new care-taker?

The best way to help your baby feel safe with someone new is to allow him to interact with the person on several occasions while you are present. It is important to let your baby take the initiative and proceed at his own pace. If the new person attempts to hold or otherwise impose herself on your baby, or if you leave before your baby is ready, he may become frightened and the process will have to be started all over again. The following example illustrates how babies initiate interactions with strangers when they are ready to do so:

> When my son was ten months old we went to a family workshop. There were many people of all ages sitting around on the floor in a big room. For quite a while at first he sat on my lap and refused to move or interact with anybody. When strangers attempted to touch him or interact with him, he turned away and clung to me. After a while, he crawled a few feet away from me, but came right back to sit in my lap some more. Then he crawled a little further away while continually checking to see if I was still there. He kept returning to me and then crawling away again, each time going a little further. Then he began crawling towards other people, touching them, and initiating interactions. After about two hours of this he was feeling entirely comfortable moving around the whole room

and letting people interact with him. When he was allowed the time and the freedom to become acquainted in his own way, he became quite friendly and outgoing. His security came from the fact that I did not move from my position on the floor, and the other people were not forcing him to interact with them before he was ready.

Each baby has his own way of become comfortable with a new person. One baby might hide behind his parent and peek out occasionally to see if the stranger is looking. This would be a good cue for the new person to initiate a game of "peek-a-boo." Another baby might begin throwing toys at the stranger. This would be a cue for the person to throw the toys back again, or comment on each one. Gradually the baby will move closer to the new person. It is best not to leave the room during the first few encounters with a new person, unless you are sure your baby feels quite safe. Once your baby allows the new person to touch him and play with him, you can try stepping out of the room for a few seconds, after explaining to your baby that you will be right back. If that separation causes no distress, you can try leaving for a few minutes. You can then gradually increase the time periods of your absence.

Even once your baby is familiar with a baby-sitter, he may need you to stay a few minutes after a baby-sitter arrives, rather than leave immediately. The length of time will be longer if you are leaving your baby in another place rather than your own home. It is important to take the time for this and wait until your baby feels comfortable before you leave.

Some people become quite upset when babies initially reject their attempts at interaction. It is hard to be rejected as it can trigger childhood memories of being rejected. Although witnessing a baby's strong attachment can make adults feel uncomfortable, this does not justify pushing babies into strangers' laps before the babies are ready to be there. In fact, this will only make the baby want to cling more to his parents. You cannot force growth and independence. Adults who feel it necessary to push babies beyond their limits in this area would benefit both themselves and their families by figuring out where their feelings of urgency are stemming from. It is of primary importance to trust babies to outgrow their dependencies at their own rate, and to let them venture forth only when they feel ready to do so. To interfere with babies in this respect is to deny them the trust, respect, and safety that they deserve.

Some parents attempt to avoid a crying scene by making their departure while the baby's back is turned or while he is busily involved with a toy. I do not recommend this, because it can lead to later problems. Your baby will soon notice that you are gone, and he will inevitably feel betrayed. If this happens repeatedly, your baby may begin to feel that the world is unpredictable, and lose his trust in you, or develop a fear of being abandoned.

It is therefore a good idea to explain everything to your baby from birth on. Tell him that you will be leaving, when you plan to return, and who will be with him. To help him understand, you can explain things in terms of your baby's experience, for example, "at nap time," "at lunch time," "when you are asleep," or "I'll come back to nurse you." Although your baby may not understand these explanations at first, it is always wise to give too many explanations rather than too few, because you don't know exactly when he begins to understand.

If you plan to have another caretaker while your baby is asleep, it is also wise to prepare him for that, even though he is not likely to see the person at all. But if you have not prepared him and he awakens, he may resist going to sleep in the future for fear that you will leave him. It is better to have the baby-sitter arrive *before* your baby falls asleep, so he will not be surprised to find a different person there if he wakes up.

If an emergency situation arises in which a stranger must take care of your baby, it is best to have someone come to stay with your baby in his own home rather than take him to a stranger's home. The presence of an older sibling can also help alleviate the trauma. If your baby cries, the baby-sitter should allow and encourage the crying to continue, without trying to distract him. She should explain to your baby where you are and when you will return, no matter how young he is.

When your baby is reunited with you following a traumatic situation, do not be surprised if he shows anger at you. This is a normal and healthy reaction. Try to accept his crying and tantrums, which may occur for many weeks following even a short separation, because he needs to express all the fear, grief, and anger at having been left. He may show increased clinging and a strong resistance to separation, and this is also quite normal. It is important to remember that babies can heal themselves of the effects of traumatic experiences. However, this situation can be avoided if you take the time to familiarize your baby with several people from birth, so that he will not be too traumatized if something unexpected should happen that requires you to separate from your baby.

What if my baby refuses to be left with anyone else after she has become attached to me?

Some babies cannot seem to develop a trusting relationship with another person, and refuse to be separated from their mother, even for one minute. These babies even refuse to stay with their fathers or grandparents whom they have known since birth. If your baby shows this form of extreme separation anxiety, consider the five possible explanations below.

The caretaker is not warm and sensitive.
Perhaps your baby refuses to be left because she senses that the person is unable to give her good quality attention. Babies who are accustomed to good, sensitive parenting will not accept attention of lower quality. Many parents find that their baby warms up immediately to certain people, but never seems to feel comfortable with others. You can trust your baby's judgment as to who is a good caretaker for her and who is not.

Your baby is feeling stressed.
Any stress will increase your baby's attachment needs. You can expect separations to be more difficult if your baby is feeling sick or tired, or if there is stress in the family caused by factors such as illness, death, financial problems, or marital disputes. Your baby will naturally be more clingy and resistant to separation during all new situations such as a trip, or following a move to a new home. You can

also expect this behavior following natural disasters such as earth-quakes, floods, or fires. If you live in an area with a high neighbor-hood crime rate or in a country at war, it is only natural for your baby to resist separating from you.

Your baby needs to cry for unrelated reasons.

Another possible explanation for extreme separation anxiety is that your baby may simply need to cry, even though it looks like a strong case of separation anxiety. Perhaps she does not cry enough with you because you tend to distract her from her feelings. In this case, your distractions will act as control patterns for her that repress her emotions. As described in Chapter 2, babies learn to repress their crying by means of repetitive behaviors called control patterns. Dif-ferent control patterns can arise in your baby depending on how you respond to her crying. If you repeatedly try to stop your baby from crying by nursing her for "comfort" (instead of holding her lovingly and allowing her to continue crying), your breasts are likely to be-come your baby's control pattern. She will therefore appear to need your constant presence, and contact with you (even without nursing) will cause her to repress the crying that she needs to do.

These control patterns can be thought of as distorted attachments. The babies become attached to objects or body parts (a blanket, their thumb, their mother's breasts), but not to whole people in a secure way. As such, these distorted attachments inhibit true intimacy and healthy attachment and growth. In addition to a general clingyness, other clues that you may be repressing your baby's crying are her reluctance to play independently and frequent night awakenings.

If you think that your body or behavior might be acting as a control pattern for your baby, this would explain her strong resis-tance to separation from you, which, in reality, is simply a need to cry. Instead of frequently nursing or rocking her for comfort, you can try to become more of a listener and less of a "soother." If you feel comfortable doing so, you could ask a familiar person to hold your baby while you stay in the room, even though your baby might pro-test and cry. A next step would be for you to leave the room. If she is with a familiar person whom you trust, you can be assured that this is probably not a new hurt, but an opportunity for her to release accumulated tensions that have nothing to do with separation anxiety. Here is an illustration:

> At 15 months of age, Amy was very much attached to her mother. She and her mother had visited me on five or six occasions, and I had interacted with Amy. She enjoyed being at my house, running around with my daughter (also a toddler), and playing with her toys. My daughter and I had been to her house several times. Amy seemed to be comfortable with me, but only when her mother was present. If her mother left the room, only for a second, Amy would cry and run after her. One morning they came to visit, and her mother reported that Amy had been awake part of the night, and that she was fussy and clingy that morning (a fairly usual occurrence). Her mother had previously decided to leave her with me for the first time, so she said good-bye and left as planned. Amy cried very hard for about 25 minutes while I held her and paid attention to her. After that she became involved in playing with some toys while sitting on my lap. This playing was interspersed with more crying at times, but by the time her mother came back, one hour later, Amy was playing happily and independently. Later that day, her mother called me up to report that Amy had been in a wonderful mood after coming home, and was neither whiny nor clingy. It seems clear from this example that Amy needed to do some crying before she even arrived at my house. She did not normally cry with her mother because her mother did not understand her crying need and did not give her the necessary undivided attention. Her mother's departure was not hurtful, but simply the trigger for some badly needed crying. Because I did not try to stop her, she was able to release tensions by crying as long as she needed to.

If your baby always clings to her mother and refuses to be left with her father or other family member whom she has known since birth, this could be an indication that she has a control pattern associated with her mother's body (assuming, of course, that the father or other relative is a warm, nurturing person). When my son was one year old, he would sometimes cry very hard when I left him with his father. He seemed to want me, and as soon as he was in my arms would stop crying. Often, his father would hold him anyway (when I wanted to take a shower, for example), and let him cry as long as he needed to. Afterwards, he would be a lot less clingy with me, and quite happy to be with his father. In fact, these crying sessions actually helped the two of them form a deeper bond with each other. (This was the period during which my nursing him was acting as a control pattern.) Some fathers feel rejected when their baby cries with them. Keep in mind that your baby may be using the opportunity to do some badly needed crying.

Your baby is having a conditioned emotional response to previous trauma.

The present situation of separation may be distressing for your baby because of a similarity to a past traumatic experience. When something triggers a memory of a past trauma, this is called a conditioned emotional response. Normally, babies will cry and heal themselves immediately following hurtful experiences, but if they do not complete their crying, these kinds of fears can occur later on.

If, sometime in the past, you left your baby with strangers, each subsequent separation will tend to trigger the feelings she experienced during the earlier separation (assuming she was not able to cry enough about it when it occurred). Every time you leave, she will remember the previous time when she felt scared. This will occur even though she is left with a familiar person, and each time it happens, she will attempt to finish the crying she needed to do at the time. In fact, your absence may be necessary in order for her to heal from this trauma. If you think this kind of fear is operating, your baby will probably benefit by being left with someone very familiar with whom she can cry until she has fully released the old, painful feelings. This very problem arose when my son was two years old. Here is how it happened and how he overcame it:

> Just after my son's s second birthday, he was being observed once a week by a University class studying language acquisition. I was present in the room with him, but one time the students wanted to hear him talk without me present. Thinking he would feel safe without me, I told him I would return in a little while, and went into another room where I could observe him through a one-way mirror. He did not cry at first, but began to look more and more unhappy until he finally burst into tears. I returned at that point, but

was unable to give him the attention necessary for him to finish the crying he needed to do. During the next two weeks he was very clingy, and refused to be left with anybody, even a well-loved aunt he had known since birth. Every time I tried to encourage him to cry about the traumatic event, he seemed very happy. He would only cry when I left. So I left him with his aunt one day, after explaining the situation to her. She held him while he cried continuously for 50 minutes. After that day he was once again quite happy to be with her, as well as his other familiar caretakers.

If your baby was separated from her mother at birth, even if only for a few hours, that situation may serve as the initial separation that will tend to trigger anxiety during later separations. All adopted babies have experienced separation trauma, so if your baby is adopted, be aware that this can affect her reaction to separations and to all new situations.

If your baby refuses to be left with someone with whom she previously felt entirely safe, something traumatic must have happened to your baby the last time she was with that person, or in another similar situation. Before leaving her with the same person again, it is wise to determine the cause of your child's distress, which could range from something as inoffensive as a new dog in the person's home, to something more serious such as abuse. Trust your baby before assuming that you know what is best. Or perhaps it has nothing to do with the caretaker at all, who could simply be wearing something that day that reminds your baby of a nurse who recently gave her an injection. If you suspect a conditioned emotional response, it may be too overwhelming for your baby to be left with that person until she has healed from the trauma that is being triggered.

Your baby is reacting to your own separation anxiety.

To make matters even more complicated, your baby can sense *your* anxiety and cry because of it. Babies are extremely sensitive to their parents' emotional states, so what looks like your baby's strong separation anxiety may be partly a reflection of your own.

According to Bowlby, it is normal for mothers to become anxious when separations from their babies last too long, just as it is normal for the babies to become anxious. Both partners, the mother and the baby, contribute to the complex regulation of the attachment system, because both know instinctively that babies need to be close to their mothers for survival and optimal development.[21] It is also normal for fathers, and anyone else who is bonded to the infant, to have similar emotions.

However, some mothers (or fathers) have stronger separation anxiety than their babies, and are unable to leave their baby, even though she might be perfectly happy to be left with familiar people. Instead of being adaptive, this can hamper your baby's development.

There are several possible reasons for overly strong parental anxiety. Some parents worry that their baby will not be well cared for in their absence. Both you and your baby will naturally feel more comfortable with a caretaker who is warm and sensitive and uses a similar approach to your own. If you are hesitant to leave your baby with someone, your baby will probably sense this and resist separating from you. It may be necessary to train your caretaker and give specific instructions and information about your approach to parenting, so that you will feel more comfortable leaving your baby.

Perhaps you feel deep terror that your baby will die if you are not with her at all times. The urge to protect your baby is normal and healthy, and it is important to be aware of possible dangers to your child's safety. However, if you find yourself worrying so much that it interferes with your baby's exploratory behavior or individuation process, your anxiety probably comes from some trauma in your own past. Perhaps you experienced a traumatic separation or death of a loved one that you have not completely grieved. This will make it hard to trust other people to care for your baby even when your baby doesn't cry.

Some parents enjoy the feeling of being needed and wanted by their baby, especially if it contradicts their own childhood experiences of feeling rejected. If your own parents made you feel unloved, having a baby strongly attached to you can bolster your self-esteem. But if you become too dependent of this relationship in order to feel good about yourself, you could unconsciously resist your child's growth towards independence.

Although your resistance to separation can have its origin in your own past, I recommend that you trust your intuition and not leave your baby until you feel comfortable doing so. Don't let anyone else convince you that your baby is too attached or you are overprotective. You are the person in the best position to decide what to do in your particular situation, and you are the one who must live with the results of your decisions. You will have many opportunities to separate from your child, and it doesn't have to happen until you are both ready.

Do babies need their mothers to be their primary caretakers?

The three most important things that babies need are milk on demand (preferably breast milk), continuity in caretakers so that the baby has the opportunity to form attachments, and good quality, individual attention. The importance of breastfeeding makes it logical that the mother be one of the primary caretakers during the first year. Traditionally, mothers have been expected to be the sole caretakers for babies, but the job of caring for a baby is so time-consuming and demanding that one person cannot be expected to do an adequate job. Caring for a baby is a 24-hour job, so mothers need a lot of help.

Although fathers cannot breastfeed, they can certainly hold and interact with the baby, change his diapers, bathe and dress him, and respond to his crying. Fathers, like mothers, can learn to do these things with skill and care, and gain much pleasure from them. In studies of father-infant interaction, researchers found that fathers were just as nurturing as mothers and just as sensitive to infant cries.[22] I strongly recommend that mothers and fathers arrange their lives so that a parent can stay home with the infant during the first few important years when babies need so much individual attention. A two or three year time commitment for each child is not much out of a total life span.

Shared parenting between mothers and fathers is not always easy. Some factors that can interfere are work schedules, men's reluctance to help, men's feelings of inadequacy as nurturers, and women's resentment of men taking over their traditional roles. Men and women are the victims of a sexist society, and many hurdles have to be overcome to make shared parenting easier. One father I interviewed had this to say about shared parenting:

> I recall feeling that I didn't know anything about how to be a parent. I had no idea how to change a diaper. I was just totally in the dark, and I really felt incompetent. I had previously had no experience taking care of a baby. And all of a sudden, I had no choice. I still feel sometimes that I'm not doing a good job. I think in general, though, I'm doing just fine. I suppose what I'm continually doing is comparing myself to my wife. I see how she treats him, the way she interacts with Nathan. I think I consider her as the expert, and I see myself not coming up to her standards, and I feel really bad. I feel that I should be interacting with him more, that I shouldn't leave it all up to her. Or that he's better off with her. It probably doesn't help the way she tends to be critical with me sometimes, like when I put clothes on him with colors that don't match. When she comments on this, I begin to feel that I don't know anything about dressing. I just haven't developed the awareness of what matches what. When my wife asked me to take care of Nathan one day a week, I recall feeling that it was going to be a burden, a responsibility, and that I wouldn't be able to get any work done. There go my Saturdays. I didn't really want to do it, but I felt obligated to do it. In retrospect I think that it was fair. It was a new concept to me. I probably conceived of myself in the roles that my parents had. The primary caretaking responsibility was always my mother's, and so I just assumed it would by my wife's.

Babies benefit from having more than one primary caretaker. The anthropologist Margaret Mead wrote: "Cross-cultural studies suggest that adjustment is most facilitated if the child is cared for by many warm friendly people."[23] It is therefore to your baby's benefit to have other caretakers in addition to you. Babies with more than one caretaker have the opportunity to form several deep attachments instead of just one, and their lives are much richer right from the start. Once babies have formed multiple attachments, they will have more than one person to feel safe with when they reach a stage of separation and stranger anxiety. Furthermore, babies with more than one caretaker run less of a risk of being neglected or mistreated when their primary caretaker is tired or irritable.

Everybody has certain strengths and weaknesses in caring for babies. Some people have more patience for reading books, and hate to change diapers, while others enjoy the care-taking routines but become bored looking at the same picture book over and over again. The advantage of several caretakers for each baby is that the baby will benefit from each person's strengths, while the effect of each person's weaknesses or lack of patience will be minimized.

Motherhood is not inherently oppressive, nor are biological differences and the division of labor based on these differences. During the hunter-gatherer era of our species, women were probably the primary caretakers for babies, as well as the gatherers of food, while men were probably the primary hunters. This made sense, as it would have been difficult for mothers to go hunting while breastfeeding.

Nowadays, however, mothers are frequently oppressed, and this assumes many forms. Pregnant women are often forced to quit their jobs. The work that mothers do is considered to be unskilled, unimportant, and demeaning. Mothers receive no salary, and are often denied a maternity leave from their previous job (especially in the United States). Mothers are expected to be the primary caretakers for babies, but they are not given enough help and are usually denied the emotional and financial support they need in order to meet their children's needs effectively. To make matters worse, mothers are the first to be criticized and blamed for their children's faults. But when children turn out to be competent and well adjusted, people attribute this to an inborn trait rather than giving mothers any credit.

Unfortunately, the media image of a liberated woman is antithetical to motherhood. Many women have accepted the male standards of what constitutes acceptable and worthwhile work, and this has led to a refusal by some radical feminists to take care of their babies or to breastfeed. These women have felt so oppressed that they have overreacted by rejecting anything that causes them to play a different role from that of a man. They have internalized the oppressive standards of a male-dominated culture. Women should not be fighting desperately to be like men. Instead, we should be striving for a culture in which we are allowed to be ourselves, develop our full human potential, and make choices. If a woman wants to become a computer programmer or a doctor, she should be allowed to acquire the education she needs to do so. Likewise, if a woman chooses to become a stay-at-home mother during part of her life, she should also be fully supported in that choice and recognized for her valuable contributions to society.

If you wish to join the work force, it is important that you not do so at the expense of your baby's well being, whether you are a mother or a father. Try to balance your need to pursue a career and earn money with your baby's need for attention. Can the job wait a year or two? Remember that your baby needs *you* much more than new toys or expensive trips. Remember also that by raising healthy children you are helping to make this a better world.

What about daycare for babies?

Studies have found that daycare during the first year can hamper a baby's development. Infants in daycare for more than 20 hours per week are more likely to show insecure patterns of attachment at one year of age, are less cooperative with adult requests, and show more aggression in social interactions with other babies.[24]

Other studies, however, have found that these negative effects occur only when babies are placed in poor quality daycare centers. Babies enrolled in high quality daycare centers, even during their first year, do not seem to be at greater risk for developmental problems.[25] Unfortunately, an in-depth assessment of 225 randomly selected infant and toddler daycare centers in the U.S. in 1993 rated only 8% of them to be of good or excellent quality. Forty percent were rated poor in quality, and the rest mediocre. The researchers concluded that, "most child care, especially for infants and toddlers, is mediocre in quality and sufficiently poor to interfere with children's emotional and intellectual development."[26] Daycare centers will hopefully improve in quality as educators learn about infants' needs.

The number of staff for each baby, as well as group size, are important considerations. The National Association for the Education of Young Children recommends a ratio of one adult for every three infants, and limiting the group size to six (with two adults) during the first year.[27] Most infant centers do not meet these recommendations. But even one adult for three infants is not really enough. What if all three need to be held or fed at the same time? One adult cannot possibly meet three infants' needs for quality, individual care.

Another problem with daycare is that, unless the center is near the mother's work place, it will be difficult for her to breastfeed her baby. Some mothers express their milk and refrigerate it so the baby can be fed her breast milk when she is at work. This is certainly better than feeding a baby cow's milk, but it is not the same as letting a baby suck at her mother's breast.

The fact that babies can survive and develop "normally" in good quality daycare centers does not mean that they are developing *optimally*. Babies need a one-to-one relationship with an adult who responds sensitively to their cues, holds them as needed, and gives them individual attention.

Human beings are not born in litters (except in the rare cases of twins or triplets), so it seems as if nature went out of her way to provide at least one adult for every baby. The contraceptive effect of breastfeeding contributes to child spacing, as does the prevalence of postpartum sexual taboos in many traditional cultures, where babies are born two or more years apart. In the prehistoric hunter-gatherer societies, the birth spacing averages were probably even longer.

After the first year, a one-to-two adult/baby ratio may be sufficient for a few hours a day, but nobody should be required to care for more than two babies under the age of two for any length of time. Once children reach the age of two-and-a-half or three, they no longer require so much individual attention. They become more sociable with other children, and can benefit from good quality group care. Even at that age, however, the adult/child ratio should be kept high.

If you must find substitute care for your infant, the best arrangement is one-to-one attention from a warm, nurturing person (such as a live-in nanny or a grandparent). If that is impossible, the next best arrangement would be to place your baby in the care of a person who has only one or two other children to care for.

If you have no choice but to place your baby in a daycare center, try to find one with a high adult/baby ratio that is clean, safe, and attractive, where the adults are affectionate with the children, and where your baby will receive consistent care from the same person.

Look for a center that allows your baby to have her own individual schedule of sleeping and eating, rather than one that tries to mold all the babies into a rigid schedule. Also be sure to make several unscheduled visits to observe the conditions of the center. Try not to put your baby in a daycare center more than 20 hours a week during her first year. When your baby is with you, give her as much individual attention as possible.

Don't be surprised if your baby cries with you after being in the care of others, even though the substitute caretaker has assured you that your baby was perfectly happy while you were gone. Babies typically save their crying for those people with whom they feel the safest. Some parents notice that their baby begins to cry the minute they come to pick her up, while others report that their baby doesn't "fall apart" until they are home. Although your baby's crying may be especially irritating to you after a full day at work, remember that your love and support during these crying times are exactly what your baby needs from you while she releases stress from her day.

How can I get help with the job of parenting?

If you find it difficult to meet your baby's needs, this is probably at least partly due to the fact that you are not receiving enough help and support. There is a cultural myth that parents should be able to raise children on their own, without any support from society. This is completely unrealistic.

In the prehistoric past, humans lived in clans that averaged about 30 people. Each baby must have received a considerable amount of attention from many caring adults, because there were probably always more adults than children.

Until fairly recently, large, extended families were very common in most cultures of the world. Before the industrial revolution in Europe, for example, many related people all lived under the same roof, or at least in the same village. Babies were given a tremendous amount of attention with this arrangement. They were breastfed on demand for several years. Adults encouraged babies to be dependent, and they frequently rocked and cuddled them and responded promptly to their cries. Toilet training was not attempted during the first year.[28]

After 1750, because of the industrial revolution, the traditional extended family began to be replaced by the nuclear family, consisting of only a mother, a father, and their children, because families had to move to be near the factories and mills. Fathers usually worked outside the home, and mothers were left alone with the household chores and the children (although in many cases the women and children worked in the factories as well). Women had less help with child rearing and household chores than ever before in the history of the human species. Married couples turned to each other as the only sources of attention and companionship, and this began to put a strain on the marital relationship.

With so many demands on the mother's time, energy, and attention, child-rearing practices began to change drastically.[29] Instead of encouraging dependence, mothers began fostering independence in their babies at an early age. Babies were still breastfed (until the invention of nursing bottles and breast milk substitutes), but scheduled feeding times were introduced for the first time. Solid foods were given at an early age, followed by early weaning. Babies were expected to sleep alone from birth. Toilet training was started very early, sometimes as early as three weeks of age. The notion of "spoiling" was introduced and became widely accepted. Parents were advised not to touch or hold their babies too much for fear of spoiling them, and to ignore them when they cried. To make matters even worse, the decline in breastfeeding caused a reduction in the natural contraceptive effect of nursing, and mothers were often forced to care for two babies who were only one year apart in age.

The deplorable child-rearing practices that have been so common in the twentieth century are therefore the result of these tremendous pressures on mothers resulting from the decline of extended families. Furthermore, there has been a breakdown of neighborhood support systems because families move so frequently that there is little time to form deep friendships. Divorces have become more frequent, along with the number of father-absent homes. Economic pressures have forced women into the work force soon after the births of their children, and this has increased the demand for infant daycare.

It is obvious that extensive social changes are needed if all babies are to receive the quality care that they need and deserve. We need better maternity and paternity leaves, with pay, as well as more part-time jobs with no loss of fringe benefits for both men and women. Shared jobs can be very helpful for parents of young children, so that parents can split one paid job and divide the work day as they wish.

We also need to find ways of using the time and experience of older people instead of forcing them to lead useless and isolated lives in retirement centers. Many old people are separated by thousands of miles from their own grandchildren and would love to spend time with babies. With the participation of these older people and perhaps also teenage volunteers, it may be possible to have daycare centers with a one-to-one adult/baby ratio.

A return to the traditional extended family is not feasible or even desirable for many people, so we need to create our own clans or tribes. Look for other parents with whom you can exchange childcare. This can be a valuable source of help, and has the advantage of not costing any money. Some families have experimented with cooperative or communal living arrangements with non-related friends. The shared housework and child care, as well as the companionship and emotional support help relieve the stresses that so commonly occur in nuclear families.

Try to form a support network for yourself, and get together as much as possible with other parents of young children. Usually just being with other parents and babies makes the job of parenting easier, and can result in a renewed ability to give good attention to your own baby. Look for organizations that sponsor playgroups, such as women's centers, community centers, adult education centers, churches, and public schools. If there are no playgroups in your community, you can start your own with friends or neighbors, and meet in private homes, a park, or a community center. Your baby will learn valuable social skills by interacting with other babies, and you will meet other parents.

If you are feeling depressed or on the verge of abusing your child, you need immediate help and support. Look for a support group or therapist, or call a telephone hotline. But most importantly, *do not isolate yourself.* Find someone to talk to.

One way to make the job of parenting easier is to take preventive measures by spacing your children at least three years apart. This will reduce the likelihood of sibling rivalry, and will also enable you to fill each baby's needs for attention. This will minimize problems with your children later one. Children who are three or more years old are not as dependent on adults for having basic physical needs filled (such as eating, dressing, toileting, etc.). They are also able to entertain themselves with other children, and understand that their parents can give them attention at certain times but not at others. A further advantage of spacing children several years apart is that the older sibling(s) can help care for the baby or play with her.

I also recommend limiting the number of children. A good guideline is to have no more children than the number of adults in the household. Two children would therefore be a reasonable limit in a home with only two adults. It makes little sense to bring children into the world if you cannot give them adequate attention and care. If you are a single parent or if you have twins, your job will be especially difficult. Try to get as much help as possible from friends, relatives, or agencies. You are always justified in asking for help when the welfare of your children is at stake.

Conclusion

Never before has the job of parenting been as important as it is today. If we are to raise children to be competent, compassionate, and non-violent, we must treat them with love, trust, and respect. If we can meet our children's needs and help them retain the ability to feel and express their emotions, then we can truly improve the world, one family at a time.

However, we cannot expect mothers and fathers to do this alone. We need economic and social policies that give top priority to families with young children. We cannot expect parents to raise children well when they have very little money, emotional support, or help, or when they lack information about children's developmental needs.

There are challenging tasks ahead for everyone, and it is never too late to begin. Together, we *can* change the world.

EXERCISES

Explore your childhood.

1. Describe your childhood relationship with your parents. Were you strongly attached to them? Were you encouraged to be independent before you were ready? Did you feel close to your parents as an adolescent?
2. Did you suffer from any traumatic separations from your parents or other people as a child? How did you feel?
3. What roles did your mother and father have? What role were you expected to assume as an adult? How do you feel about this?

Express your feelings about your baby.

1. Do you feel that your baby is too strongly or too weakly attached to you? How do you feel if your baby clings and resists separating from you?
2. Have other people ever tried to give you advice or commented about your baby's attachment behavior? How did it make you feel?
3. How do you feel when you are separated from your baby? Do you feel that your own separation anxiety is too strong or too weak?

Nurture yourself.

1. Are you getting enough help with the job of parenting? If not, try to find ways of obtaining the help and support that you need.
2. If you do not have a healthy attachment to your own parents (and if they are still alive), take steps to improve your relationship with them before it is too late. This can greatly benefit both you and your baby.
3. What social or economic changes would you like to see that would make the job of parenting easier for you? What can you do to bring those changes about?

APPENDIX

A Letter From Australia

I have received hundreds of letters from parents around the world thanking me for writing *The Aware Baby*, and explaining how it has changed their lives. The following letter, from a woman in Australia, is particularly powerful in its ability to inform, inspire, and reassure other parents. It is printed here with permission.

Dear Dr. Solter,

Before having children, I had a very firm view that leaving babies to cry in their rooms was the basis of all the insecurity in this world. As an adult I have yet to encounter another individual who does not experience some sort of insecurity in his/her life. To me crying meant expressing an unmet need that the baby was begging the parents to meet. Once that need was met, the baby would no longer need to cry. Ignoring that cry was in effect saying to children that their needs were not important, that they were not important, and that they were unworthy. I felt that this is the message that I and all of my peers had experienced and were still experiencing in adulthood: an inability to accept our true value because it was made very plain to us from day one of life that our feelings didn't count.

I also felt very strongly (and still feel) that current parenting practices are designed to separate a baby (child) from both the mother and the father, as though there were something wrong with a child totally relying on his/her parents for everything. I had many parents tell me that independence had to be taught. I differed in that I thought independence was something children strived for when they felt confident in their abilities. To put it crudely: by pushing a child away from you he/she will only push harder to come back, but by holding a child close to you, you give him/her the security to push away.

This was my basic philosophy when I gave birth to my first child. I had never heard the term Attachment Parenting. Breastfeeding was quite a success (my daughter weaned herself at two years and eight months). My plan of action with my daughter was to keep our home calm, and to hold my baby whenever she needed or wanted to be held. I would respond to, and comfort, my baby's every cry. I would let my child know how much I loved her, how much she meant to me. She would never get the message that I had something better to do than to care for her. I was (and still am) a strong believer in loving touch and baby massage.

Once I had my darling baby home I found that answering my baby's cries was the easy part. My husband, who was raised in a very similar manner to myself, but with even less respect, had difficulty in accepting my level of commitment to our child. In the first few weeks of life my daughter always seemed to wake up crying the second we sat down to dinner. I would immediately pick my child up and comfort her. My husband, who was raised on a strict routine, with no permissible deviation, began to question this and to express the opinion that she would have to learn to "wait" until we had eaten. For the sake of harmony I sat at the table one evening and ate with tears streaming down my face, silently crying for my baby's pain. This was a good lesson for both of us. My husband learned to reheat meals, and I learned to express myself before things got out of hand.

My daughter never seemed to be able to get enough of the breast. I was often feeding her for an hour at a time. She would often cry for no discernible reason, and would awaken screaming. I was very distressed, and I felt that I was doing something wrong, as I am sure all new mothers do. I was told it was colic and that it would pass. She didn't seem to want to sleep during the day and would cry if I tried to lay her down anywhere. I carried her for months, well, for years really. She was very alert during the day and loved to be outside and doing something as long as she was connected to me.

I tried every remedy in every book I could get my hands on to help her sleep, except, of course, anything that involved her doing it on her own. Nothing worked. She cried a large part of the day, but the nighttime crying was the worst. She would start screaming in her sleep as though she was in terrible agony. The only thing to settle her was the breast, but she seemed to reject any touch. She tolerated the baby massage for a few months but I eventually had to stop it, as it became so obvious that she hated it. If I kissed her she moved her head away. The only contact she wanted with me was the breast, and to be held in an upright position. She needed to be on me or my husband at all times or she would become distressed. Comforting her was a real challenge.

The advice I was getting from books and those around me was advice I did not want and that I knew in my heart I could not follow. I am sure you have heard it all: "You are spoiling that baby, put her down," "Leave her to cry; she will learn soon enough," "If you don't want her waking in the night for a feed, just don't feed her. Let her cry it out. She's only waking because you are feeding her" (this at 4 months), "Give her solids, that should make her sleep," "Put her on the bottle. She obviously isn't getting enough from you."

I began to feel very low and quite a failure. My baby just did not fit the mold. She was not sleeping anywhere near the guidelines, usually about half, and sometimes a third, of what the books told me to expect. When she was about four or five months old I found a book about attachment-style parenting in the library, and that at least helped me to feel as though I was doing the right things. But I still wasn't able to have a "happy" baby. I began to become obsessed with her lack of sleep, and I felt that was what was preventing her from being a relaxed and happy baby.

By the time my little one was six months old I began to fall apart. I was crumbling under the strain and from lack of sleep. My husband began to express his impatience and anger at the constant crying, and I became tense every time she started to cry, as I knew it would anger him and reinforce my feelings of failure. Now I had an unhappy husband *and* an unhappy baby.

Then I found your book in the library (*The Aware Baby*). As I read it, it made so much sense to me. I certainly could relate to its message. My little one had had a traumatic birth experience (a breech birth). She was easily overstimulated and very sensitive. Whilst reading your book I came to the realisation that crying was not "bad."

What a revelation for me! I had always taken her crying as a reflection on my bad parenting skills and my inability to get her to sleep. I felt that her crying apparently for no reason was her way of telling me that I wasn't doing enough. To be quite frank, I felt that I *was* doing enough, and I had begun to resent my inability to make my baby "happy" and her seeming inability to be "happy".

I could really relate to past hurts resurfacing, especially for my husband, when my baby cried. This became far more of an issue for me once I finally began to allow my little one to cry and to be supportive of that crying. I began slowly, and, to be honest, my heart had a great deal of trouble accepting the crying for what it is rather than for what I felt it was (a reflection on my lack of parenting skills).

My little one needed to do a great deal of crying, and, to some extent, she still does. She has an extremely intense temperament. It took me a great deal of time to completely accept your ideas and be able to apply them successfully, due mostly to my own personal resistance. I had to work very hard at overcoming this so I could be a complete parent to my child. Because of the time factor, and the fact that I had for so long tried to suppress her need to cry, she had definitely received the message, in no uncertain terms, from both her father and me, that crying was not okay. (He took much longer than I to accept crying as a perfectly normal and acceptable part of our child's expression.) This meant extra work for all of us. We had to relearn a lot. We had to learn ways to encourage rather than to repress. We had to reassure our daughter that what she was doing was what she needed to be doing, and that we were now here for her and wanted to help her through it. It took a lot of work, and we are still working on this with her.

My second daughter, on the other hand, whom we have been able to treat appropriately from the beginning, does not try to suppress her tears, and the benefits of a good cry are far more apparent with her. I have also applied your approach to tantrums with both of my children, with great success.

The most important lesson that you were able to teach me was that intense feelings are valid. They do have a place and a meaning to our children, and they are healthy and essential for our children's emotional well-being. Feelings are important, and we as parents should encourage those feelings and allow our little ones to vent on their own levels, not by a standard acceptable to the parent. I can certainly verify that my children are a lot more relaxed, confident, and sane because you showed me the way to respect and honor the instincts that they were born with. Having applied your approach to my children, I can see the empathy and caring that they are able to show to each other, their parents, and others. I do not believe that they would be able to do this if they were forced to carry around all that excess baggage of emotional hurt.

So I would like to thank you for your books. You saved my sanity at a very trying time in my life. But more than that, you helped us all as a family to have a better understanding of ourselves and our needs. Your books enabled me to see past my own hurts, to deal with them, to help me stop the cycle, and to let my children grow up the way that I had imagined was possible. I believe now that they will be able to grow without insecurities, and to know that their feelings do matter and that they have every right to express and purge those feelings. You have made a major and very positive impact on my life and that of my family.

Carmel

A few years later, I contacted Carmel to ask her permission to reprint her letter in this book, and she sent me the following update:

The child I described in my letter to you is now six-and-a-half years old. Only last Saturday evening she was very tired, and, after a very full day, had some tears to express. As she lay in bed she started to cry, and I said to her, "You've had a very big day, darling. Why don't you have a good cry." Her tears flowed freely for about five to ten minutes while I smiled down at her and gently caressed her brow. When she had finished, she smiled up at me, closed her eyes, and dropped into a peaceful and deep sleep.

Without your help, we could never have come this far. You have given us a very precious gift, one I shall always be grateful for.

Carmel

REFERENCES

References for the Introduction

1. Konner, M.J. (1977). Infancy among the Kalahari Desert San. In P.H. Leiderman, S.R. Tulin, and A. Roselfeld (Eds.), *Culture and Infancy: Variations in the Human Experience*, 287-327. New York: Academic Press.
2. Liedloff, J. (1975). *The Continuum Concept*. Addison-Wesley, Inc.
3. LeVine, R.A., Dixon, S., LeVine, S., Richman, A., Leiderman, P.H., Keefer, C., and Brazelton, T.B. (1994). *Child Care and Culture: Lessons From Africa*. Cambridge: Cambridge University Press.
4. deMause, L. (1974). *The History of Childhood*. The Psychohistory Press.
5. Nelson, C.A. & Carver, L.J. (1998). The effects of stress and trauma on brain and memory; a view from developmental cognitive neuroscience. *Development and Psychopathology*, 10(4), 793-809.
   Bremner, J.D. (1999). Does stress damage the brain? *Biological Psych.*, 45(7), 797-805.

References for Chapter 1

1. Stott, D.H. (1973). Follow-up study from birth of the effects of pre-natal stresses. *Developmental Medicine and Child Neurology*, 15, 770-787.
   Van den Bergh, B.R.H. (1990). The influence of maternal emotions during pregnancy on fetal and neonatal behavior. *Pre- and Perinatal Psychology Journal*, 5(2), 119-130.
   Glynn, L.M., Wadhwa, P.D., & Sandman, C.A. (2000). The influence of corticotropin-releasing hormone on fetal development and parturition. *Journal of Prenatal and Perinatal Psychology and Health*, 14 (3-4), 243-256.
2. Zuckerman, B., Bauchner, H., Parker, S., & Cabral, H. (1990). Maternal depressive symptoms during pregnancy, and newborn irritability. *Journal of Developmental and Behavioral Pediatrics*, 11, 190-194.
   Lundy, B.L., Jones, N.A., Field, T., Nearing, G., Davalos, M., Pietro, P.A., Schanberg, S., Kuhn, C. (1999). Prenatal depression effects on neonates. *Infant Behavior and Development*, 22(1), 119-129.
3. Verny, T. (1981). *The Secret Life of the Unborn Child*. New York: Dell.
   Chamberlain, D.B. (1998a). Prenatal Receptivity and Intelligence. *Journal of Prenatal and Perinatal Psychology and Health*, vol. 12(3-4), 95-117.
4. DeCasper, A. & Spence, M. (1986). Prenatal speech influences newborns' perception of speech sounds. *Infant Behavior and Development*, 9, 133-150.
5. Chamberlain, D.B. (1997). Early and very early parenting: New territories. *Journal of Prenatal and Perinatal Psychology and Health*, 12(2).
   Manrique, B., Contasti, M., Alvarado, M.A., Zypman, M., Palma, N., Ierrobino, M.T.,

Ramirez, I., & Carini, D. (1998). A controlled experiment in prenatal enrichment with 684 families in Caracas, Venezuela: results to age six. *Journal of Prenatal and Perinatal Psychology and Health*, 12 (3-4), 209-234.

Panthuraamphorn, C., Dookchitra, D., & Sanmaneechai, M. (1998). Environmental influences on human brain growth and development. *Journal of Prenatal and Perinatal Psychology and Health,* 12 (3-4), 163-174.

Lafuente, M.J., Grifol, R., Segarra, J., Soriano, J., Gorba, M.A., & Montesinos, A. (1998). Effects of the firststart method of prenatal stimulation on psychomotor development: the first six months. *Journal of Prenatal and Perinatal Psychology and Health*, 12 (3-4), 197-208.

6. Verny, T. (1991). *Nurturing the Unborn Child*. New York: Delacorte Press.

7. Janov, A. (1983). *Imprints: The Lifelong Effects of the Birth Experience*. New York: Coward-McCann, Inc.

Salk, L., Lipsitt, L.P., Sturner, W.Q., Reilly, B.M., & Levat, R.H. (1985). Relationship of maternal and perinatal conditions to eventual adolescent suicide. *Lancet*, 8429, 624-627.

Jacobson, B. Eklund, G., Hamberger, L., Linnarsson, D. Sedvall, G., Valverius, M. (1987). Perinatal origin of adult self-destructive behavior. *Acta Psychiatr. Scand.*, 76(4), 364-371.

Lewis, S.W. & Murray, R.M. (1987). Obstetric complications, neurodevelopmental deviance, and risk of schizophrenia. *Journal of Psychiatric Research*, 21(4), 413-421.

Jacobson, B., Nyberg, K., Gronbladh, L., Eklund, G., Bygdeman, M., Rydberg, U. (1990). Opiate addiction in adult offspring through possible imprinting after obstetric treatment. *British Medical Journal*, 301 (6760), 1067-1070.

Roedding, J. (1991). Birth trauma and suicide: A study of the relationship of near-death experiences at birth and later suicidal behavior. *Pre- and Perinatal Psychology Journal*, 6(2), 145-167.

Batchelor, E.S., Jr., Dean, R.S., Gray, J.W., and Wench, S. (1991). Classification rates and relative risk factors for perinatal events predicting emotional/behavioral disorders in children. *Pre- and Perinatal Psychology Journal*, 5(4), 327-346.

Kandel, E. & Mednick, S. (1991). Perinatal complications predict violent offending. *Criminology*, 29(3), 519-529.

Raine, A., Brennan, P., Mednick, S.A. (1994). Birth complications combined with early maternal rejection at age 1 year predispose to violent crime at age 18 years. *Archives of General Psychiatry*, 51(12), 984-988.

Jones, P.B., Rantakallio, P., Hartikainen, A.L., Isohanni, M., Sipila, P. (1998). Schizophrenia as a long-term outcome of pregnancy, delivery, and perinatal complications: a 28-year follow-up of the 1966 north Finland general population cohort. *American Journal of Psychiatry*, 155(3), 355-364.

8. Janov, A. (1983). (See 7)

Emerson, W. (1998). Birth Trauma: The Psychological Effects of Obstetrical Interventions. *Journal of Prenatal and Perinatal Psychology and Health*, 13(1), 11-44.

9. Janov, A. (1983). (See 7)

10. Chamberlain, D.B. (1998). *The Mind of Your Newborn Baby*. Berkeley, CA: North Atlantic Books.

11. Taddio, A., Katz, J., Ilersich, A.L., Koren, G. (1997). Effect of neonatal circumcision on pain response during subsequent routine vaccination. *Lancet*, 1:349 (9052), 599-603.

12. Janov, A. (1983). (See 7)

Chamberlain, D.B. (1998). (See 10)

13. Noble, E. (1993). *Primal Connections*. Simon and Schuster.

14. Gordon, N.P., Walton, D. McAdam, E., Derman, J., Gallitero, G., Garrett, L. (1999). Effects of providing hospital-based doulas in health maintenance organization hospitals. *Obstet. Gynecol.* 93(3), 422-426.

15. Klaus, M.H. & Kennell, J.H. (1997). The doula: an essential ingredient of childbirth rediscovered. *Acta Paediatrica*, Oct. 86 (10), 1034-1036.
16. Kitzinger, S. (1987). *Your Baby, Your Way*. New York: Pantheon Books.
17. Bradley, R.A. *Husband-Coached Childbirth*. (1965). New York: Harper & Row.
18. Klaus, M.H. & Kennell, J.H. (1976). *Maternal-Infant Bonding*. Saint Louis: The C.V. Mosby Company.
19. Klaus, M. (1997). Paper presented at the 8th International Congress of the Association for Pre- and Perinatal Psychology and Health, San Francisco.
20. Greenberg, M. & Morris, N. (1974). Engrossment: the newborn's impact upon the father. *American Journal of Orthopsychiatry*, 44, 520-531.
21. Klaus, M.H. & Kennell, J.H. (1976). (See 18)
22. Klaus, M.H. & Kennell, J.H. (1976). (See 18)
23. Myers, B.J. (1987). Mother-Infant Bonding as a Critical Period. In M.H. Bornstein (Ed.), *Sensitive Periods in Development: Interdisciplinary Perspectives*. Hillsdale, New Jersey: Lawrence Erlbaum & Associates.
24. Panuthos, C. (1983). The Psychological Effects of Cesarean Deliveries. *Mothering*, 26, 61-65.
25. Ludington-Hoe, S.M., Thompson, C., Swinth, J., Hadeed, A.J., and Anderson, G.C. (1994). Kangaroo Care: Research Results and Practical Implications and Guidelines. *Neonatal Network*, Vol. 13 (1), 19-27.
    Tessier, R., Cristo, M., Velez, S. Giron, M., de Calume, Z.F., Ruiz-Palaez, J.G., Charpak, Y., Charpak, N. (1998). Kangaroo mother care and the bonding hypothesis. *Pediatrics*, 102 (2), 17.
26. Newton, N. (1971). Psychological differences between breast and bottle feeding. *The American Journal of Clinical Nutrition*, 24, 993-1004.
    Klaus, M. (1997). (See 19)
27. Montagu, A. (1971). *Touching: The Human Significance of the Skin*. New York: Columbia University Press.
28. Martin, R.D. (1990). *Primate Origins and Evolution: A Phylogenetic Reconstruction*. Princeton University Press.
29. Gardner, L.I. (1972). Deprivation dwarfism. *Scientific American*, 227, 76-82.
30. Sapolsky, R. (1994). *Why Zebras Don't Get Ulcers*. New York: W.H. Freeman & Co.
31. Brazelton, T.B. (1992). *Touchpoints: Your Child's Emotional and Behavioral Development*. Addison-Wesley Publishing House.
32. Spitz, R. (1945). Hospitalism: an inquiry into the genesis of psychiatric conditions in early childhood. *Psychoanalytic Study of the Child*, 1, 53-74.
    Provence, S. & Lipton, R.C. (1962). *Infants in Institutions*. International Universities Press.
    Kaler, S.R. & Freeman, B.J. (1994). Analysis of environmental deprivation: cognitive and social development in Romanian orphans. *Journal of Child Psychology and Psychiatry*, 35, 769-781.
33. Carlson, M., Dragomir, C., Earls, F., Farrell, M., Macovei, O., Nystrom, P., & Sparling, J. (1995). Effects of social deprivation on cortisol regulation in institutionalized Romanian infants. *Abstracts of the Society for Neuroscience*, 21, 524.
34. Van der Kolk. (1987). *Psychological Trauma*. Washington, DC: Amer. Psychiatric Press.
35. Restak, R.M. (1979). *The Brain: The Last Frontier*. Doubleday & Co., Inc.
36. Liedloff, J. (1975). *The Continuum Concept*. Addison-Wesley Publishing Company, Inc.
37. Casler, L. (1965). The study of the effects of extra tactile stimulation on the development of institutionalized infants. *Genetic Psychology Monographs*, 71, 137-175.
38. Field, T.M., Schanberg, S.M., Scarfidi, F., Bauer, C.R., Vega-Lahr, N., Garcia, R., Nystrom, J., & Kuhn, C.M. (1986). Tactile/kinesthetic stimulation effects on preterm neonates. *Pediatrics* 77, 654-658.

39. Acolet, D., Medi, N., Giannakoulopoulos, X., Bond, C., Weg, W., Clow, A., Glover, V. (1993). Changes in plasma cortisol and catecholamine concentrations in response to massage in premature infants. *Archives of Diseases in Childhood*, 68, 29-31.
40. Gray, L., Watt, L., Blass, E.M. (2000). Skin-to-skin contact is analgesic in healthy newborns. *Pediatrics* 105(1): e14.
41. Leboyer, F. (1976). *Loving Hands: The Traditional Indian Art of Baby Massage*. New York: Alfred A. Knopf.
42. Lipton, E.L., Steinschneider, A. & Richmond, J.B. (1960). Autonomic function in the neonate II. Physiologic effects of motor restraint. *Psychosomatic Medicine*, 22, 57-76
43. Korner, A., Guilleminault, C., Van den Hoed, J., Baldwin, R.B. (1978). Reduction of sleep apnea and bradycardia in preterm infants of oscillating water beds: a controlled polygraphic study. *Pediatrics*, 61(4), 528-533.
    Clark, D.L., Cordero, L., Goss, K.C. & Manos, D. (1989). Effects of rocking on neuromuscular development in the premature infant. *Biological Neonate*, 56(6), 306-314.
    Sammon, M.P. & Darnall, R.A. (1994). Entrainment of respiration to rocking in premature infants: coherence analysis. *Journal of Applied Physiology*, 77(3), 1548-1554.
44. Malcuit, G., Pomerleau, A., Brosseau, N. (1988). Cardiac and behavioral responses to rocking stimulations in one- and three-month-old infants. *Perceptual and Motor Skills*, 66(1), 207-217.
    Grosswater, J. Sottiaux, M., Rebuffat, E., Simon, T., Vandeweyer, M., Kelmanson, I., Blum, D., & Kahn, A. (1995). Reduction in obstructive breathing events during body rocking: a controlled polygraphic study in preterm and full-term infants. *Pediatrics*, 96(1), 64-68.
45. Salk, L. (1973). Role of the heartbeat in the relationship between mother and infant. *Scientific American*, (May), 24-29.
46. Cohn, J.F. & Tronick, E.Z. (1983). Three-month-old infants' reactions to simulated maternal depression. *Child Development*, 54, 185-193.
47. Small, M. (1998). *Our Babies, Ourselves: How Biology and Culture Shape the Way we Parent*. New York: Anchor Books.
48. DeCasper, A. & Fifer, W.P. (1980). Of human bonding: newborns prefer their mothers' voices. *Science*, 208, 1174-1176.
49. Ainsworth, M.D., Bell, S.M., Stayton, D.J. (1972). Individual differences in the development of some attachment behaviors. *Merrill-Palmer Quarterly*, Vol. 18(2), 123-143.
50. Provence, S. & Lipton, R.C. (1962). (See 32)
51. Bell, S.M. & Ainsworth, M.D. (1972). Infant crying and maternal responsiveness. *Child Development*, 43, 1171-1190.

References for Chapter 2

1. St. James-Roberts, I. & Halil, T. (1991). Infant crying patterns in the first year: normal community and clinical findings. *J. of Child Psychology and Psychiatry*, 32 (6), 951-968.
2. Barr, R.G., Konner, M., Bakeman, R., & Adamson, L. (1991). Crying in !Kung San infants: A test of the cultural specificity hypothesis. *Developmental Medicine and Child Neurology*, 33(7), 601-610.
3. St. James-Roberts, I., Bowyer, J., Varghese, S., Sawdon, J. (1994). Infant crying patterns in Manali and London. *Child Care, Health and Development*, 20(5), 323-337.
4. St. James-Roberts, I. & Halil, T. (1991). (See 1)
5. Wessel, M.A. (1954). Paroxysmal fussing in infancy, sometimes called "colic." *Pediatrics*, 14, 421-434.

6. St. James-Roberts, I., Conroy, S., Wilsher, C. (1998). Stability and outcome of persistent infant crying. *Infant Behavior and Development*, 21(3), 411-435.
7. Miller, A.R. & Barr, R.G. (1991). Infantile colic: is it a gut issue? *Pediatric Clinics of North America*, 38, 1407-1423.
8. Spock, B. & Parker, S.J. (1998). *Dr. Spock's Baby and Child Care* (7th edition). New York: Pocket Books.
9. Jakobsson, I., Lothe, L., Ley, D., Borschel, M.W. (2000). Effectiveness of casein hydrolysate feedings in infants with colic. *Acta Pediatrica*, 89(1), 18-21.
10. Stewart, A.H., et al. (1954). Excessive infant crying (colic) in relation to parent behavior. *American Journal of Psychiatry*, 110, 687-694.
    Lakin, M. (1957). Personality factors in mothers of excessively crying (colicky) babies. *Monographs of the Society for Research in Child Development*, 22, 1-48.
11. Miller, A.R., Barr, R.G., & Eaton, W.O. (1993). Crying and motor behavior of six-week-old infants and postpartum maternal mood. *Pediatrics*, 92(4), 551-558.
12. St. James-Roberts, I., Conroy, S., Wilsher, K. (1998). Links between maternal care and persistent infant crying in the early months. Thomas Coram Res. Unit, Univ. of London.
13. Brazelton, T.B. (1969). *Infants and Mothers: Differences in Development.* New York: Dell Publishing, Inc.
14. Frey, II, W.H. & Langseth, M. (1985). *Crying: The Mystery of Tears*. Winston Press.
15. Vaughn, B. & Sroufe, L.A. (1979). The temporal relationship between infant heart rate acceleration and crying in an aversive situation. *Child Development*, 50, 565-567.
16. Karle, W., Corriere, R., & Hart, J. (1973). Psychophysiological changes in abreaction therapy. Study I: Primal Therapy. *Psychotherapy: Theory, Research and Practice*, 10, 117-122.
    Woldenberg, L., Karle, W., Gold, S., Corriere, R., Hart, J., & Hopper, M. (1976). Psychophysiological changes in feeling therapy. *Psychological Reports*, 39, 1059-1062.
17. Frey, II, W.H. & Langseth, M. (1985). (See 14)
18. deZegher, F., Vanhole, C., Van den Berghe, G., Devlieger, H., Eggermont, E., Veldhuis, J.D. (1994). Properties of thyroid stimulating hormone and cortisol secretion by the human newborn on the day of birth. *Journal of Clinical Endocrinology and Metabolism*, 79(2), 576-581.
    Lewis, M. & Ramsey, D. (1995). Stability and change in cortisol and behavioral response to stress during the first 18 months of life. Developmental Psychobiology, 28(8), 419-428.
19. Gunnar, M.R. (1988). Adrenocortical activity and behavioral distress in human newborns. *Developmental Psychobiology*, 21(4), 297-310.
    Gunnar, M.R., Larson, M.C., Hertsgaard, L., Harris, M.L., & Brodersen, L. (1992). The stressfulness of separation among nine-month-old infants: effects of social context variables and infant temperament. *Child Development*, 63, 290-303.
20. Zuckerman, B., Bauchner, H., Parker, S., & Cabral, H. (1990). Maternal depressive symptoms during pregnancy, and newborn irritability. *Journal of Developmental and Behavioral Pediatrics*, 11, 190-194.
21. Kitzinger, S. (1989). *The Crying Baby*. Viking.
22. Kitzinger, S. (1989). (See 21)
23. Bernal, J.F. (1973). Night waking in infants during the first 14 months. *Developmental Medicine and Child Neurology*, 15(6), 760-769.
    Keller, H., Lohaus, A., Volker, S., Cappenberg, M., Chasiotis, A. (1998). Relationships between infant crying, birth complications, and maternal variables. Child Care Health Development, 24(5), 377-394.
24. Hunziger, V.A. & Barr, R.G. (1986). Increased carrying reduces infant crying: A randomized controlled trial. Pediatrics, 77, 641-648.
25. James, W. (1890). *The Principles of Psychology*. Vol. 1. New York: Holt.

26. Barnard, K.E. (1973). The effects of stimulation on the sleep behaviors of the premature infant. In M. Batty (Ed.), *Western Journal for Communicating Nursing Research*, Vol. 6.
27. Brazelton, T.B. (1985). Application of cry research to clinical perspectives. In B.M. Lester and C.F.Z. Boukydis (Eds.), *Infant Crying: Theoretical and Research Perspectives*. New York: Plenum Press.
28. Lucassen, P.L., Assendelft, W.J., Gubbels, J.W., van Eijk, J.T., van Geldrop, W.J., Neven, A.K. (1998). Effectiveness of treatments for infantile colic: systematic review. Institute for Research in Extramural Medicine, Free University, Amsterdam, The Netherlands.
29. Lester, B.M. & Boukydis, C.F. (1985). *Infant Crying: Theoretical and Research Perspectives*. New York: Plenum Press.
30. Gunnar et al. (1992). (See 19)
31. Cohn, J.F. & Tronick, E.Z. (1983). Three-month-old infants' reactions to simulated maternal depression. *Child Development*, 54, 185-193.
32. Papousek, M. & von Hofacker, N. (1998). Persistent crying in early infancy: a non-trivial condition of risk for the developing mother-infant relationship. *Child Care, Health and Development*, 24(5), 395-424.
33. Poole, S.R. (1991). The infant with acute, unexplained, excessive crying. *Pediatrics*, 88(3), 450-455.
34. Michelsson, K. & Michelsson, O. (1999). Phonation in the newborn infant cry. *International Journal of Pediatric Otorhinolaryngology*, 49, Suppl.1, S297-301.
35. Brown, B. & Rosenbaum, L. (1983). *Stress effects of IQ*. Paper presented at the meeting of the American Association for the Advancement of Science, Detroit.
36. Carlson, M., Dragomir, C., Earls, F., Farrell, M., Macovei, O., Nystrom, P., & Sparling, J. (1995). Effects of social deprivation on cortisol regulation in institutionalized Romanian infants. *Abstracts of the Society for Neuroscience*, 21, 524.
37. Bremner, J.D. & Narayan, M. (1998). The effects of stress on memory and the hippocampus throughout the life cycle: implications for childhood development and aging. *Developmental Psychopathology*, Vol. 10(4), 871-885.
38. Frey, II, W.H. & Langseth, M. (1985). (See 14)
39. Welch, M.A. (1983). Retrieval from autism through mother/child holding therapy. In E.A. Tinbergen (Ed.), *Autistic Children: New Hope for a Cure*. London: George Allen & Unwin.
40. Lovaas, O.I. (1987). Behavioral treatment and normal educational and intellectual functioning in young autistic children. *Journal of Consulting and Clinical Psych.*, 55(1), 3-9.
Sheinkopf, S.J. & Siegel, B. (1998). Home-based behavioral treatment of young children with autism. *Journal of Autism and Developmental Disorders*, 28(1), 15-23.
41. Maurice, C. (1993). *Let Me Hear Your Voice: A Family's Triumph Over Autism*. New York: Alfred A. Knopf, Inc.
42. Magid, K. & KcKelvey, C.A. (1987). *High Risk: Children Without a Conscience*. New York: Bantam Books.
Keck, G.C. & Kupecky, R.M. (1995). *Adopting the Hurt Child*. Pinon Press, Colorado Springs, Colorado.
Myeroff, R., Mertlich, G., & Gross, J. (1999). Comparative effectiveness of holding therapy with aggressive children. *Child Psychiatry and Human Development*, 29(4), 303-313.
43. Gunnar, M.R. (1988). (See 19)
44. Murray, A. (1979). Infant crying as an elicitor of parental behavior: An examination of two models. *Psychological Bulletin*, 86, 191-215.
Frodi, A. (1985). When empathy fails: Aversive infant crying and child abuse. In B.M. Lester and C.F.Z. Boukydis (Eds.). *Infant Crying: Theoretical and Research Perspectives*. New York: Plenum Press.
45. Weston, J. (1968). The pathology of child abuse. In R. Helfer and C. Kempe (Eds.). *The Battered Child*. Chicago: University of Chicago Press.

References for Chapter 3

1. Mata, L.J. & Wyatt, R.G. (1971). Host resistance to infection. *American Journal of Clinical Nutrition*, 24, 976-986.
   Wilson, A.C., Forsyth, J.S., Greene, S.A., Irvine, L., Hau, C., Howie, P.W. (1998). Relation of infant diet to childhood health: seven year follow up of cohort of children in Dundee infant feeding study. *British Medical Journal*, 316(7124), 21-25.
2. Baumslag, N. & Michels, D.L. (1995). *Milk, Money, and Madness: The Culture and Politics of Breastfeeding*. Westport, Connecticut: Bergin & Garvey.
3. Lucas, A., Morley, R., Cole, T.J., Lister, G., Leeson-Payne, C. (1992). Breast milk and subsequent intelligence quotient of children born preterm. *Lancet*, 339(8788), 261-264.
4. Klaus, M.H. & Klaus, P. (1998). *Your Amazing Newborn*. Perseus Books.
5. Newton, N. (1968). Breast Feeding. Psychology Today, 34.
6. Brazelton, T.B. (1992). *Touchpoints: Your Child's Emotional and Behavioral Development*. Addison-Wesley.
7. Konner, M & Worthman, C. (1980). Nursing frequency, gonadal function, and birth spacing among !Kung hunter-gatherers. *Science*, 207, 788-791.
8. LeVine, R.A., Dixon, S., LeVine, S., Richman, A., Leiderman, P.H., Keefer, C.H. & Brazelton, T.B. (1994). *Child care and culture: Lessons from Africa*. New York, NY: Cambridge University Press.
9. Barr, R., Konner, M., Bakeman, R., & Adamson, L. (1991). Crying in !Kung infants: A test of the cultural specificity hypothesis. *Developmental Medicine and Child Neurology*, 33, 601-610.
10. Levine, R.A. (1977) Child rearing as cultural adaptation. In P.H. Leiderman, S.R. Tulkin, A. Rosenfeld (Eds.), *Culture and Infancy: Variations in the Human Experience*. New York: Academic Press.
11. Konner, M. (1977). Infancy among the Kalahari Desert San. In P.H. Leiderman, S.R. Tulkin, A. Rosenfeld (Eds.), *Culture and Infancy: Variations in the Human Experience*. New York: Academic Press.
    Ainsworth, M.S. (1977). Infant development and mother-infant interaction among the Ganda and American families. In P.H. Leiderman, S.R. Tulkin, A. Rosenfeld (Eds.), *Culture and Infancy: Variations in the Human Experience*. New York: Academic Press.
    Shostak, M. (1981). *Nisa: The Life and Words of a !Kung Woman*. New York: Vintage Books.
12. Small, M. (1998). *Our Babies, Ourselves: How Biology and Culture Shape the Way we Parent*. New York: Anchor Books.
13. Small, M. (1998). (See 12)
14. Woolridge, M.W. & Fisher, C. (1988). Colic, "overfeeding," and symptoms of lactose malabsorption in the breast-fed baby: a possible artifact of feed management? *Lancet*, 2(8607), 382-384.
15. Munroe, R., Munroe, R., Whiting, B.B. (1981). *Handbook of Cross-Cultural Human Development*. New York: Garland Publishers.
16. Mead, M. & Newton, M. (1967). Cultural patterning of perinatal behavior. In S.A. Richardson & A.F. Guttmacher (Eds.). *Childbearing: Its Social and Psychological Aspects*. Baltimore: Williams & Williams Co.
17. Woolridge, M.W. & Fisher, C. (1988). (See 14)
18. Baumslag, N. & Michels, D.L. (1995). (See 2)
19. Ostwald, P.F. & Murry, T. (1985). The communicative and diagnostic significance of infant sounds. In B.M. Lester and C.F.Z. Boukydis (Eds.). *Infant Crying: Theoretical and Research Perspectives*. New York: Plenum Press.

20. Beal, V.A. (1957). On the acceptance of solid foods, and other food patterns, of infants. *Pediatrics, 20, 448.*
21. Wilson et al. (1998). (See 1)
22. Davis, C. (1928). Self-selection of diet by newly weaned infants. *American Journal of Diseases of Children,* 36, 651-679.
23. Williams, R.J. (1956). *Biochemical Individuality.* New York: John Wiley & Sons, Inc.
24. Spock, B. & Parker, S.J. (1998). Dr. Spock's Baby and Child Care (7th edition). New York: Pocket Books.
25. Hirschmann, J.R. & Zaphiropoulos, L. (1993). *Preventing Childhood Eating Problems: A Practical, Positive Approach to Raising Kids Free of Food and Weight Conflicts.* Gurze Designs & Books.

References for Chapter 4

1. Renggli, F. (1992). *Selbstzerstörung aus Verlassenheit: Die Pest als Ausbruch einer Massenpsychose im Mittelalter.* Rasch und Röhring Verlag.
2. Renggli, F. (1992). (See 1)
3. Thevenin, T. (1987). *The Family Bed: An Age Old Concept in Childrearing.* Wayne, NJ: Avery Publishing Group, Inc. (First published in 1976).
   Sears, W. & Sears, M. (1993). *The Baby Book: Everything you Need to Know About Your Baby from Birth to Age Two.* Little, Brown & Company.
   Granju, K.A. & Kennedy, B. (1999). *Attachment Parenting: Instinctive Care for Your Baby and Young Child.* Pocket Books.
4. Freud, A. (1965). *Normality and Pathology in Childhood.* New York: International Universities Press.
5. Scott, J.P. (1967). The process of primary socialization in canine and human infants. In J. Hellmuth (Ed.), *Exceptional Infant. Vol. 1: The Normal Infant.* Seattle: Special Child Publications.
6. Mosko, S., Richard, C., & McKenna, J. (1997). Infant arousals during mother-infant bed sharing: implications for infant sleep and sudden infant death syndrome research. *Pediatrics,* 100(5), 841-849.
7. Mosko et al. (1997). (See 6)
8. Rognum, O.T. (1995). *Sudden Infant Death Syndrome: New Trends in the Nineties.* Oslo, Norway: Scandinavian University Press.
9. Drago, D.A. & Dannenberg, A.L. (1999). Infant Mechanical Suffocation Deaths in the United States, 1980-1997. *Pediatrics,* 103 (5), e59.
10. Drago, D.A. & Dannenberg, A.L. (1999). (See 9)
11. Janov, A. (1973). *The Feeling Child.* New York: Simon & Schuster.
12. Barry, H. III & Paxson, L.M. (1971). Infancy and Early Childhood: Cross-Cultural Codes 2. *Ethnology,* 10, 466-509.
13. Newson, J. & Newson, E. (1963). *Infant Care in an Urban Community.* Chicago: Aldine.
14. Provence, S. & Lipton, R.C. (1962). *Infants in Institutions.* New York: International Universities Press, Inc.15. Wolf, A.W. & Lozoff, B. (1989). Object attachment, thumbsucking, and the passage to sleep. *J. of the American Academy of Child and Adolescent Psychiatry,* 28(2), 287-292.
15. Wolf, A.W. & Lozoff, B. (1989). Object attachment, thumbsucking, and the passage to sleep. *J. of the American Academy of Child and Adolescent Psychiatry,* 28(2), 287-292.
16. Newson, J. & Newson, E. (1963). (See 13)
17. Elias, M.F., Nicolson, N.A., Bora, C., & Johnston, J. (1986). Sleep/wake patterns of breast-

fed infants in the first 2 years of life. *Pediatrics*, 77(3), 322-329.
18. Armstrong, T. (1995). *The Myth of the ADD Child*. Dutton.
19. Mayr, D.F. & Boelderl, A.R. (1993). The pacifier craze: collective regression in Europe. *The Journal of Psychohistory*, 21(2), 143-156.
20. Kitzinger, S. (1985). *The Crying Baby*. Viking.

References for Chapter 5

1. Devlin, B., Daniels, D. M., Roeder, K. (1997). The heritability of IQ. *Nature*, Jul. 31, 388(6641), 468-471.
2. Olds, D.L., Henderson, C.R. Jr., & Tatelbaum, R. (1994). Intellectual impairment in children of women who smoke cigarettes during pregnancy. *Pediatrics*, 93(2), 221-227.
   Goldschmidt, L., Richardson, G.A., Stoffer, D.S., Geva, D., & Day, N.L. (1996). Prenatal alcohol exposure and academic achievement at age six: a nonlinear fit. *Alcohol Clin. Exp. Res.* 20(4), 763-770.
   Richardson, G.A. (1998). Prenatal cocaine exposure. A longitudinal study of development. *Annals of the New York Academy of Science*, 846, 144-152.
3. Field, T. (1998). Maternal depression effects on infants and early interventions. *Preventive Medicine*. 27(2), 200-203.
4. Glynn, L.M., Wadhwa, P.D., Sandman, C.A. (2000). The influence of corticotropin-releasing hormone on fetal development and parturition. *Journal of Prenatal and Perinatal Psychology and Health*, 14(3-4), 243-256.
5. Lipton, B.H. (1998). Nature, nurture and the power of love. *Journal of Prenatal and Perinatal Psychology and Health*, 13(1), 3-10.
6. Rosenzweig, M.R., Bennett, E.L., & Daimond, M.C. (1972). Brain changes in response to experience. *Scientific American*, 226, 22-29.
7. Tamis-LeMonda, C. & Bornstein, M.H. (1987). Is there a "sensitive period" in human development? In M.H. Bornstein (Ed.), *Sensitive Periods in Development: Interdisciplinary Perspectives*. Hillsdale, IL: Lawrence Erlbaum & Associates.
8. Montessori, M. (1967). *The Absorbent Mind*. New York: Holt, Rinehart, & Winston.
9. Tamis-LeMonda, C. & Bornstein, M.H. (1987). (See 7)
10. Tamis-LeMonda, C. & Bornstein, M.H. (1987). (See 7)
11. Piaget, J. (1947). *The Psychology of Intelligence*. London: Routledge & Kegan Paul.
12. Condry, J. & Condry, S. (1976). Sex differences: A study of the eye of the beholder. *Child Development*, 47, 812-819.
    Condry, S.M., Condry, J.C. & Pogatschnik, L.W. (1983). Sex differences: A study of the ear of the beholder. *Sex Roles*, 9, 697-704.
13. Beal, C. (1994). *Boys and Girls: The development of gender roles*. New York: Mcgraw-Hill.
14. Ainsworth, M.D. & Bell, S.M. (1974). Mother-Infant Interaction and the Development of Competence. In K. Connolly & J. Bruner (Eds.), *The Growth of Competence*. London: Academic Press, Inc.
    Barnard, K.E., Bee, H.L., & Hammond, M.A. (1984). Home environment and cognitive development in a healthy, low-risk sample: The Seattle Study. In A.W. Gottfried (Ed.), *Home Environment and Early Cognitive Development*. Orlando, FL: Academic Press.
15. Piaget, J. (1952). *The Origins of Intelligence in Children*. New York: International Universities Press, Inc.
16. Yakota, F. & Thompson, K.M. (2000). Violence in G-Rated Animated Films. *Journal of the American Medical Association*, 283(20), 2716-2720.

17. Meltzoff, A.N. (1988). Imitation of televised models by infants. *Child Development*, 59, 1221-1229.
18. Kagan, J. (1994). *Galen's Prophecy*. New York: Basic Books.
19. Fantz, R.L. (1964). Visual experience in infants: Decreased attention to familiar patterns relative to novel ones. *Science*, 146, 668-670.
    Uzgiris, I.C. & Hunt, J.M. (1970). Attentional preference and experience: II. An exploratory longitudinal study of the effect of visual familiarity and responsiveness. *Journal of Genetic Psychology*, 117(1), 109-121.
20. McCall, R.B. & Kagan, J. (1967). Stimulus-schema discrepancy and attention in the infant. *Journal of Experimental Child Psychology*, 5, 381-390.
21. White, B.L. (1978). *Experience and Environment: Major Influences on the Development of the Young Child.* Volume 2. Englewood Cliffs, New Jersey: Prentice-Hall Inc.
22. Holt, J. (1983). *How Children Learn* (revised edition). Dell Publishing, Inc.
23. Piaget, J. (1952). (See 15)
24. Snow, C. & Ferguson, C.A. (Eds.) (1977). *Talking to Children: Language Input and Acquisition*. Cambridge, MA: Cambridge University Press.
    Bornstein, M.H. (1985). How infant and mother jointly contribute to developing cognitive competence in the child. *Proceedings of the National Academy of Sciences*, 82, 7470-7473.
25. Carlson, E.A., Jacobvitz, D., Sroufe, L.A. (1995). A developmental investigation of inattentiveness and hyperactivity. *Child Development*, 66, 37-54.
26. Kohn, A. (1993). *Punished by Rewards: The Trouble With Gold Stars, Incentive Plans, A's, Praise, and Other Bribes*. Houghton Mifflin, New York.
27. Lepper, M.R., Greene, D., & Nisbett, R.E. (1973). Undermining children's intrinsic interest with extrinsic reward: A test of the overjustification hypothesis. *Journal of Personality and Social Psychology*, 28(1), 129-137.
28. Montessori, M. (1967). (See 8)
29. Jernberg, A.M. (1993). Attachment Formation. In C.E. Schaefer (Ed.), *The Therapeutic Powers of Play*. Northvale, NJ: Aronson.
30. Sroufe, L.A. & Wunsch, J.P. (1972). The development of laughter in the first year of life. *Child Development*, 43, 1326-1344.
31. Provence, S. & Lipton, R.C. (1962). *Infants in Institutions*. New York: International Universities Press.

References for Chapter 6

1. Barnett, D., Kidwell, S.L. & Leung, K.H. (1998). Parenting and preschooler attachment among low-income urban African American families. *Child Development*, 69(6), 1657-1671.
2. Straus, M.A. (1993). Corporal punishment of children and depression and suicide in adulthood. In Joan McCord (Ed.), *Coercion and Punishment in Long Term Perspective*. New York: Cambridge University Press.
    MacMillan, H.L., Boyle, M.H., Wong, M.Y., Duku, E.K., Fleming. J.E., & Walsh, C.A. (1999). Slapping and spanking in childhood and its association with lifetime prevalence of psychiatric disorders in a general population sample. *Canadian Medical Association Journal*, 161(7), 805-809.
3. Ainsworth, M.D. & Bell, S.M. (1974). Mother-infant interaction and the development of competence. In K. Connolly & J. Bruner (Eds.), *The Growth of Competence*. London: Academic Press, Inc.

4. Dornbusch, S.M., Ritter, P.L., Leiderman, P.H., Roberts, D.F., & Fraleigh, M.J. (1987). The relation of parenting style to adolescent school performance. *Child Development*, 58, 1244-1257.

Smith, J.R. & Brooks-Gunn, J. (1997). Correlates and consequences of harsh discipline for young children. *Archives of Pediatric and Adolescent Medicine*, 141(8), 777-786.

5. Azrin, N.H. & Holz, W.C. (1966). Punishment. In W.K. Honig (Ed.), *Operant Behavior*. New York: Appleton-Century Crofts.

6. Caesar, P.L. (1988). Exposure to violence in the families-of-origin among wife-abusers and maritally nonviolent men. *Violence Victim*, 3(1), 49-63.

Straus, M.A. (1991). Discipline and deviance: physical punishment of children and violence and other crime in adulthood. *Social Problems*, 38(2), 101-123.

Straus, M.A., Sugarman, D.B., & Giles-Sims, J. (1997). Spanking by parents and subsequent antisocial behavior of children. *Archives of Pediatric & Adolescent Medicine*, 151(8), 761-767.

7. Hoffman, M.L. & Saltzstein, D. (1967). Parent discipline and the child's moral development. *Journal of Personality and Social Psychology*, 5, 45-57.

Stayton, D.J., Hogan, R. & Ainsworth, M.D. (1971). Infant obedience and maternal behavior: the origins of socialization reconsidered. *Child Development*, 42, 1057-1069.

Brenner, V. & Fox, R.A. (1998). Parental discipline and behavior problems in young children. *Journal of Genetic Psychology*, 159(2), 251-156.

8. Azrin, N.H. & Holz, W.C. (1966). (See 5)

9. Siqueland, E.R. & Lipsitt, L.P. (1966). Conditioned head-turning in human newborns. *Journal of Experimental Child Psychology*, 3, 356-376.

10. Kohn, A. (1993). *Punished by Rewards: The Trouble With Gold Stars, Incentive Plans, A's, Praise, and Other Bribes*. Houghton Mifflin, New York.

11. Miller, A. (1983). *For Your Own Good: Hidden Cruelty in Child-Rearing and the Roots of Violence*. New York: Farrar, Straus & Giroux.

12. Milgram, S. (1974). *Obedience to Authority*. New York: Harper & Row.

13. Stayton et al. (1971). (See 7)

14. Gordon, T. (1976). *P.E.T. in Action*. Wyden Books.

15. Sears, R.R., Maccoby, E.E. & Levin, H. (1957). *Patterns of Child Rearing*. Evanston, Illinois: Row & Peterson.

16. Gordon, T. (2000). *Parent Effectiveness Training: The Proven Program for Raising Responsible Children*. New York: Three Rivers Press.

17. Piaget, J. (1952). *The Origins of Intelligence in Children*. New York: International Universities Press, Inc.

18. Braine, M.D.S. (1963). The ontogeny of English phrase structure: The first phase. *Language*, 39, 1-13.

19. Wipfler, P. (1989). *Listening: A Tool for Powerful Parenting*. The Parents Leadership Institute. Palo Alto, CA.

Solter, A. (1998). *Tears and Tantrums*. Goleta, CA: Shining Star Press.

20. Bronson, W.C. (1974). Competence and the growth of personality. In K. Connolly & J. Bruner (Eds.), *The Growth of Competence*. London: Academic Press, Inc.

21. Brazelton, T.B. (1962). A child-oriented approach to toilet training. *Pediatrics*, 29, 121-128.

22. Matson, J.L. (1975). Some practical considerations for using the Foxx and Azrin rapid method of toilet training. *Psychological Reports*, 37(2), 350.

23. Spitz, R.A. (1962). Autoerotism reexamined: The role of early sexual behavior patterns in personality formation. *The Psychoanalytic Study of the Child*, 17, 283-315.

24. Levine, M.I. (1951). Pediatric observations on masturbation in children. *The Psychoanalytic Study of the Child*, 6, 117-124.

25. Spitz, R.A. (1962). (See 23)
26. Janov, A. (1973). *The Feeling Child*. New York: Simon & Schuster.
27. Coohey, C. & Braun, N. (1997). Toward an integrated framework for understanding child physical abuse. *Child Abuse and Neglect*, 21(11), 1081-1094.
    Hall, L.A., Sachs, B., & Rayens, M.K. (1998). Mothers' potential for child abuse: the roles of childhood abuse and social resources. *Nursing Research*, 47(2), 87-95.
28. Krugman, R.D. (1983). Fatal child abuse: Analysis of 24 cases. *Pediatrician*, 12(1), 68-72.
29. Weston, J. (1968). The pathology of child abuse. In R. Helfer & C. Kempe (Eds.), *The Battered Child*. Chicago: University of Chicago Press.

References for Chapter 7

1. Spitz, R.A. (1965). *The First Year of Life*. New York: International Universities Press.
2. Ainsworth, M.D. & Wittig, B.A. (1969). Attachment and exploratory behavior of one-year-olds in a strange situation. In B.M. Foss (Ed.), *Determinants of infant Behaviour,* Vol. IV. New York: John Wiley & Sons.
   Bowlby, J. (1988). *A Secure Base*. Basic Books, Inc.
3. Tennes, K.H. & Lampl, E.E. (1964). Stranger and separation anxiety in infancy. *Journal of Nervous and Mental Diseases,* 139, 247-254.
4. Schaffer, H.R. & Emerson, P.E. (1964). The development of social attachments in infancy. *Monograph of the Society for Research in Child Development.* Vol. 29.
5. Tronick, E.Z., Morelli, G.A., Ivey, P.K. (1992). The Efe forager infant and toddler's pattern of social relationships: multiple and simultaneous. *Developmental Psychology,* 28 (4), 568-577.
6. Fox, N.A., Kimmerly, N.L., Y Schafer, W.D. (1991). Attachment to mother/Attachment to father: A meta-analysis. *Child Development,* 62, 210-225.
7. Dunn, J. (1984). *Sisters and Brothers*. Cambridge, MA: Harvard University Press.
8. Gunnar, M.R., Larson, M.C., Hertsgaard, L., Harris, M.L., & Brodersen, L. (1992). The stressfulness of separation among nine-month-old infants: effects of social context variables and infant temperament. *Child Development,* 63, 290-303.
9. Tennes, K.H. & Lampl, E.E. (1964). Stranger and separation anxiety in infancy. *Journal of Nervous and Mental Diseases,* 139, 247-254.
   Schaffer, H.R. (1966). The onset of fear of strangers and the incongruity hypothesis. *Journal of Child Psychology, Psychiatry and Allied Disciplines,* 7, 95-106.
   Morgan, G.A. & Ricciuti, H.N. (1969). Infants' response to strangers during the first year of life. In B. Foss (Ed.), *Determinants of Infant Behaviour,* Vol. IV. New York: John Wiley & Sons, Inc.
10. Dennis, W. (1940). Does culture appreciably affect patterns of infant behaviour? *Journal of Social Psychology,* 12,305-317.
    Ainsworth, M.D. (1963). The development of infant-mother interaction among the Ganda. In B.M. Foss (Ed.), *Determinants of infant Behaviour, Vol.* 11. New York: John Wiley & Sons.
    Lester, B.M., Kotelchuck, M., Spelke, E., Sellers, M.J., Klein, R.E. (1974). Separation protest in Guatemalan infants: cross-cultural and cognitive findings. *Developmental Psychology, 10(1),* 7985.
    Fox, N. (1975). Separation distress in kibbutz reared children. Unpublished manuscript, Harvard University.
    Kearsley, R.B., Zelazo, P.R., Kagan, J. & Hartmann, R. (1975). Differences in separation

protest between day care and home reared infants. *Journal of Pediatrics,* 55, 171-175.

11. Provence, S. & Lipton, R.C. (1962). *Infants in Institutions.* New York: International Universities Press, Inc.

12. Ainsworth, M.D., Bell, S.M., & Stayton, D.J. (1971). Individual differences in strange-situation behavior of one-year-olds. In H.R. Schaffer (Ed.), The *Origins of human Social Relations.* London & New York: Academic Press.

13. Cicchetti, D. Togosch, F.A., Toth, S.L. (1998). Maternal depressive disorder and contextual risk: contributions to the development of attachment insecurity and behavior problems in toddlerhood. *Developmental Psychopathology,* 10(2), 283-300.

14. Sroufe, L.A., Fox, N.E., & Pancake, V.R. (1983). Attachment and dependency in developmental perspective. *Child Development,* 54,1615-1627.

15. Elicker, J., Englund, M., & Sroufe, L.A. (1992). Predicting peer competence and peer relationships in childhood from early parent-child relationships. In R. Parke & G. Ladd (Eds.), *Family-Peer Relationships: Modes of Linkage.* Hillsdale, NJ: Erlbaum.

16. Bowlby, J. (1982,,1973, 1980). *Attachment and Loss. Vol. I.- Attachment, Vol. II.- Separation, Vol. III.- Loss, Sadness and Depression.* New York: Basic Books.

17. Bower, T.G.R. (1977). *A Primer of infant Development.* W.H. Freeman & Company.

18. Bowlby, J. (1951). *Maternal Care and Mental Health.* World Health Organization, Monograph Series No. 2, Palais des Nations, Geneva.

19. Main, M. (1996). Introduction to the special section on attachment and psychopathology: 2. Overview of the field of attachment. *Journal of Consulting and Clinical Psychology.* Vol. 64(2), 237-243.

20. Vaughn, B., Igeland, B., Sroufe, L.A., & Waters, E. (1979). Individual differences in infant-mother attachment at twelve and eighteen months: Stability and change in families under stress. *Child Development, 50,* 971-975.

21. Bowlby, J. (1982). *Attachment and Loss. Vol. I.- Attachment.* New York: Basic Books.

22. Parke, R.D. & O'Leary, S.E. (1976). Father-mother-infant interaction in the newborn period: Some findings, some observations and some unresolved issues. In K. Riegel & J. Meacham *(Eds.), The Developing Individual in a Changing World, Vol. II.- Social and Environmental Issues.* The Hague: Mouton.

Yogman, M.W. (1990). Male parental behavior in human and nonhuman primates. In N.A. Krasnegor & R.S. Bridges (Ed.), *Mammalian Parenting.* Oxford University Press.

23. Mead, M. (1954). Some theoretical considerations on the problem of mother-child separation. *American Journal of Orthopsychiatry,* 24(3), 471-483.

24. Belsky, J. (1990). Developmental risk associated with infant day care. In S. Chehrazi (Ed.), *Psychosocial Issues in Day Care.* Washington, DC: American Psychiatric Press.

25. Howes, C. (1990). Can the age of entry into child care and the quality of child care predict adjustment in kindergarten? *Developmental Psychology,* 26, 292-303.

26. Cost, Quality, and Outcomes Study Team. (1995). Cost, Quality, and Child Outcomes in Child Care Centers: Key Findings and Recommendations. *Young Children,* 50(4). Washington, DC: National Association for the Education of Young Children.

27. NAEYC (1993). Research into action: The effects of group size, ratios, and staff training on child care quality. *Young Children,* 48(1), 65-67.

28. Ryerson, A. (1961). Medical advice on child rearing *1550-1900. Harvard Educational Review.* 31(3), 302-323.

29. Ryerson, A. (1961). (See 28)

INDEX

About the Author

Aletha Solter, Ph.D., is a Swiss/American developmental psychologist, mother of two grown children, international speaker, workshop leader, and consultant. She studied with Dr. Jean Piaget at the University of Geneva, Switzerland, where she earned a Master's Degree in human biology. She holds a Ph.D. in psychology from the University of California at Santa Barbara. She is the author of three books, two workbooks, and numerous articles for parents and professionals. See page 270 for a description of her books.

Dr. Solter has been working with parents, children, and professionals since 1978, and has given talks and led workshops in eight different countries. She founded The Aware Parenting Institute (www.awareparenting.com) in 1990, in order to promote the philosophy of child rearing based on her work. Aware Parenting consists of attachment-style parenting, non-punitive discipline, and acceptance of emotional release. Parents who follow this approach raise children who are bright, compassionate, non-violent, and drug-free. There is a growing list of certified Aware Parenting instructors who are helping to spread this philosophy around the world.

Dr. Solter is available for talks, workshops, and private consultations, and can be reached at the address below.

The Aware Parenting Institute
P.O. Box 206
Goleta, CA 93116
U.S.A.

Phone & Fax: (805) 968-1868
e-mail: solter@awareparenting.com
web site: www.awareparenting.com

Books by Aletha Solter

The Aware Baby
The first edition was published in 1984. It has been translated into Dutch, French, German, Hebrew, and Italian.

"I have recommended this book to thousands of parents and professionals, with outstanding results."
-William R. Emerson, Ph.D., pioneer in infant and child psychotherapy.

Helping Young Children Flourish
The sequel to *The Aware Baby*, this book covers the age range from two to eight years, and has been translated into French, German, Hebrew, and Italian. These first two books together provide a comprehensive description of the Aware Parenting philosophy.

"It is a wonderful book! I recommend it highly."
-Violet Oaklander, Ph.D., Gestalt Play Therapist, author of *Windows to Our Children*.

Tears and Tantrums: what to do when babies and children cry
This book is based on Dr. Solter's popular workshop on crying, and covers the age range from birth to eight years. It has been translated into Dutch, French, and German.

"This book will give readers more confidence as parents or caregivers, because it provides them with specific skills that will bring rewards that all parents value, namely, children who are healthier, both physically and psychologically."
-Thomas Gordon, Ph.D., founder of Gordon Training International and author of *Parent Effectiveness Training*.

The Aware Baby Workbook
Helping Young Children Flourish Workbook
These workbooks contain exercises, fill-in blanks, and handy summary charts. They can be used alone or in a group setting.

ORDER FORM

These books can be ordered through any bookstore or the Internet. To order them directly from the publisher, please fill out this form and send it with your payment (U.S. check or international money order) to Shining Star Press, P.O. Box 206, Goleta, California 93116, U.S.A.

Shipping fees for inside the U.S.: Book rate: add $1.50 to your order for the first book, 50 cents for each additional book. Allow up to 30 days for delivery. For priority mail, add $4.00 for the first book, $1.00 for each additional book.

Shipping fees outside the U.S.: International book rate for all countries (surface mail): add $2.50 to your order for the first book, $1.00 for each additional book. Allow 30 to 90 days for delivery. For airmail to other countries, please see our web site for current shipping fees.

Please inquire about our discount rates for bulk orders.

Phone and fax: (805) 968-1868

e-mail: publisher@awareparenting.com

These prices are subject to change. Please see our web site for current prices.

www.awareparenting.com

- -

Number
of copies:

_____ The Aware Baby ($15.95) .... $_____

_____ Helping Young Children Flourish ($11.95) .... $_____

_____ Tears and Tantrums ($12.95) .... $_____

_____ The Aware Baby Workbook ($10.00) .... $_____

_____ Helping Young Children Flourish Workbook ($10.00) $_____

Subtotal .... $_____
Sales tax (California residents only) .... $_____
Shipping fee (see above) .... $_____
Total amount enclosed .... $_____

Name and address (please print):

_____

_____

_____

_____